Foundation Unit 3

PREPARING LEDGER BALANCES AND AN INITIAL TRIAL BALANCE

For assessments in December 2005 and June 2006

Combined Text and Kit

In this May 2005 third edition

- Clear language and presentation
- Lots of diagrams and flowcharts
- Activities checklist to tie in each activity to specific knowledge and understanding, performance criteria and/or range statement
- Up to date for developments in the subject as at 1 April 2005
- This Text **combines the old Interactive Text and Practice and Revision Kit** for this Unit

FOR DECEMBER 2005 AND JUNE 2006 SKILLS TESTS AND EXAMS

First edition May 2003
Third edition May 2005

ISBN 0 7517 2256 1 (previous ISBN 0 7517 1594 8)

British Library Cataloguing-in-Publication Data
A catalogue record for this book
is available from the British Library

Published by

BPP Professional Education
Aldine House, Aldine Place
London W12 8AW

www.bpp.com

Printed in Great Britain by Ashford Colour Press

All our rights reserved. No part of this publication may be reproduced, stored in a retrieval system or transmitted, in any form or by any means, electronic, mechanical, photocopying, recording or otherwise, without the prior written permission of BPP Professional Education.

We are grateful to the Lead Body for Accounting for permission to reproduce extracts from the Standards of Competence for Accounting, and to the AAT for permission to reproduce extracts from the mapping and Guidance Notes.

©
BPP Professional Education
2005

Contents

Introduction

How to use this Combined Text and Kit – Foundation qualification structure – Unit 3 Standards of competence – Exam technique – Assessment strategy – Building your portfolio

	Page	Answers to activities

PART A — Revise bookkeeping and balance bank transactions

1	Revision of basic bookkeeping	3	145
2	Recording, summarising and posting transactions	15	148
3	Bank reconciliations	41	152

PART B — Control accounts

4	Sales ledger control account	61	154
5	Purchase ledger control account	81	158
6	Other control accounts	93	160

PART C — Initial trial balance

7	The correction of errors	101	160
8	From ledger accounts to initial trial balance	113	161

PART D — Filing

9	Filing	127	165

INTRODUCTION

	Page	Answers to activities

PART E Answers to activities 145

PART F Practice activities 169 213

PART G Full skills based assessments 235 291

PART H Full exam based assessments 325 363

PART I Lecturers' Resource Pack activities 385

Glossary and Index 435

Review form & free prize draw

Order form

> **IMPORTANT**
>
> From June 2006, the exam for Unit 11 (Drafting Financial Statements) will be based on international accounting standards. In addition, recently issued UK accounting standards have adopted international accounting terminology. Therefore students will increasingly meet international accounting terms in the workplace and in their reading of the accounting press. For this reason, this text shows the international equivalents of UK accounting terms when they are first introduced. There is also a glossary of UK/International accounting terms at the back of the text.

Introduction

How to use this Combined Text and Kit

Aims of this Combined Text and Kit

> To provide the knowledge and practice to help you succeed in the assessment for Foundation Unit 3 *Preparing Ledger Balances and an Initial Trial Balance*.

To complete the assessments successfully you need a thorough understanding in all areas covered by the standards of competence.

> To tie in with the other components of the BPP Effective Study Package to ensure you have the best possible chance of success.

Combined Text and Kit

Parts A to D cover all you need to know for assessment for Unit 3 *Preparing Ledger Balances and an Initial Trial Balance*. Numerous activities throughout the text help you practise what you have just learnt.

When you have understood and practised the material in parts A to D and reviewed the answers to activities in Part E, you will have the knowledge and experience to tackle Parts F to I of this Combined Text and Kit which include the following.

- Part F: Practice activities
- Part G: Full skills based assessments
- Part H: Full exam based assessments

These parts of the text aim to get you through the assessments, whether in the form of the AAT simulation or in the workplace.

Passcards

These short memorable notes are focused on key topics for Unit 3, designed to remind you of what the Combined Text and Kit has taught you.

INTRODUCTION

Recommended approach to this Combined Text and Kit

(a) To achieve competence in Unit 3 (and all the other units), you need to be able to do **everything** specified by the standards. Study parts A to D very carefully and do not skip any of it.

(b) Learning is an **active** process. Do **all** the activities as you work through parts A to D of the text so you can be sure you really understand what you have read.

(c) Before you work through Parts F to I of this Combined Text and Kit, check that you still remember the material using the following quick revision plan for each of the chapters in parts A to D.

  (i) Read and learn the **key learning points**, which are a summary of the chapter.

  (ii) Do the **quick quiz** again. If you know what you're doing, it shouldn't take long.

(d) Once you have completed your quick revision plan for each chapter, you are ready to tackle parts F to I of the Combined Text and Kit.

  (i) Try the **Practice Activities**. These are short activities, linked into the Standards of Competence, to reinforce your learning and consolidate the practice that you have had doing the activities in parts A to D of this Combined Text and Kit.

  (ii) Then do the **Skills Based Assessments**. This are pitched at the level you can expect when you do a full skills based assessment, they do cover most of the performance criteria of the elements indicated.

  (iii) **Attempt the Exam Based Assessments**. These will help you develop techniques in approaching the assessments and allocating time correctly. For guidance on this, please see Exam Based Assessment Technique on page (xvi).

(e) Go through the **Passcards** as often as you can in the weeks leading up to your assessment.

This approach is only a suggestion. You or your college may well adapt it to suit your needs.

Remember this is a **practical** course.

(a) Try to relate the material to your experience in the workplace or any other work experience you may have had.

(b) Try to make as many links as you can to your study of the other Units at Foundation level.

(c) Keep this Combined Text and Kit – (hopefully) you will find it invaluable in your everyday work too!

Lecturers' Resource Pack activities

Part K of this Combined Text and Kit includes a number of chapter-linked activities without answers. We have also included one skills based assessment and one exam based assessment, all without answers. The answers for this section are in the BPP Lecturers' Resource Pack for this Unit.

Foundation qualification structure

The competence-based Education and Training Scheme of the Association of Accounting Technicians is based on an analysis of the work of accounting staff in a wide range of industries and types of organisation. The Standards of Competence for Accounting which students are expected to meet are based on this analysis.

The AAT approved new standards of competence in 2002, which take effect from 1 July 2003. This Text reflects the **2003 standards.**

The Standards identify the key purpose of the accounting occupation, which is to operate, maintain and improve systems to record, plan, monitor and report on the financial activities of an organisation, and a number of key roles of the occupation. Each key role is subdivided into units of competence, which are further divided into elements of competences. By successfully completing assessments in specified units of competence, students can gain qualifications at NVQ/SVQ levels 2, 3 and 4, which correspond to the AAT Foundation, Intermediate and Technician stages of competence respectively.

Whether you are competent in a Unit is demonstrated by means of:

- *Either* an Exam (set and marked by AAT assessors)
- *Or* a Skills Test (where competence is judged by an Approved Assessment Centre to whom responsibility for this is devolved)
- Or *both* Exam *and* Skills Test

Below we set out the overall structure of the Foundation (NVQ/SVQ Level 2) stage, indicating how competence in each Unit is assessed.

All units are assessed by Skills Test, and Unit 3 is also assessed by Exam.

INTRODUCTION

NVQ/SVQ Level 2 – Foundation

All units are mandatory.

Unit 1 Recording Income and Receipts

Element 1.1	Process documents relating to goods and services supplied
Element 1.2	Process receipts

Skills test *only*

Unit 2 Making and Recording Payments

Element 2.1	Process documents relating to goods and services received
Element 2.2	Process payments

Skills test *only*

Unit 3 Preparing Ledger Balances and an Initial Trial Balance

Element 3.1	Balance bank transactions
Element 3.2	Prepare ledger balances and control accounts
Element 3.3	Draft an initial trial balance

Exam *and* skills test

Unit 4 Supplying Information for Management Control

Element 4.1	Code and extract information
Element 4.2	Provide comparisons on costs and income

Skills test *only*

Unit 21 Working with Computers

Element 21.1	Use computer systems and software
Element 21.2	Maintain the security of data

Skills test *only*

Unit 22 Contribute to the Maintenance of a Healthy, Safe and Productive Working Environment

Element 22.1	Monitor and maintain a safe, healthy and secure working environment
Element 22.2	Monitor and maintain an effective and efficient working environment

Skills test *only*

Unit 23 Achieving Personal Effectiveness

Element 23.1	Plan and organise your own work
Element 23.2	Maintain good working relationships
Element 23.3	Improve your own performance

Skills test *only*

Unit 3 Standards of competence

The structure of the Standards for Unit 3

The Unit commences with a statement of the **knowledge and understanding** which underpin competence in the Unit's elements.

The Unit of Competence is then divided into **elements of competence** describing activities which the individual should be able to perform.

Each element includes:

(a) A set of **performance criteria.** This defines what constitutes competent performance.

(b) A **range statement.** This defines the situations, contexts, methods etc in which competence should be displayed.

(c) **Evidence requirements.** These state that competence must be demonstrated consistently, over an appropriate time scale with evidence of performance being provided from the appropriate sources.

(d) **Sources of evidence.** These are suggestions of ways in which you can find evidence to demonstrate that competence. These fall under the headings: 'observed performance; work produced by the candidate; authenticated testimonies from relevant witnesses; personal account of competence; other sources of evidence.'

The elements of competence for Unit 3 *Preparing Ledger Balances and an Initial Trial Balance* are set out below. Knowledge and understanding required for the unit as a whole are listed first, followed by the performance criteria and range statements for each element.

Unit 3: Preparing Ledger Balances and an Initial Trial Balance

What is the unit about?

This unit relates to the internal checks involved in an organisation's accounting processes. The first element is primarily concerned with comparing individual items on the bank statement with entries in the cash book, and identifying any discrepancies. This involves recording details from the relevant primary documentation in the cash book, manual and computerised, and calculating the totals and balances of receipts and payments. You are also required to identify any discrepancies, such as differences identified by the matching process, and prepare a bank reconciliation statement.

The second element requires you to total the relevant accounts and to reconcile the control accounts, within a computerised and a manual accounting system. You are also required to resolve or refer any discrepancies and to ensure security and confidentiality.

The third element involves drafting an initial trial balance manually and producing a trial balance from a computerised accounting system. You will be expected to identify and rectify discrepancies, which may occur in a manual accounting system, and create a suspense account where necessary.

INTRODUCTION

Knowledge and understanding

The business environment

1. Types of business transactions and the documents involved (Elements 3.1 & 3.2)
2. General principles of VAT (Element 3.1)
3. General bank services and operation of bank clearing system (Element 3.1)
4. Function and form of banking documentation (Element 3.1)

Accounting methods

5. Double entry bookkeeping, including balancing accounts (Elements 3.1, 3.2 & 3.3)
6. Methods of coding (Elements 3.1, 3.2 & 3.3)
7. Capital and revenue expenditure (Element 3.1)
8. Operation of manual accounting systems (Elements 3.1, 3.2 & 3.3)
9. Operation of computerised accounting systems including output (Elements 3.1, 3.2 & 3.3)
10. The use of the cash book and petty cash book as part of the double entry system or as books of prime entry (Elements 3.1, 3.2 & 3.3)
11. Identification of different types of errors (Element 3.1)
12. Relationship between the accounting system and the ledger (Elements 3.1 & 3.2)
13. Petty cash procedures: imprest and non imprest methods: analysis (Element 3.2)
14. Methods of posting from primary records to ledger accounts (Element 3.2)
15. Inter-relationship of accounts - double entry system (Elements 3.2 & 3.3)
16. Use of journals (Elements 3.2 & 3.3)
17. Reconciling control accounts with memorandum accounts (Element 3.2)
18. Function and form of the trial balance (Element 3.3)

The organisation

19. Relevant understanding of the organisation's accounting systems and administrative systems and procedures (Elements 3.1, 3.2 & 3.3)
20. The nature of the organisation's business transactions (Elements 3.1, 3.2 & 3.3)
21. Organisational procedures for filing source information (Elements 3.1, 3.2 & 3.3)

Element 3.1 Balance bank transactions

Performance criteria		Chapters in this Text
A	Record details from the relevant primary documentation in the cash book and ledgers	2,3
B	Correctly calculate totals and balances of receipts and payments	2,3
C	Compare individual items on the bank statement and in the cash book for accuracy	3
D	Identify discrepancies and prepare a bank reconciliation statement	3

Range statement

1. Primary documentation: credit transfer; standing order and direct debit schedules; bank statement
2. Cash book and ledgers: manual; computerised
3. Discrepancies: differences identified by the matching process
4. Bank reconciliation statement: manual; computerised

Element 3.2 Prepare ledger balances and control accounts

Performance criteria		Chapters in this Text
A	Make and record authorised adjustments	4,5,7
B	Total relevant accounts in the main ledger	4,5
C	Reconcile control accounts with the totals of the balance in the subsidiary ledger	4,5,6
D	Reconcile petty cash account with cash in hand and subsidiary records	6
E	Identify discrepancies arising from the reconciliation of control accounts and either resolve or refer to the appropriate person	4,5,6
F	Ensure documentation is stored securely and in line with the organisation's confidentiality requirements	9

Range statement

1. Record: manual journal; computerised journal
2. Adjustments: to correct errors; to write off bad debts
3. Control accounts: sales ledger; purchase ledger; non-trade debtors; manual; computerised
4. Discrepancies: manual sales ledger and manual purchases ledger control account not agreeing with subsidiary ledger; cash in hand not agreeing with subsidiary record or control account

Element 3.3 Draft an initial trial balance

Performance criteria		Chapters in this Text
A	Prepare the draft initial trial balance in line with the organisation's policies and procedures	8
B	Identify discrepancies in the balancing process	8
C	Identify reasons for imbalance and rectify them	8
D	Balance the trial balance	8

Range statement

1. Trial balance: manual; computerised
2. Discrepancies in a manual accounting system: incorrect double entries; missing entries and wrong calculations
3. Rectify imbalances in a manual accounting system by: adjusting errors; creating a suspense account

INTRODUCTION

Exam technique

Completing exams successfully at this level is half about having the knowledge, and half about doing yourself full justice on the day. You must have the right **technique**.

The day of the exam

1. Set at least one **alarm** (or get an alarm call) for a morning exam.
2. Have **something to eat** but beware of eating too much; you may feel sleepy if your system is digesting a large meal.
3. Allow plenty of **time to get to where you are sitting the exam**; have your route worked out in advance and listen to news bulletins to check for potential travel problems.
4. **Don't forget** pens, pencils, rulers, erasers.
5. Put **new batteries** into your calculator and take a spare set (or a spare calculator).
6. **Avoid discussion** about the exam assessment with other candidates outside the venue.

Technique in the exam

1. **Read the instructions (the 'rubric') on the front of the exam carefully**

   Check that the format hasn't changed. It is surprising how often assessors' reports remark on the number of students who do not attempt all the tasks.

2. **Read the paper twice**

   Read through the paper twice - don't forget that you are given 15 minutes' reading time. Check carefully that you have got the right end of the stick before putting pen to paper. Use your 15 minutes' reading time wisely.

3. **Check the time allocation for each section of the exam**

   Time allocations are given for each section of the exam. When the time for a section is up, you should go on to the next section.

4. **Read the task carefully and plan your answer**

   Read through the task again very carefully when you come to answer it. Plan your answer to ensure that you **keep to the point**. Two minutes of planning plus eight minutes of writing is virtually certain to produce a better answer than ten minutes of writing. Planning will also help you answer the assessment efficiently, for example by identifying workings that can be used for more than one task.

5. **Produce relevant answers**

   Particularly with written answers, make sure you **answer what has been set**, and not what you would have preferred to have been set. Do not, for example, answer a question on **why** something is done with an explanation of **how** it is done.

6. **Work your way steadily through the exam**

   Don't get bogged down in one task. If you are having problems with something, the chances are that everyone else is too.

7   **Produce an answer in the correct format**

The assessor will state **in the requirements** the format which should be used, for example in a report or memorandum.

8   **Do what the assessor wants**

You should ask yourself what the assessor is expecting in an answer; many tasks will demand a combination of technical knowledge and business commonsense. Be careful if you are required to give a decision or make a recommendation; you cannot just list the criteria you will use, but you will also have to say whether those criteria have been fulfilled.

9   **Lay out your numerical computations and use workings correctly**

Make sure the layout is in a style the assessor likes.

Show all your **workings** clearly and explain what they mean. Cross reference them to your answer. This will help the assessor to follow your method (this is of particular importance where there may be several possible answers).

10 **Present a tidy paper**

You are a professional, and it should show in the **presentation of your work**. You should make sure that you write legibly, label diagrams clearly and lay out your work neatly.

11 **Stay until the end of the exam**

Use any spare time **checking and rechecking** your script. Check that you have answered all the requirements of the task and that you have clearly labelled your work. Consider also whether your answer appears reasonable in the light of the information given in the question.

12 **Don't worry if you feel you have performed badly in the exam**

It is more than likely that the other candidates will have found the exam difficult too. As soon as you get up to leave the venue, **forget** that exam and think about the next - or, if it is the last one, celebrate!

13 **Don't discuss an exam with other candidates**

This is particularly the case if you **still have other exams to sit**. Even if you have finished, you should put it out of your mind until the day of the results. Forget about exams and relax!

INTRODUCTION

Assessment strategy

This Unit is assessed by **skills test** and **exam**.

Skills test

A skills test is a means of collecting evidence of your ability to **carry out practical activities** and to **operate effectively in the conditions of the workplace** to the standards required. Evidence may be collected at your place of work, or at an Approved Assessment Centre by means of simulations of workplace activity, or by a combination of these methods.

If the Approved Assessment Centre is a **workplace**, you may be observed carrying out accounting activities as part of your normal work routine. You should collect documentary evidence of the work you have done, or contributed to, in an **accounting portfolio**. Evidence collected in a portfolio can be assessed in addition to observed performance or where it is not possible to assess by observation.

Where the Approved Assessment Centre is a **college or training organisation**, devolved assessment will be by means of a combination of the following.

(a) Documentary evidence of activities carried out at the workplace, collected by you in an **accounting portfolio**.

(b) Realistic **simulations** of workplace activities. These simulations may take the form of case studies and in-tray exercises and involve the use of primary documents and reference sources.

(c) **Projects and assignments** designed to assess the Standards of Competence.

If you are unable to provide workplace evidence you will be able to complete the assessment requirements by the alternative methods listed above.

Possible assessment methods

Where possible, evidence should be collected in the workplace, but this may not be a practical prospect for you. Equally, where workplace evidence can be gathered it may not cover all elements. The AAT regards performance evidence from simulations, case studies, projects and assignments as an acceptable substitute for performance at work, provided that they are based on the Standards and, as far as possible, on workplace practice.

There are a number of methods of assessing accounting competence. The list below is not exhaustive, nor is it prescriptive. Some methods have limited applicability, but others are capable of being expanded to provide challenging tests of competence.

Assessment method	Suitable for assessing
Performance of an accounting task either in the workplace or by simulation: eg preparing and processing documents, posting entries, making adjustments, balancing, calculating, analysing information etc by manual or computerised processes	**Basic task competence.** Adding supplementary oral questioning may help to draw out underpinning knowledge and understanding and highlight your ability to deal with contingencies and unexpected occurrences
General case studies. These are broader than simulations. They include more background information about the system and business environment	Ability to **analyse a system** and suggest ways of modifying it. It could take the form of a written report, with or without the addition of oral or written questions
Accounting problems/cases: eg a list of balances that require adjustments and the preparation of final accounts	Understanding of the **general principles of accounting** as applied to a particular case or topic
Preparation of flowcharts/diagrams. To illustrate an actual (or simulated) accounting procedure	**Understanding of the logic** behind a procedure, of controls, and of relationships between departments and procedures. Questions on the flow chart or diagram can provide evidence of underpinning knowledge and understanding
Interpretation of accounting information from an actual or simulated situation. The assessment could include non-financial information and written or oral questioning	**Interpretative competence**
Preparation of written reports on an actual or simulated situation	**Written communication skills**
Analysis of critical incidents, problems encountered, achievements	Your ability to handle **contingencies**
Listing of likely errors eg preparing a list of the main types of errors likely to occur in an actual or simulated procedure	Appreciation of the range of **contingencies** likely to be encountered. Oral or written questioning would be a useful supplement to the list
Outlining the organisation's policies, guidelines and regulations	Performance criteria relating to these aspects of competence. It also provides evidence of competence in **researching information**
Objective tests and short-answer questions	**Specific knowledge**
In-tray exercises	Your **task-management ability** as well as technical competence
Supervisors' reports	**General job competence**, personal effectiveness, reliability, accuracy, and time management. Reports need to be related specifically to the Standards of Competence
Analysis of work logbooks/diaries	**Personal effectiveness**, time management etc. It may usefully be supplemented with oral questioning
Formal written answers to questions	**Knowledge and understanding** of the general accounting environment and its impact on particular units of competence
Oral questioning	**Knowledge and understanding** across the range of competence including organisational procedures, methods of dealing with unusual cases, contingencies and so on. It is often used in conjunction with other methods

INTRODUCTION

Exam

An exam is a means of collecting evidence that you have the **essential knowledge and understanding** which underpins competence. It is also a means of collecting evidence across the **range of contexts** for the standards, and of your ability to **transfer skills**, knowledge and understanding to different situations. Thus, although exams contain practical tests linked to the performance criteria, they also focus on the underpinning knowledge and understanding. You should, in addition, expect each exam to contain tasks taken from across a broad range of the standards.

Unit 3 Ledger Balances and Initial Trial Balance

With the introduction of the New Standards for the Level 2 NVQ/SVQ in Accounting, there will be a single Exam Based Assessment which will be based on Unit 3 *Preparing Ledger Balances and an Initial Trial Balance.*

The exam will be in two sections and of three hours duration in total. In addition a reading time of 15 minutes will be allowed. It will be based on an organization which operates a manual accounting system consisting of a main ledger and subsidiary ledgers. The exam will always use the terms main ledger but other organisations may refer to it as the general ledger or nominal ledger. Equally, the subsidiary ledgers may be referred to as the sales and purchases ledgers in other organisations. The subsidiary ledger control accounts will be referred to as the sales ledger control account, purchases ledger control account and non-trade debtors control account in the exam. Candidates can assume that the control accounts will be contained in the main ledger forming part of the double entry. The individual accounts of debtors and creditors will be in the subsidiary ledgers and will therefore be regarded as memoranda accounts.

Section 1 will always ask candidates to enter opening balances into accounts, record transactions from books of prime entry, balance off accounts and complete an initial trial balance. The books of prime entry given could be a selection from sales and sales returns day books **or** purchases and purchases returns day books, cash book and journal. In the past feedback from Centres and candidates has indicated that it is confusing to include both sales and purchases day books as books of prime entry. As there is only enough room/time available to feature one subsidiary ledger, and in response to this feedback, the exam at Foundation level will give extracts from the sales/sales returns day books **or** purchases/purchases returns day books, but not both.

Centres and candidates should note that this section requires the candidate to balance all of the accounts, and so candidates should possess the necessary skills to produce neatly and accurately balanced accounts, with balances clearly labelled. In previous exams task 1.3 asked the candidate to 'balance the accounts showing clearly the balances carried down and brought down'. Now this instruction is split into two tasks. In task 1.3 the candidate will be required to balance the account showing clearly the balance carried down. Task 1.4 will ask the candidate to clearly show the balance brought down. This is indicative of the importance placed on this aspect of competence at this level.

The candidate will be asked to transfer the balances calculated in the first part of section 1 to the trial balance, and then to transfer the remaining balances from a given list. Candidates should total the debit and credit columns of the trial balance, which should be equal. A trial balance with an imbalance will never be tested in section 1, therefore the trial balance should always balance.

Candidates are advised to take 90 minutes to complete section 1. Whilst the aim should be to produce a trial balance with the total of the debit and credit columns equal, candidates should not sacrifice checking time, or time allocated for section 2, in an attempt to discover the reason for an imbalance. On completion of both sections, if the candidate is still within the three hours time allowed, it is at this point that they should revisit section 1 and make further checks for accuracy.

Section 2 will always contain a mixture of 10 questions and tasks, some of which will be short-answer, and some requiring a longer response. Typical examples of the tasks which a candidate can expect are, control account reconciliations, preparation of journal entries, creation or clearance of a suspense account either in an account or through the journal, completion of banking and business documentation and the preparation of a bank reconciliation statement. Centres should note that candidates will always be asked to start the bank reconciliation statement with the statement balance, and reconcile this to the balance in the cash book.

INTRODUCTION

It should be noted that the following areas are included in the 2003 standards of competence for this unit, which were not included, or explicitly stated, in the previous standards (2000). This indicates that these topics are now examinable.

Performance criteria

- Bank reconciliation statement (3.1)

Range

- Direct debit schedules and bank statements as source documents (3.1)
- Non-trade debtors control account (3.2)
- Suspense account (3.3)

Knowledge and understanding

- General principles of VAT
- Methods of coding
- Capital and revenue expenditure
- The use of the cash book and petty cash book as part of the double entry system or as books of prime entry
- Petty cash procedures: imprest and non imprest methods; analysis

Building your portfolio

What is a portfolio?

A portfolio is a collection of work that demonstrates what the owner can do. In AAT language the portfolio demonstrates **competence**.

A painter will have a collection of his paintings to exhibit in a gallery, an advertising executive will have a range of advertisements and ideas that she has produced to show to a prospective client. Both the collection of paintings and the advertisements form the portfolio of that artist or advertising executive.

Your portfolio will be unique to you just as the portfolio of the artist will be unique because no one will paint the same range of pictures in the same way. It is a very personal collection of your work and should be treated as a **confidential** record.

What evidence should a portfolio include?

No two portfolios will be the same but by following some simple guidelines you can decide which of the following suggestions will be appropriate in your case.

(a) **Your current CV**

This should be at the front. It will give your personal details as well as brief descriptions of posts you have held with the most recent one shown first.

(b) **References and testimonials**

References from previous employers may be included especially those of which you are particularly proud.

(c) **Your current job description**

You should emphasise financial **responsibilities and duties**.

(d) **Your student record sheets**

These should be supplied by AAT when you begin your studies, and your training provider should also have some if necessary.

(e) **Evidence from your current workplace**

This could take many forms including **letters, memos, reports** you have written, **copies of accounts** or **reconciliations** you have prepared, **discrepancies** you have investigated etc. Remember to obtain permission to include the evidence from your line manager because some records may be sensitive. Discuss the performance criteria that are listed in your Student Record Sheets with your training provider and employer, and think of other evidence that could be appropriate to you.

(f) **Evidence from your social activities**

For example you may be the treasurer of a club in which case examples of your cash and banking records could be appropriate.

(g) **Evidence from your studies**

Few students are able to satisfy all the requirements of competence by workplace evidence alone. They therefore rely on simulations to provide the remaining evidence to complete a unit. If you are not working or not working in a relevant post, then you may need to rely more heavily on simulations as a source of evidence.

(h) **Additional work**

Your training provider may give you work that specifically targets one or a group of performance criteria in order to complete a unit. It could take the form of questions, presentations or demonstrations. Each training provider will approach this in a different way.

(i) **Evidence from a previous workplace**

This evidence may be difficult to obtain and should be used with caution because it must satisfy the 'rules' of evidence, that is it must be current. Only rely on this as evidence if you have changed jobs recently.

(j) **Prior achievements**

For example you may have already completed the health and safety unit during a previous course of study, and therefore there is no need to repeat this work. Advise your training provider who will check to ensure that it is the same unit and record it as complete if appropriate.

How should it be presented?

As you assemble the evidence remember to **make a note** of it on your Student Record Sheet in the space provided and **cross reference** it. In this way it is easy to check to see if your evidence is **appropriate**. Remember one piece of evidence may satisfy a number of performance criteria so remember to check this thoroughly and discuss it with your training provider if in doubt.

To keep all your evidence together a ring binder or lever arch file is a good means of storage.

When should evidence be assembled?

You should begin to assemble evidence **as soon as you have registered as a student**. **Don't leave it all** until the last few weeks of your studies, because you may miss vital deadlines and your resulting certificate sent by the AAT may not include all the units you have completed. Give yourself and your training provider time to examine your portfolio and report your results to AAT at regular intervals. In this way the task of assembling the portfolio will be spread out over a longer period of time and will be presented in a more professional manner.

What are the key criteria that the portfolio must fulfil?

As you assemble your evidence bear in mind that it must be:

- **Valid**. It must relate to the Standards.
- **Authentic**. It must be your own work.
- **Current**. It must refer to your current or most recent job.
- **Sufficient**. It must meet all the performance criteria by the time you have completed your portfolio.

INTRODUCTION

What are the most important elements in a portfolio that cover Unit 3?

You should remember that the unit is about **ledger balances** and **initial trial balance**. Therefore you need to produce evidence not only demonstrating that you can carry out certain tasks, but also you must show that you can supply the required information.

For Element 3.1 *Balance bank transactions* you need to show that you can deal with receipts and payments in the cash book in the correct manner. This will include, for example, being able to carry out a bank reconciliation.

To fulfil the requirements of Element 3.2 *Prepare ledger balances and control accounts* you need to demonstrate that you can identify and report on differences between the subsidiary ledger accounts and the control accounts in the main ledger, eg sales ledger control account and the sales ledger balances in the subsidiary ledger.

For Element 3.3 *Draft an initial trial balance* you need to show that you can balance off ledger accounts and then transfer the balances correctly to an initial trial balance. You also need to be able to identify errors and correct for wrong calculations, missing entries and incorrect double entry.

Finally

Remember that the portfolio is **your property** and **your responsibility**. Not only could it be presented to the external verifier before your award can be confirmed; it could be used when you are seeking **promotion** or applying for a more senior and better paid post elsewhere. How your portfolio is presented can say as much about you as the evidence inside.

> For further information on portfolio building, see the BPP Text *Building Your Portfolio*. This can be ordered using the form at the back of this Text or via the Internet: www.bpp.com/aat

PART A

Revise bookkeeping and balance bank transactions

chapter 1

Revision of basic bookkeeping

Contents

1 Introduction
2 Basics of double entry
3 Capital and revenue items
4 Documenting business transactions

Knowledge and understanding

1 Types of business transactions and the documents involved
2 General principles of VAT
5 Double entry bookkeeping, including balancing accounts
7 Capital and revenue expenditure
20 The nature of the organisation's business transactions

> **Important note**
> The knowledge and understanding points in Unit 3 are mainly the same as for Units 1 and 2. However do not neglect these knowledge and understanding points, as these subjects can be included in the Unit 3 exam eg methods of coding, general principles of VAT, filing.

1 Introduction

Most of the knowledge and understanding points in Unit 3 are duplicates of those in Units 1 and 2. This allows the examiner to **include them in the Unit 3 exam**.

Therefore do not overlook this chapter. It is **vital** if you are going to prove yourself **competent**. It also lays the foundations for more detailed topics later in this Combined Text and Kit.

If you have any problems understanding the material in this chapter, please revise these topics in the BPP Combined Text and Kit for Units 1 and 2.

2 Basics of double entry

2.1 Double entry

Assets are represented by **debits** and liabilities by **credits**. For every debit entry, there is an equal credit entry and so:

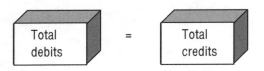

We will use this when preparing a trial balance in Part C. The following should be revision. If not, revise Chapter 5 of the BPP Combined Text and Kit for Units 1 and 2.

ASSET ACCOUNT		LIABILITY ACCOUNT	
DEBIT	**CREDIT**	**DEBIT**	**CREDIT**
Increase	Decrease	Decrease	Increase

DRAWINGS		CAPITAL ACCOUNT	
DEBIT	**CREDIT**	**DEBIT**	**CREDIT**
Increase	Decrease	Decrease	Increase

EXPENDITURE		INCOME	
DEBIT	**CREDIT**	**DEBIT**	**CREDIT**
Increase	Decrease	Decrease	Increase

Remember the following:

Capital is the amount of money invested in the business by the owner(s) and so is a liability owed by the business to the owner(s).

Drawings decrease capital and so are **debits**.

Profit increases capital and so is a **credit**.

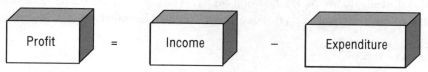

So **income** increases profit and is a **credit**.

Expenditure decreases profit and is a **debit**.

2.2 Double entry bookkeeping

Double entry bookkeeping is based on the idea that every transaction creates two entries: a debit and a credit.

If a bank accepts cash from a customer, two things happen: the bank's cash increases and the amount owed to a customer increases.

In accountancy terms, the entries in the bank's accounts are:

    DEBIT: Cash
    CREDIT: Amount owed to customers (creditors)

When a business pays one of its suppliers the entries are:

    DEBIT: Amount owed to creditors
    CREDIT: Cash

Activity 1.1

What are the entries for the following transactions? Ignore VAT for the moment.

Transactions	DEBIT (Dr)	CREDIT (Cr)
Owner puts £500 into the business		
Cash sales of £1,000		
Purchases of £2,500 made on credit		
Credit sales made totalling £5,000		
£2,000 received from debtor		
Business expenses paid of £750		
Drawings made of £1,000		

Tutorial note. If you find this activity difficult, postings are revised in Chapter 2.

3 Capital and revenue items

3.1 The balance sheet

A **balance sheet** is a statement of the assets, liabilities and capital of a business at a given moment in time.

The balance sheet is divided into two halves, showing **capital** in one half and **net assets** (**assets** less **liabilities**) in the other. It reflects the accounting equation, in that **one half must equal the other.**

	£
NAME OF BUSINESS	
BALANCE SHEET AS AT (DATE)	
Assets	X
Less liabilities	(X)
Net assets	X
Capital	X

There are two types of assets.

Fixed (non-current) asset	Current asset
For continuing use in the business not sale	Generally for use within one year
Make a profit over more than one accounting period (eg plant and machinery)	Cash or other assets (stock, debtors) which can be turned into cash within a year

Liabilities in the balance sheet are either **current** (due to be paid within a short period, usually one year) or **long-term**.

3.2 The profit and loss account (income statement)

The profit and loss account (income statement) is a statement which matches the **income** earned in a period with the **expenses** incurred in earning it.

It has the following format:

Sales	X
Less cost of sales	(X)
Gross profit	X
Expenses	(X)
Net profit	X

Activity 1.2

(a) What is the purpose of the balance sheet?

(b) What are:
  (i) Fixed (non-current) assets?
  (ii) Current assets?

(c) What are:
  (i) Current liabilities?
  (ii) Long-term (non-current) liabilities?

3.3 Capital and revenue expenditure

Some items appear in the balance sheet (**capital items**) and some appear in the profit and loss account (income statement) (**revenue items**). You need to tell them apart.

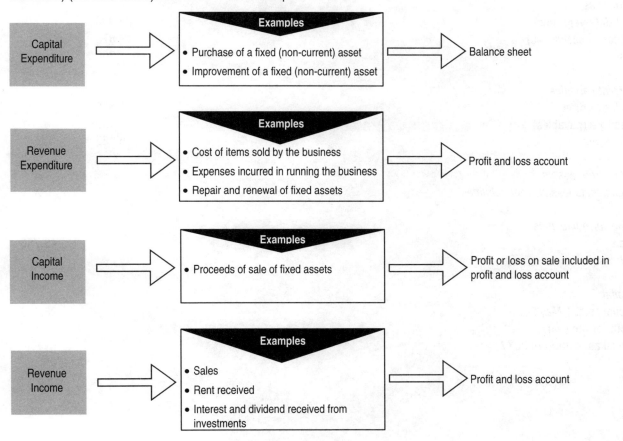

Activity 1.3

What is the difference between capital and revenue expenditure? Why is the distinction important?

Activity 1.4

Set out below are the balance sheet and profit and loss account of Spock Enterprises as at 30 April 20X7.

SPOCK ENTERPRISES
BALANCE SHEET AS AT 30 APRIL 20X7

	£	£
Fixed assets		
Freehold premises		87,500
Fixtures and fittings		14,000
Motor vehicles		15,750
		X
Current assets		
Stocks (inventories)	28,000	
Debtors (receivables)	875	
Cash	700	
	X	
Current liabilities		
Bank overdraft	3,500	
Creditors (payables)	3,150	
Tax payable	6,125	
	X	
Net current assets		X
Total assets less current liabilities		X
Long-term liabilities		
Loan		43,750
Net assets		X
Capital		
Capital as at 1 May 20X6		76,300
Profit for the year		X
Capital as at 30 April 20X7		X

SPOCK ENTERPRISES
PROFIT AND LOSS ACCOUNT FOR THE YEAR ENDED 30 APRIL 20X7

	£	£
Sales		243,775
Cost of sales		152,425
Gross profit		X
Other income		3,500
		X
Selling and distribution expenses	25,725	
Administration expenses	25,900	
Finance expenses	29,225	
		X
Net profit		X

Task

Fill in the missing numbers in the spaces marked with an 'X'. Start with the balance sheet and work down as far as 'net assets'. Insert this figure in the space labelled 'capital as at 30 April 20X7'. You should then be able to work out the other missing numbers.

Tutorial note. Before looking at the solution, check for yourself whether your answer is right by comparing the 'net profit' figure in the profit and loss account with the 'profit for the year' figure in the balance sheet. If your answer is correct, the two figures should be the same.

4 Documenting business transactions

4.1 Documents

- Invoice
- Credit note
- Letter of enquiry
- Quotation
- Sales/purchase order
- Stock (inventory) lists
- Supplier lists
- Staff time sheets
- Goods received/delivered notes
- Till receipts

These two are the most important. Learn their contents in detail. They may be used in multi-part stationery sets.

You will have met most of these documents in Units 1 and 2.

Activity 1.5

List the documents which you would expect to change hands when you have a new roof installed in your house.

The purpose of the **accounting system** is to record, summarise and present the information contained in the documents generated by transactions.

4.2 Discounts

There are two types of discount which you must be able to deal with.

- **Trade discounts** (a reduction in the cost of the goods)
- **Cash discounts** (a reduction in the amount payable for the goods)

Activity 1.6

John Smith, the proprietor of Smith Electrical, is interested in purchasing 60 halogen toasters. The toasters normally sell for £50 but you are able to offer a 20% trade discount and, in addition, a settlement discount of 5%, provided that payment is made within 14 days. John Smith asks you to give him a verbal quotation of exactly how much he would have to pay for the toasters.

Tasks

(a) Clearly showing your workings, calculate how much in total Smith Electrical would have to pay for the toasters if payment was made within 14 days of the sale. Ignore VAT.

(b) Calculate how much would have to be paid if payment was *not* made within 14 days. Ignore VAT.

4.3 VAT

VAT is often thought to be difficult, but the rules for the types of transactions you will deal with are very straightforward.

Rule 1 There are three **rates** of VAT: standard rate (17½%), lower rate (5%) and zero rate. (Any task will always show the VAT rate to be used.)

Rule 2 **Input tax** is paid on goods and services bought by a business; **output tax** is charged on goods and services sold.

Rule 3 Some goods are **exempt** from VAT.

Rule 4 Gross price = net price + VAT.

1: REVISION OF BASIC BOOKKEEPING

Rule 5   VAT included in a gross price can be calculated using the VAT fraction: 17.5/117.5 or 7/47.

Rule 6   Total VAT shown on an invoice should be rounded **down** to the nearest 1p, so £32.439 would be shown as £32.43.

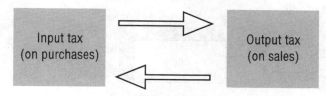

4.3.1 VAT and discounts

When a cash discount is offered, VAT is computed on the amount of the invoice *less* the discount (at the highest rate offered), even if the discount is not taken.

Activity 1.7

Electromarket Ltd, an electrical goods retailer, ordered 20 clock radios from Timewatch Ltd. The radios cost £10 each, plus VAT at 17.5%. Timewatch Ltd offers a 5% discount for payment within 10 days. By mistake, Timewatch Ltd supplied 25 clock radios and issued an invoice for 25. On being informed of its mistake, Timewatch issued a credit note for the 5 radios which were returned.

Tasks

(a)   Calculate the VAT shown on the invoice.
(b)   Calculate the VAT shown on the credit note.

PART A REVISE BOOKKEEPING AND BALANCE BANK TRANSACTIONS

Key learning points

-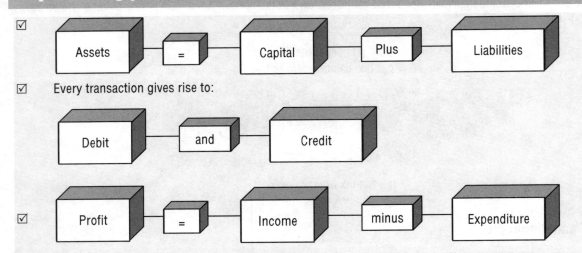

- Every transaction gives rise to:

- A **balance sheet** shows the assets, liabilities and capital at a given moment in time.
- The **profit and loss account** matches income with expenses incurred in earning it.
- **Capital expenditure** is expenditure to improve or acquire fixed assets. It creates or increases fixed assets in the balance sheet.
- **Revenue expenditure** is for maintenance or the trade of the business. It is charged to the profit and loss account.
- VAT on sales is **output tax**. VAT on purchases is **input tax**.
- If output tax exceeds input tax, balance is paid to C+E. If input tax exceeds output tax, balance is repaid by C+E to the business.
- VAT is **always** calculated on the **full discounted** price regardless of whether the discount is taken.
- **VAT** is collected by a business on behalf of HM Customs and Excise (C&E).

Quick quiz

1. What is the accounting equation?

   A Assets + Liabilities = Capital

   B Assets + Capital = Liabilities

   C Assets = Capital + Liabilities

   D Assets = Capital – Liabilities

2. What is a balance sheet?

3. Name two types of discount and distinguish between them.

4. VAT is calculated on the price less _____. *Complete the blanks (2 words).*

Answers to quick quiz

1. **C** Assets = Capital + Liabilities

2. A balance sheet is a statement of the assets, liabilities and capital of a business at a given moment in time.

3. (i) Trade discount is a reduction in the cost of goods.
   (ii) Cash discount is a reduction in the amount payable for the goods.

4. VAT is calculated on the price less **cash discount**.

PART A   REVISE BOOKKEEPING AND BALANCE BANK TRANSACTIONS

Activity checklist

This checklist shows which performance criteria, range statement or knowledge and understanding point is covered by each activity in this chapter. Tick off each activity as you complete it.

Activity

1.1	☐	This activity deals with knowledge and understanding point 5: double entry bookkeeping.
1.2	☐	This activity deals with knowledge and understanding point 7: capital and revenue expenditure.
1.3	☐	This activity deals with knowledge and understanding point 7: capital and revenue expenditure.
1.4	☐	This activity deals with knowledge and understanding point 7: capital and revenue expenditure.
1.5	☐	This activity deals with knowledge and understanding point 1: types of business transactions and the documents involved.
1.6	☐	This activity deals with knowledge and understanding point 1: types of business transactions.
1.7	☐	This activity deals with knowledge and understanding point 2: general principles of VAT.

chapter 2

Recording, summarising and posting transactions

Contents

1. The problem
2. The solution
3. Recording business transactions: an overview
4. The sales day books
5. The purchase day books
6. The cash book
7. The main ledger
8. Double entry book-keeping
9. Posting from the day books

Performance criteria

3.1.A Record details from the relevant primary documentation in the cash book and ledgers
3.1.B Correctly calculate the totals and balances of receipts and payments

Knowledge and understanding

5   Double entry bookkeeping, including balancing accounts
10 Use of the cash book and petty cash book as part of the double entry system or as books of prime entry
12 Relationship between the accounting system and the ledger
14 Methods of posting from primary records to ledger accounts
15 Inter-relationship of accounts – double entry system
19 Relevant understanding of the organisation's accounting systems

1 The problem

Any business produces a lot of documents in the course of trading.

- Invoices for sales and purchases
- Credit notes
- Remittance advices and cheques received
- Petty cash receipts
- Cheque stubs for payments
- Electronic receipts and payments

It is impossible to know how a business is performing by just looking at the **source documents** (the **primary documentation**).

2 The solution

- **Record** each transaction
- **Summarise** a period's transactions
- **Post** the summary to the ledger

This chapter is mainly revision of topics already dealt with in Units 1 and 2. However these subjects are vitally important if you are going to understand bank reconciliations (see Chapter 3) and control accounts (Part B). Finally a trial balance (Part C) could not be prepared without this knowledge.

3 Recording business transactions: an overview

3.1 Why do we need to record source documents?

A business sends out and receives *many* source documents.

The details on these source documents need to be recorded, otherwise the business might forget to ask for some money, or forget to pay some, or even accidentally pay something twice.

It needs to **keep records of source documents** – of transactions – so that it knows what is going on.

3.2 How do we record them?

Books of prime entry form the record of all the documents sent and received by the business.

Book of prime entry	Documents recorded	Summarised and posted to
Sales day book/Sales returns day book	Sales invoices, credit notes sent	Sales (receivables) ledger/control account in main ledger
Purchase day book/Purchase returns day book	Purchase invoices, credit notes received	Purchase (payables) ledger/control account in main ledger
Cash book	Bank transactions	Main ledger
Petty cash book	Notes and coin paid and received	Main ledger
Journal	Adjustments	Main ledger

The journal will be dealt with in Chapter 7.

Activity 2.1

State which books of prime entry the following transactions would be entered into.

(a) Your business pays A Brown (a supplier) £450.
(b) You send D Steptoe (a customer) an invoice for £650.
(c) You receive an invoice from A Brown for £300.
(d) You pay D Steptoe £500.
(e) F Jones (a customer) returns goods to the value of £250.
(f) You return goods to J Green to the value of £504.
(g) F Jones pays you £500.

TERMINOLOGY ALERT

The AAT uses specific terminology.

Main ledger – this is the same as **general or nominal ledger**.

Subsidiary ledger – this is the same as:

- **Sales (debtors or receivables) ledger AND**
- **Purchases (creditors or payables) ledger**

In this text we will use the terms sales ledger and purchases ledger rather than subsidiary ledger because you need to tell them apart. Be prepared to meet 'subsidiary ledger' in a simulation or exam.

3.3 Summarising source documents

Ledger used	Need for summary
Subsidiary ledgers Sales ledger Purchases ledger	Summaries need to be kept of all the transactions undertaken with an **individual** supplier or customer - invoices, credit notes, cash - so that a net amount due or owed can be calculated.
Main ledger (a) Sales ledger control account (b) Purchases ledger control account	Summaries need to be kept of the **total** transactions undertaken with all suppliers and customers, so a total for debtors and a total for creditors can be calculated.

We will look at control accounts in more detail later in this Text.

3.4 Posting to the ledgers

Have a look at the diagram on the next page. It shows how items are **posted** to (**entered in**) the ledgers, ultimately to arrive at the financial statements.

Don't worry that some of the terms are unfamiliar. Keep referring back to this diagram as you work through the Text. It will soon make sense.

In Units 1 and 2 you covered the sales and purchase day books and the cash book. We will revise these briefly before going on to see how transactions are posted to the ledgers.

4 The sales day books

4.1 Sales Day book

The **sales day book** is a list of all invoices sent out to **customers** each day.

The following is an extract from a sales day book. Ignore VAT for the moment.

SALES DAY BOOK

Date	Invoice number (2)	Customer	Sales ledger Code	Total amount invoiced £
20X7				
Jan 10	247	James Ltd	J14	105.00
	248	Steptoe & Son	S8	86.40
	249	Talbot & Co	T6	31.80
	250	John Silvertown	S9	1,264.60
				1,487.80

(1) The column called 'sales ledger code' identifies that particular customer in the sales ledger.

2: RECORDING, SUMMARISING AND POSTING TRANSACTIONS

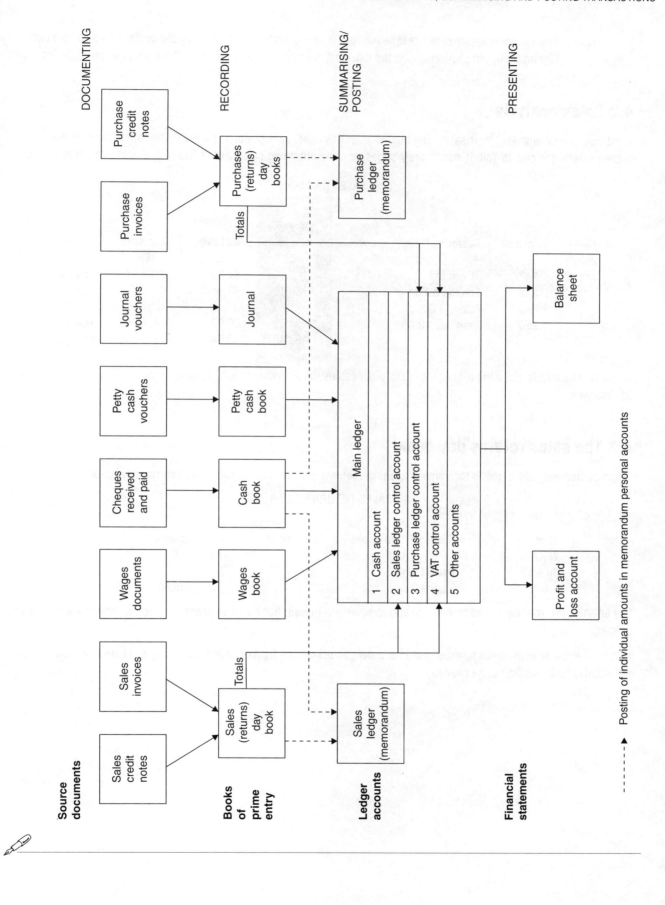

(2) The invoice number is the **unique number** given to each sales invoice by the business's sales system. Listing them out sequentially in the sales day book helps us to see that all the invoices are included.

4.2 Sales analysis

Most businesses 'analyse' their sales. The business, in this case, sells boots and shoes. The sale to Steptoe was entirely boots, the sale to Talbot was entirely shoes, and the other two sales were a mixture of both. VAT is at 17.5%.

SALES DAY BOOK

Date 20X7	Invoice	Customer	Sales ledger code	Total amount invoiced £	Boot sales £	Shoe sales £	VAT £
Jan 10	247	James Ltd	J14	105.00	60.00	29.37	15.63
	248	Steptoe & Son	S8	86.40	73.54		12.86
	249	Talbot & Co	T6	31.80		27.07	4.73
	250	John Silvertown	S9	1,264.60	800.00	276.26	188.34
				1,487.80	933.54	332.70	221.56

This sort of analysis gives the managers of the business useful information which helps them to decide how best to run the business.

4.3 The sales returns day book

When customers return goods for some reason, the returns are recorded in the **sales returns day book**.

SALES RETURNS DAY BOOK

Date 20X7	Customer and goods	Sales ledger code	Amount £
30 April	Owen Plenty		
	3 pairs 'Texas' boots	P7	135.00

Not all sales returns day books analyse what goods were returned, but it makes sense to keep as complete a record as possible.

If there are few returns, sales returns could be shown as **bracketed figures in the sales day book**. In this case, a sales returns day book would not be needed.

5 The purchase day books

5.1 Purchase day book

The **purchase day book** is the record of all the invoices received from **suppliers.**

An extract from a purchase day book might look like this (assuming VAT @ 17.5%).

PURCHASE DAY BOOK

Date	Supplier (2)	Purchase ledger code (1)	Total amount invoiced	Purchases (3)	Stationery	VAT
20X7			£	£	£	£
Mar 15	Sugar & Spice	S31	315.00	268.09		46.91
	F Seager	S46	29.40	25.03		4.37
	ABC	A42	116.80		99.41	17.39
	Shabnum Rashid	R12	100.00	85.11		14.89
			561.20	378.23	99.41	83.56

(1) The 'purchase ledger code' is a reference to the individual supplier in the purchase ledger.

(2) There is no 'invoice number' column, because the purchase day book records **other people's invoices**, which have all sorts of different numbers. Sometimes, however, a purchase day book may allocate an internal number to an invoice.

(3) Like the sales day book, the purchase day book analyses the invoices which have been sent in. In this example, three of the invoices related to goods which the business intends to re-sell (called simply 'purchases') and the other invoice was for stationery.

5.2 The purchase returns day book

The **purchase returns day book** records credit notes received for goods sent back to the suppliers.

The business expects a **credit note** from the supplier. In the meantime it may send the supplier a **debit note**, indicating the amount it expects its total debt to be reduced.

An extract from the purchase returns day book might look like this.

PURCHASE RETURNS DAY BOOK

Date	Supplier and goods	Purchase ledger code	Amount
20X7			£
29 April	Boxes Ltd		
	300 cardboard boxes	B27	46.60

Again, purchase returns could be shown as **bracketed figures** in the purchase day book.

6 The cash book

6.1 The cash book

The **cash book** is used to keep a cumulative record of money received and money paid out by the business **via its bank account**.

This could be money received **on the business premises** in notes, coins and cheques which are subsequently banked. There are also receipts and payments made by bank transfer, standing order, direct debit, BACS and, in the case of bank interest and charges, directly by the bank.

One part of the cash book is used to record **receipts**, and another part to **record payments**. Below is a summary of what a cash book looks like. We have received £100 from a customer and paid £90 to a supplier. These amounts will be analysed in the cash book and posted to the general ledger.

LEFT HAND SIDE: RECEIPTS					RIGHT HAND SIDE: PAYMENTS				
Date	Narrative	Discount allowed	Total receipt	Analysis	Date	Narrative	Discount received	Total payment	Analysis
		£10	£100	£100			£7	£90	£90

Note the following points about this cash book.

(a) It represents two sides of a **ledger account**: the left hand receipts side is DEBIT, the right hand payments side is CREDIT.

(b) It is a **two-column cash book** - on the debit side there are two columns: one column for total receipts and one for discounts allowed; on the credit side there are also two columns – one for total payments and one for discounts received.

(c) Discounts allowed and received are **memorandum columns** only - they do not represent cash movements.

(d) On each side, the 'analysis' can be one or more columns; **the total of the analysis columns *always* equals the total column**.

The best way to see how the cash book works is to follow through an example. **Note that in this example we are going to ignore VAT,** in order to simplify the workings.

Example: Cash book

On 1 September 20X7, Liz Cullis had £900 in the bank. During the day, Liz had the following receipts and payments.

(a) Cash sale: receipt of £80
(b) Payment from credit customer Hay: £400 less discount allowed £20
(c) Payment from credit customer Been: £720
(d) Payment from credit customer Seed: £1,000 less discount allowed £40
(e) Cash sale: receipt of £150
(f) Cash received for sale of machine: £200
(g) Payment to supplier Kew: £120
(h) Payment to supplier Hare: £310
(i) Payment of telephone bill: £400
(j) Payment of gas bill: £280
(k) Payment of £1,500 to Hess for new plant and machinery

If you look through these transactions, you will see that six of them are receipts and five of them are payments.

Now we will calculate Liz's closing balance.

Solution

The cash book for Liz Cullis is shown on the following page.

6.2 Balancing the cash book

You will remember this from Units 1 and 2.

At the beginning of the day there is a debit **opening balance** of £900 on Liz Cullis's cash book. During the day, the total receipts and payments were as follows.

	£
Opening balance	900
Receipts (3,390 – 900)	2,490
	3,390
Payments	(2,610)
Closing balance	780

The **closing balance** of £780 represents the excess of receipts over payments. It means that Liz Cullis still has cash available at the end of the day, so she 'carries it down' at the end of 1 September from the payments side of the cash book, and 'brings it down' at the beginning of 2 September to the receipts side of the cash book.

In other words, the cash book is balanced just like any other ledger account, as we saw in Units 1 and 2.

PART A   REVISE BOOKKEEPING AND BALANCE BANK TRANSACTIONS

LIZ CULLIS: CASH BOOK

RECEIPTS

Date 20X7	Narrative		Discount allowed £	Total £	Receipts from customers £	Cash sales £	Other £
1 Sept	Balance b/d *			900			
	(a) Cash sale			80		80	
	(b) Customer pays: Hay	SL96	20	380	380		
	(c) Customer pays: Been	SL632		720	720		
	(d) Customer pays: Seed	SL501	40	960	960		
	(e) Cash sale			150		150	
	(f) Non-current asset sale			200			200
			60	3,390	2,060	230	200
2 Sept	Balance b/f **						

* (= opening balance)
** (= new opening balance)

PAYMENTS

Date 20X7	Narrative		Total £	Payments to suppliers £	Expenses £	Fixed assets £
1 Sept	(g) Supplier paid: Kew	PL543	120	120		
	(h) Supplier paid: Hare	PL76	310	310		
	(i) Telephone expense		400		400	
	(j) Gas expense		280		280	
	(k) Plant and machinery		1,500			1,500
			2,610	430	680	1,500
			780			
			3,390	430	680	1,500

Note: In order to cross cast the receipts section the opening balance of £900 should be deducted from the total column. The discount allowed of £60 is a memorandum item only and is not included.

6.3 Bank statements

Weekly or monthly, a business will receive a **bank statement**. Bank statements should be used to check that the amount shown as a balance in the cash book agrees with the amount on the bank statement, and that no cash has 'gone missing'.

This is called a **bank reconciliation** (see Chapter 3).

6.4 Petty cash book

The **petty cash book** keeps a cumulative record of the **small amounts** of cash received into and paid out of the cash float.

You have already covered it in Units 1 and 2.

7 The main ledger

7.1 The main ledger

The **main ledger** summarises the financial affairs of a business. It contains details of assets, liabilities and capital, income and expenditure and so profit and loss.

It consists of a large number of different **ledger accounts**, each account having its own purpose or 'name' and an identity or code. Other names for the main ledger are the **nominal ledger** or **general ledger**.

7.2 Posting to the main ledger

Transactions are **posted** to accounts in the main ledger from the books of prime entry.

Posting is often done in total (ie all sales invoices in the sales day book for a day are added up and the total is posted to the sales ledger control account). However individual transactions are also posted (eg purchase of fixed assets).

PART A   REVISE BOOKKEEPING AND BALANCE BANK TRANSACTIONS

Here are some examples of ledger accounts in the main ledger.

Ledger account	Fixed asset	Current asset	Current liability	Long-term liability	Capital	Expense	Income
Plant and machinery at cost	✓						
Motor vehicles at cost	✓						
Proprietor's capital					✓		
Purchases of raw materials						✓	
Stock of raw materials		✓					
Sales ledger control		✓					
Purchases ledger control			✓				
Wages and salaries						✓	
Rent and rates						✓	
Advertising expenses						✓	
Bank charges						✓	
Motor expenses						✓	
Telephone expenses						✓	
Sales							✓
Cash		✓					
Bank overdraft			✓				
Bank loan				✓			

7.3 The format of a ledger account

If a ledger account is kept in an actual book rather than as a computer record, it usually looks like this.

ADVERTISING EXPENSES

Date	Narrative	Ref	£	Date	Narrative	Ref	£
20X7							
15 April	AbFab Agency for quarter to 31 March	PL 348	2,500				

There are two sides to the account, and an account heading on top, and so it is convenient to think in terms of 'T' accounts.

NAME OF ACCOUNT

DEBIT SIDE	£	CREDIT SIDE	£

We have already seen this with Liz Cullis's cash book. We will now go on to use the cash book to demonstrate the double-entry bookkeeping.

8 Double entry book-keeping

8.1 Double entry

As we saw in Chapter 1, every financial transaction gives rise to two accounting entries, one a debit and the other a credit.

The following may help you to remember how entries are posted.

Debits	**C**redits
increase	increase
Expenses	**L**iabilities
Assets	**I**ncome
Drawings	**C**apital
decrease	decrease
Liabilities	Assets
DEAD	**CLIC**

8.2 Cash transactions

The cash book is a good starting point for understanding double entry. Remember:

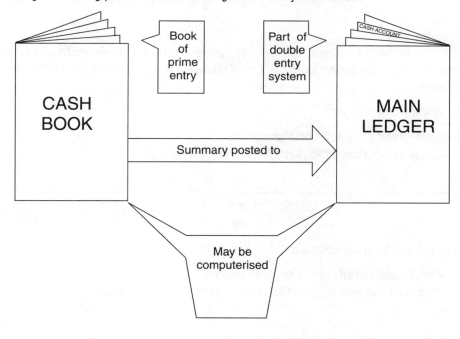

PART A   REVISE BOOKKEEPING AND BALANCE BANK TRANSACTIONS

Here are the main cash transactions.

Cash transactions	DR	CR
Sell goods for cash	Cash	Sales
Buy goods for cash	Purchases	Cash
Pay an expense	Expense a/c	Cash

Example: Double entry for cash transactions

In the cash book of a business, the following transactions have been recorded.

(a)   A cash sale (ie a receipt) of £2,000
(b)   Payment of a rent bill totalling £150
(c)   Buying some goods for cash at £100
(d)   Buying office furniture for cash at £2,000

How would these four transactions be posted to the ledger accounts? For that matter, which ledger accounts should they be posted to? Don't forget that each transaction will be posted twice, in accordance with the rule of double entry.

Solution

(a)   The two sides of the transaction are:

   (i)   Cash is received (**debit** entry in the cash account as the asset of cash is increased)
   (ii) Sales increase by £2,000 (**credit** entry in the sales account as income increases)

SALES ACCOUNT

	£		£
		Cash a/c	2,000

(Note how the entry in the cash account (at the end of this solution) is cross-referenced to the sales account and vice-versa. This enables a person looking at one of the accounts to trace where the other half of the double entry can be found.)

(b)   The two sides of the transaction are:

   (i)   Cash is paid (**credit** entry in the cash account)
   (ii) Rent expense increases by £150 (**debit** entry in the rent account)

RENT ACCOUNT

	£		£
Cash a/c	150		

(c)   The two sides of the transaction are:

   (i)   Cash is paid (**credit** entry in the cash account)
   (ii) Purchases increase by £100 (**debit** entry in the purchases account)

PURCHASES ACCOUNT

	£		£
Cash a/c	100		

(d) The two sides of the transaction are:

(i) Cash is paid (**credit** entry in the cash account)

(ii) Assets – in this case, shelves – increase by £2,000 (**debit** entry in office furniture account)

OFFICE FURNITURE (ASSET) ACCOUNT

	£		£
Cash a/c	2,000		

If all four of these transactions related to the same business, the **summary cash account** would end up looking like this.

CASH ACCOUNT

	£		£
Sales a/c	2,000	Rent a/c	150
		Purchases a/c	100
		Office furniture a/c	2,000

Activity 2.2

In the cash book of a business, the following transactions have been recorded on 7 April 20X7.

(a) A cash sale (ie a receipt) of £60
(b) Payment of rent totalling £4,500
(c) Buying some goods for cash at £3,000
(d) Buying some shelves for cash at £6,000

Task

Draw the appropriate ledger ('T') accounts and show how these four transactions would be posted to them.

8.3 Credit transactions

Not all transactions are settled immediately in cash.

(a) A business purchases goods on **credit terms**, so that the suppliers are **creditors** of the business until settlement is made in cash.

(b) The business grants credit terms to its customers, who are **debtors** of the business.

PART A REVISE BOOKKEEPING AND BALANCE BANK TRANSACTIONS

No entries can be made in the cash book, because initially no cash has been received or paid. Where then can the details of the transactions be posted?

The solution to this problem is to use **ledger accounts for debtors and creditors**.

CREDIT TRANSACTIONS	DR	CR
Sell goods on credit terms	Debtors	Sales
Receive cash from debtor	Cash	Debtors
Net effect = cash transaction	Cash	Sales
Buy goods on credit terms	Purchases	Creditors
Pay cash to creditor	Creditors	Cash
Net effect = cash transaction	Purchases	Cash

The net effect in the ledger accounts is the same as for a cash transaction - the only difference is that there has been a time delay during which the debtor/creditor accounts have been used.

Example: Credit transactions

(a) The business sells goods on credit to a customer Mr A for £2,000.
(b) The business buys goods on credit from a supplier B Ltd for £100.

How and where are these transactions posted in the ledger accounts?

Solution

(a)

DEBTORS ACCOUNT

	£		£
Sales a/c	2,000		

SALES ACCOUNT

	£		£
		Debtors account (Mr A)	2,000

(b)

CREDITORS ACCOUNT

	£		£
		Purchases a/c	100

PURCHASES ACCOUNT

	£		£
Creditors a/c (B Ltd)	100		

Example continued: When cash is paid to creditors or by debtors

The business paid £100 to B Ltd one month after the goods were acquired. The two sides of this new transaction are:

(a) Cash is paid (**credit** entry in the cash account).
(b) The amount owing to creditors is reduced (**debit** entry in the creditors account).

CASH ACCOUNT

	£		£
		Creditors a/c (B Ltd)	100

CREDITORS ACCOUNT

	£		£
Cash a/c	100		

If we now bring together the two parts of this example, the original purchase of goods on credit and the eventual settlement in cash, we find that the accounts appear as follows.

CASH ACCOUNT

	£		£
		Creditors a/c	100

PURCHASES ACCOUNT

	£		£
Creditors a/c	100		

CREDITORS ACCOUNT

	£		£
Cash a/c	100	Purchases a/c	100

The **two entries in the creditors account cancel each other out**, indicating that no money is owing to creditors. We are left with a credit entry of £100 in the cash account and a debit entry of £100 in the purchases account. These are exactly the same entries as a **cash** purchase of £100.

Similar reasoning applies when a **customer settles his debt**. In the example above, when Mr A pays his debt of £2,000 the two sides of the transaction are:

- Cash is received (debit entry in the cash account)
- The amount owed by debtors is reduced (credit entry in the debtors account)

CASH ACCOUNT

	£		£
Debtors a/c (Mr A)	2,000		

DEBTORS ACCOUNT

	£		£
		Cash a/c	2,000

The accounts recording this sale to, and payment by, Mr A now appear as follows.

CASH ACCOUNT

	£		£
Debtors a/c	2,000		

SALES ACCOUNT

	£		£
		Debtors a/c	2,000

DEBTORS ACCOUNT

	£		£
Sales a/c	2,000	Cash a/c	2,000

The **two entries in the debtors account cancel each other out**, while the entries in the cash account and sales account reflect the same position as if the sale had been made for cash.

Activity 2.3

Identify the debit and credit entries in the following transactions.

(a) Bought a machine on credit from A, cost £8,000
(b) Bought goods on credit from B, cost £500
(c) Sold goods on credit to C, value £1,200
(d) Paid D (a creditor) £300
(e) Collected £180 from E, a debtor
(f) Paid wages £4,000

(g) Received rent bill of £700 from landlord G
(h) Paid rent of £700 to landlord G
(i) Paid insurance premium £90

Activity 2.4

Your business, which is not registered for VAT, has the following transactions.

(a) The sale of goods on credit
(b) Credit notes to credit customers upon the return of faulty goods
(c) Daily cash takings paid into the bank

Task

For each transaction complete the following grid:

Transaction	Original documents	Book of prime entry	Main ledger entry	
			Dr	Cr
(a)				
(b)				
(c)				

9 Posting from the day books

9.1 Sales day book to sales ledger control account

Earlier we used four transactions entered into the sales day book.

SALES DAY BOOK

Date 20X7	Invoice	Customer	Sales ledger ref	Total amount invoiced £	Boot sales £	Shoe sales £	VAT £
Jan 10	247	James Ltd	SL 14	105.00	60.00	29.37	15.63
	248	Steptoe & Son	SL 8	86.40	73.54		12.86
	249	Talbot & Co	SL 6	31.80		27.07	4.73
	250	John Silvertown	SL 9	1,264.60	800.00	276.26	188.34
				1,487.80	933.54	332.70	221.56

We post the total of the **total amount invoiced column** to the **debit** side of the **sales ledger control account**. The **credit** entries would be to the different **sales accounts,** (boot sales and shoe sales) and **VAT control account**.

The posting to the sales ledger control account is usually just the total amount, but could be analysed as shown here.

PART A REVISE BOOKKEEPING AND BALANCE BANK TRANSACTIONS

SALES LEDGER CONTROL ACCOUNT (SLCA)

	£		£
Boot sales	933.54		
Shoes sales	332.70		
VAT Control	221.56		
	1,487.80		

BOOT SALES

	£		£
		SLCA	933.54

SHOE SALES

	£		£
		SLCA	332.70

VAT CONTROL

	£		£
		Sales ledger control account (SLCA)	221.56

That is why the analysis of sales is made, and why we analyse items in other books of prime entry.

Do we know how much we are owed by individual debtors? The answer is no. Therefore we keep two sets of accounts running in parallel – **sales ledger control account** in the main ledger and the memorandum **sales ledger** (individual debtor accounts). **The sales ledger was covered in detail in Unit 1**.

REMEMBER!

Only the sales ledger control account is actually part of the double-entry system. The **individual** customers' transactions are posted to the sales ledger from the sales day book, as a memorandum.

9.2 Purchase day book to purchase ledger control account

Here is the page of the purchase day book which we saw in Section 5.1.

PURCHASE DAY BOOK

Date 20X7	Supplier	Purchase ledger ref	Total amount invoiced £	Purchases £	Expenses £	VAT £
Mar 15	Sugar & Spice	PL 31	315.00	268.09		46.91
	F Seager	PL 46	29.40	25.03		4.37
	ABC	PL 42	116.80		99.41	17.39
	Shabnum Rashid	PL 12	100.00	85.11		14.89
			561.20	378.23	99.41	83.56

This time we will post the total of the total amount invoiced column to the credit side of the purchase ledger control account. The debit entries are to the different expense accounts and VAT.

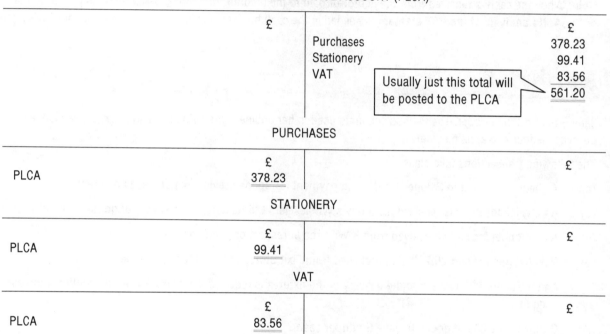

Again, we keep a separate record of how much we owe individual creditors by keeping two sets of accounts running in parallel – **the purchase ledger control account** in the main ledger, part of the double-entry system, and the memorandum **purchase ledger** (individual creditors accounts). We enter individual creditors transactions in their purchase ledger account from the purchase day book. **The purchase ledger was covered in detail in Unit 2**.

9.3 Section summary

CREDIT TRANSACTIONS	DR		CR	
	Memorandum	*Main ledger**	*Main ledger**	*Memorandum*
Sell goods to John Silvertown	Sales ledger: John Silvertown	SLCA (gross amount)	Sales (net) VAT	– –
Receive cash from John Silvertown	–	Cash a/c	SLCA	Sales ledger: John Silvertown
Buy goods from Sugar & Spice	–	Purchases (net) VAT	PLCA (gross amount)	Purchase ledger: Sugar & Spice
Pay cash to Sugar & Spice	Purchase ledger: Sugar & Spice	PLCA	Cash a/c	–

*Individual transactions included in **totals** posted from books of prime entry.

Note: When the cash is received from the debtor or paid to the creditor, the **total gross amount** is posted to the SLCA or PLCA. **No analysis of the VAT element** is needed in the cash book as this was done when the invoice was posted.

Activity 2.5

Jane Smith is a sole trader. The various accounts used in her business are held in a cash book, a sales ledger, a purchase ledger and a main ledger.

The following transactions take place.

(a)   A cheque is issued to P Jones for £264 in payment for goods previously purchased on credit.

(b)   An invoice for £850 is received from Davis Wholesalers Ltd relating to the supply of goods on credit.

(c)   A credit note for £42 is received from K Williams in respect of goods returned.

(d)   New fixtures costing £5,720 are purchased from Fixit Stores and paid for by cheque.

(e)   An invoice for £25 relating to the delivery of the fixtures is received from Fixit Stores and settled immediately by cheque.

(f)   G Cullis sells £85 of goods to Jane Smith for cash.

(g)   An invoice is issued to R Newman for £340 relating to the purchase by him of goods on credit.

(h)   An insurance premium of £64 is paid to Insureburn Ltd by cheque.

(i)   A cheque for £40 received previously from J Baxter, a credit customer, is now returned unpaid by the bank.

Task

For each transaction in Jane Smith's books complete the following table:

| | Main ledger | | Subsidiary ledger | |
	DR	CR	DR	CR
(a)				
(b)				
(c)				
(d)				
(e)				
(f)				
(g)				
(h)				
(i)				

Activity 2.6

Your business has the following transactions.

(a) The purchase of goods on credit
(b) Allowances to credit customers upon the return of faulty goods (sales returns)
(c) Refund from petty cash to an employee of an amount spent on entertaining a client

Task

For each transaction identify clearly:

(a) The original document(s)
(b) The book of prime entry for the transaction
(c) The postings in the double entry system

Key learning points

- Business transactions are initially recorded on **source documents**. Records of the details on these documents are made in books of prime entry.

- The main **books of prime entry** are as follows.
    - Sales day book
    - Purchase day book
    - Cash book
    - Petty cash book
    - Journal

- Most accounts are contained in the **main ledger** (or **general or nominal ledger**).

- The rules of double entry state that every financial transaction gives rise to **two accounting entries**, one a **debit**, the other a **credit**. It is vital that you understand this principle.

- A **debit** is one of:
    - An increase in an asset
    - An increase in an expense
    - A decrease in a liability

- A **credit** is one of:
    - An increase in a liability
    - An increase in income
    - A decrease in an asset

- The **sales ledger** and **purchase ledger** are **subsidiary ledgers** which contain **memorandum** accounts for each individual debtor and creditor. They do not (usually) form part of the double entry system.

Quick quiz

1. Books of prime entry record all the documented _____ undertaken by the business. *Complete the blank.*
2. What is recorded in the sales day book?
3. A debit entry on an asset account decreases the asset. True or false?
4. What is the double entry when goods are sold for cash?
5. What is the double entry when goods are purchased on credit?

Answers to quick quiz

1. Books of prime entry record all the documented **transactions** undertaken by the business.
2. The sales day book records the invoices sent out to customers each day.
3. False. It increases the asset balance.
4. *Debit* Cash; *Credit* Sales.
5. *Debit* Purchases; *Credit* Purchase ledger control account.

Activity checklist

This checklist shows which performance criteria, range statement or knowledge and understanding point is covered by each activity in this chapter. Tick off each activity as you complete it.

Activity		
2.1		This activity deals with knowledge and understanding point 19: relevant understanding of the organisation's accounting systems.
2.2		This activity deals with knowledge and understanding point 5: double entry bookkeeping and performance criteria 3.1.B
2.3		This activity deals with knowledge and understanding point 5: double entry bookkeeping and performance criteria 3.1.A
2.4		This activity deals with knowledge and understanding point 5: double entry bookkeeping and performance criteria 3.1.A
2.5		This activity deals with knowledge and understanding point 5: double entry bookkeeping and performance criteria 3.1.A
2.6		This activity deals with knowledge and understanding point 5: double entry bookkeeping and performance criteria 3.1.A

PART A REVISE BOOKKEEPING AND BALANCE BANK TRANSACTIONS

chapter 3

Bank reconciliations

Contents

1. The problem
2. The solution
3. Bank reconciliations
4. The bank statement
5. How to perform a bank reconciliation
6. Reconciliations on a computerised system
7. Bank services and types of account

Performance criteria

- 3.1.A Record details from the relevant primary documentation in the cash book and ledgers
- 3.1.B Correctly calculate totals and balances of receipts and payments
- 3.1.C Compare individual items on the bank statement and in the cash book for accuracy
- 3.1.D Identify discrepancies and prepare a bank reconciliation statement

Range statement

- 3.1.1 Primary documentation: credit transfer; standing order and direct debit schedules; bank statement
- 3.1.2 Cash book and ledgers: manual; computerised
- 3.1.3 Discrepancies: differences identified by the matching process
- 3.1.4 Bank reconciliation statement: manual; computerised

Knowledge and understanding

- 3 General bank services and operation of bank clearing system
- 4 Function and form of banking documentation
- 11 Identification of different types of errors

PART A   REVISE BOOKKEEPING AND BALANCE BANK TRANSACTIONS

1 The problem

By now you'll be familiar with the cash book. But this is a record of the amount of cash the business **thinks** it has in the bank.

You, too, may have an idea of what your bank balance should be. But then you get your bank statement, and the amount is rather different…

2 The solution

A bank reconciliation compares entries in the cash book and the bank statement and identifies differences.

3 Bank reconciliations

3.1 Why is a bank reconciliation necessary?

Why might your own estimate of your bank balance be different from the amount shown on your bank statement? There are three common explanations.

Cause of difference	Explanation
Errors	Errors in calculation, or in recording income and payments, are as likely to have been made by yourself as the bank. These **errors must be corrected**.
Bank charges or bank interest	The bank might deduct interest on an overdraft or charges for its services, which you are not informed about until you receive the bank statement. **These should be accounted for in your records**.
Timing differences	(a) **Cheques recorded as received** and paid-in but not yet 'cleared' and added to your account by the bank. This will be resolved in a very short time when the cheques are eventually cleared. (b) **Payments made by cheque** and recorded, but not yet banked by the payee. Even when they are banked, it takes a day or two for the banks to process them and for the money to be deducted from your account. These are known as **unpresented cheques**.

4 The bank statement

It is common practice for a bank to issue a monthly **statement** to each customer, itemising:

- The **balance** on the account **at the beginning** of the month
- Deposits and receipts due to the customer during the month
- **Payments** made by the customer during the month
- The **balance** the customer has on his account **at the end of the month**

REMEMBER!

If you have money in your account, **the bank owes you that money**, and you are a **creditor** of the bank. (If you are in 'credit', you have money in your bank account.)

However, in your books of account, if you have money in your account it is an asset (a **debit** balance) and the bank owes you that money (is your **debtor**).

If a business has £8,000 in the bank. It will have a debit balance in its own cash book, but the bank statement will show a credit balance of £8,000.

The bank's records are a 'mirror image' of the customer's own records, with debits and credits reversed. It is similar to a supplier's statement, which records the supplier's sales but the customer's purchases.

4.1 What does a bank statement look like?

An example of a bank statement is shown below; nearly all bank statements will look something like this.

Southern Bank CONFIDENTIAL

200 BROMFORD AVENUE
LONDON
E11 8TH

Account: ABC & CO.
4 THE MEWS
LONDON E4 2P2

SHEET NO 52 (d)

Telephone 020 8359 3100

20X2 Statement date 13 JUN 20X2 (a) Account no 9309823 (b)

Date	Details	Withdrawals	Deposits	Balance (£)
(c) 11MAY	Balance from Sheet no. 51 (d)			(f) 787.58
14MAY	000059 (g)	216.81		570.77
22MAY	000058	157.37		413.40
24MAY	000060	22.00		391.40
29MAY	LION INSURANCE DD (i)	87.32		
	CATS238/ 948392093 DD	1,140.10		
	LB HACKBETH CC SO (j)	54.69		
	COUNTER CREDIT 101479 (h)		469.86	
	INTEREST (l)	9.32		
	CHARGES (k)	30.00		460.17 O/D
13JUN	Balance to Sheet no. 53			(f) 460.17 O/D

(e) **Key**
SO Standing Order DV Dividend CC Cash &/or Cheques Auto Withdrawals AC Automated cash PY Payroll Interest - see over
EC Eurocheque TR Transfer CP Card Purchases DD Direct Debit OD Overdrawn

PART A   REVISE BOOKKEEPING AND BALANCE BANK TRANSACTIONS

Letter	Item	Explanation
(a)	Statement date	Only transactions which have passed through your account **up to this date** (and since the last statement date) will be shown on the statement.
(b)	Account number	This number is required on the statement, particularly if the bank's customer has **more than one account**.
(c)	Date	This shows the date any transaction **cleared** into or out of your account. You may have made the transaction earlier.
(d)	Sheet number	Each bank statement received will have a number. The numbers run in **sequential order**; this shows if a statement is missing.
(e)	Key	Not all bank statements will have a key to the abbreviations they use but it is helpful when one is provided. Note the following. • **Dividends** can be paid directly into a bank account. • **Automated cash** is a withdrawal from an automated teller machine - unusual for a business. • **Card purchase** is a purchase by debit card, again unusual for a business.
(f)	Balance	Most statements show a balance as at the end of each day's transactions.
(g)	Cheque numbers	The number is the same as that which appears on the individual cheque. Numbers are necessary to help you to **identify items** on the statement: you could not do so if only the amount of the cheque appeared.
(h)	Paying-in slip numbers	The need for these numbers is the same as for cheques.
(i)	Direct debit payments and receipts	The **recipient** of the direct debit payment is usually identified, either in words or by an account number.
(j)	Standing order payments and receipts	Again, the recipient is identifiable.
(k)	Charges	Based on the **number of transactions** (cheques, receipts and so on) which have been processed through your account in a given period (usually a quarter).
(l)	Interest	Interest is charged on the amount of an **overdrawn balance** for the period it is overdrawn.

Activity 3.1

The bank statement of Gary Jones Trading Ltd for the month of February 20X7 is shown below.

Task

You are required to explain briefly the shaded items on the statement.

Southern Bank   CONFIDENTIAL

Clapham Common Branch
Clapham Common
London SW6

Account: Four Corners Trading Ltd
3 Barnes Street
Clapham SW6

SHEET NO 72

Telephone 020 7728 4213

20X7   Statement date 28 February 20X7   Account no 01140146

Date	Details		Withdrawals	Deposits	Balance (£)
	Balance brought forward				1,225.37
1 Feb	Cheque	800120	420.00		805.37
4 Feb	Cheque	800119	135.40		669.97
7 Feb	Bank giro credit	Pronto Motors		162.40	
7 Feb	Credit			380.75	
7 Feb	BACS	7492	124.20		1,088.92
9 Feb	Cheque	800121	824.70		264.22
11 Feb	Cheque	800122	323.25		59.03 OD
14 Feb	Credit			522.70	463.67
19 Feb	Credit			122.08	585.75
21 Feb	BACS		124.20		
21 Feb	Direct debit	Swingate Ltd	121.00		340.55
23 Feb	Bank giro credit	Bord & Sons		194.60	535.15
25 Feb	Cheque	800123	150.00		385.15
27 Feb	Credit			242.18	627.33
28 Feb	Bank charges		15.40		611.93
28 Feb	Balance to Sheet no.	73			611.93

5 How to perform a bank reconciliation

5.1 The reconciliation

The **cash book and bank statement will rarely agree at a given date**. Several procedures should be followed to ensure that the reconciliation between them is performed correctly.

Step 1   Identify the cash book balance and the bank balance (from the bank statement) on the date to which you wish to reconcile.

Step 2   Cross cast the cash book for the period since the last reconciliation and identify and note any errors found. It is important to cross cast the cash book as a means of verifying that the balance is correct.

Step 3   Examine the bank statements for the same period and identify those items which appear on the bank statement but which have not been entered in the cash book.

- Standing orders and direct debits (into and out of the account)
- Dividend receipts from investments
- Bank charges and interest

Make a list of all those found.

Step 4   Identify all reconciling items due to timing differences.

(a)   Some cheque payments entered in the cash book have not yet been presented to the bank, or 'cleared', and so do not yet appear on the bank statement.

(b)   Cheques received, entered in the cash book and paid into the bank, but which have not yet been cleared and entered in the account by the bank, do not yet appear on the bank statement.

5.2 What does a bank reconciliation look like?

ADJUSTED CASH BOOK BALANCE

	£	£
Cash book balance brought down		X
Add: correction of understatement	X	
receipts not entered in cash book (standing orders, direct debits)	X	
		X
Less: correction of overstatement	X	
payments/charges not entered in cash book (standing orders, direct debits)	X	
		(X)
Corrected cash book balance		A

BANK RECONCILIATION	£
Balance per bank statement	X
Add: cheques paid in and recorded in the cash book but not yet credited to the account by the bank (**outstanding lodgements**)	X
Less: cheques paid by the business but not yet presented to the business's bank for settlement (**unpresented cheques**)	(X)
Balance per cash book	A

Example: Bank reconciliation

At 30 September 20X3 the debit balance in the cash book of Dotcom Ltd was £805.15. A bank statement on 30 September 20X3 showed Dotcom Ltd to be in credit by £1,112.30.

On investigation of the difference between the two sums, three things come to light.

(a) The cash book had been added up wrongly on the debit side; it should have been £90.00 more.
(b) Cheques paid in but not yet credited by the bank amounted to £208.20.
(c) Cheques drawn but not yet presented to the bank amounted to £425.35.

We need to show the correction to the cash book and show a statement reconciling the balance per the bank statement to the balance in the cash book.

Solution

BANK RECONCILIATION 30.9.X3

	£	£
Cash book balance brought down		805.15
Add: correction of adding-up		90.00
Corrected balance		**895.15**
Balance per bank statement		1,112.30
Add: cheques paid in, recorded in the cash book, but not yet credited to the account by the bank	208.20	
Less: cheques paid by the company but not yet presented to the company's bank for settlement	(425.35)	
		(217.15)
Balance per cash book		**895.15**

The reconciling items noted here will often consist of several transactions which can either be listed on the face of the reconciliation or listed separately. In particular, there may be a **great many outstanding cheques** if this is a busy business account.

PART A REVISE BOOKKEEPING AND BALANCE BANK TRANSACTIONS

To sum up, you can see here that the reconciliation falls into **two distinct steps**:

Step 1   Correct the cash book.

Step 2   Reconcile the bank balance to the corrected cash book balance.

Activity 3.2

The cash book of Gary Jones Trading Ltd for February 20X7 is set out below.

CASH BOOK

Receipts				Payments			
Date	Details			Date	Details	Cheq no	
20X7			£	20X7			£
1/2	Balance b/d		1,089.97	1/2	Rent	800120	420.00
3/2	Pronto Motors		162.40	4/2	R F Lessing	800121	824.70
3/2	Cash sales		380.75	4/2	Wages	BACS	124.20
11/2	Cash sales		522.70	11/2	British Gas plc	800122	323.25
16/2	Cash sales		122.08	18/2	D Waite	800123	150.00
24/2	Cash sales		242.18	18/2	Wages	BACS	124.20
28/2	Warley's Ltd		342.50	23/2	S Molesworth	800124	207.05
				25/2	Fogwell & Co	800125	92.44
				28/2	Balance c/d		596.74
			2,862.58				2,862.58
	Balance b/d		596.74				

Task

Using the information from the bank statement (Activity 3.1), complete the cash book entries for the month. (The transactions to be entered are those which appear on the bank statement but are not to be found in the cash book as shown above.) You do not need to reproduce the whole of the cash book given above. Use the balance b/d figure as your starting point.

The following additional information is available. The difference between the opening bank balance at 1 February per the cash book of £1,089.97 and the opening balance at 1 February per the bank statement of £1,225.37 CR is explained by the cheque number 800119 for £135.40 which was recorded in the cash book in January and presented on 7 February.

Activity 3.3

Prepare a bank reconciliation statement for Gary Jones Trading as at 28 February 20X7 using the information given in Activities 3.1 and 3.2.

5.3 Timing and frequency of the bank reconciliation

When and how often a company's bank reconciliation is performed depends on several factors.

Factor	Considerations
Frequency and volume of transactions	The more transactions there are, then the greater the likelihood of error.
Other controls	If there are very few checks on cash other than the reconciliation, then it should be performed quite often. (Other checks would include agreeing receipts to remittance advices.)
Cash flow	If the company has to keep a very close watch on its cash position then the reconciliation should be performed as often as the information on cash balances is required. Most companies do a reconciliation at the end of each month. If a company is very close to its overdraft limit, then it might need to do a weekly reconciliation.

Activity 3.4

At your firm, Gemfix Engineering Ltd, a new trainee has been asked to prepare a bank reconciliation statement as at the end of October 20X7. At 31 October 20X7, the company's bank statement shows an overdrawn balance of £142.50 DR and the cash book shows a favourable balance of £24.13.

You are concerned that the trainee has been asked to prepare the statement without proper training for the task. The trainee prepares the schedule below and asks you to look over it.

	£
Balance per bank statement (overdrawn)	142.50
Overdraft interest on bank statement, not in cash book	24.88
Unpresented cheques (total)	121.25
Cheque paid in, not credited on bank statement	(290.00)
Error in cash book*	27.00
	25.63
Unexplained difference	(1.50)
Balance per cash book	24.13

*Cheque issued for £136.00, shown as £163.00 in the cash book.

The trainee says that he was not able to reconcile the difference completely, but was pleased that he was able to 'get it down' to £1.50. He feels that there is no need to do any more work now since the difference remaining is so small. He suggests leaving the job on one side for a week or so in the hope that the necessary information will come to light during that period.

Tasks

(a) So that you can show the trainee how a bank reconciliation ought to be performed, prepare:

    (i) A statement of adjustments to be made to the cash book balance

    (ii) A corrected bank reconciliation statement as at 31 October 20X7

(b) Explain to the trainee why it is important to prepare bank reconciliations regularly and on time.

5.4 Stopped cheques

When you have received a cheque and banked it but it has already been stopped by the drawer, then the bank will not process it.

    (a) You have already written the receipt in your cash book, but now it must be taken out again.

    (b) This can be shown in the cash book as a deduction from receipts or an addition to payments, whichever is easier.

If you have written a cheque to someone and then subsequently you stop it, you must remove the payment from the cash book. If the reversal of the entry is not carried out then it will appear as a reconciling item on the bank reconciliation.

5.5 Out of date cheques

Banks consider cheques 'stale' after six months. Cheques which have been written but which have not been presented to the bank will continue to appear on a reconciliation month after month.

Step 1 Every time the reconciliation is performed you should check whether the oldest outstanding cheques are over six months old.

Step 2 Cancel or 'write back' such cheques in the cash book; they will then cease to be reconciling items.

Step 3 Notify the bank to stop the cheque as a precaution.

Step 4 Raise a new cheque.

5.6 Standing orders and direct debit schedule

Never just accept that a standing order or direct debit appearing on the bank statement is correct. The organisation must keep an up to date schedule of all current standing orders and direct debit.

Whenever a bank reconciliation is carried out, you must check all payments and/or receipts under standing order or direct debit to this schedule.

- The bank may use the wrong amount, particularly if the order or debit has been changed recently.
- The bank may pay an order or debit that has been recently cancelled.
- The bank may miss an order or debit that has been recently set up.
- The business may need to cancel an order or debit that has been overlooked.

Activity 3.5

On 1 October 20X0, Talbot Windows received a bank statement for the month of September 20X0.

(a) Update the cash book, checking items against the bank statement and against the standing order schedule. Total the cash book, showing clearly the balance carried down.

(b) Prepare a reconciliation statement.

WEST BANK plc

220 High Street, Bolton, BL9 4BQ

To: Talbot Windows   Account No 48104039   30 September 20X0

STATEMENT OF ACCOUNT

DATE 20X0	DETAILS	DEBIT £	CREDIT £	BALANCE £
1 Sept	Balance b/f			13,400
4 Sept	Cheque No 108300	1,200		12,200
1 Sept	Counter credit		400	12,600
8 Sept	Credit transfer Zebra Sales		4,000	16,600
10 Sept	Cheque No 108301	470		16,130
16 Sept	Standing order West Council	300		15,830
24 Sept	Bank charges	132		15,698
25 Sept	Standing order Any Bank	400		15,298
30 Sept	Cheque No 108303	160		15,138
30 Sept	Credit transfer Bristol Ltd		2,000	17,138
30 Sept	Salaries	9,024		8,114

CASH BOOK

Date 20X0	Details	Bank £	Date 20X0	Cheque No	Details	Bank £
1 Sept	Balance b/f	13,400	1 Sept	108300	J Hibbert	1,200
1 Sept	L Peters	400	5 Sept	108301	Cleanglass	470
28 Sept	John Smith	2,400	25 Sept	108302	Denham Insurers	630
29 Sept	KKG Ltd	144	29 Sept	108303	Kelvin Ltd	160
					Salaries	9,024

> **Schedule of current standing orders**
>
> 1. Monthly, on 16th of the month, £300.00 to West Council regarding rates.
>
> 2. Monthly, on 25th of month, £400.00 to Any Bank for hire purchase agreement.
>
> *J. Maclean*
>
> Chief Accountant

6 Reconciliations on a computerised system

In essence there is **no difference between reconciling a manual cash book and reconciling a computerised cash book**.

6.1 Computer controls over cash

In theory many of the same errors could occur in a computerised cash book as in a manual one. However, the computer will have **programme controls** built in to prevent or detect many of the errors.

Error	Programme control
Casting (addition)	Computers are programmed to add up correctly.
Updating from ledgers	When money is received from debtors, it will be posted to the sales ledger. The computer will then automatically update the bank account in the main ledger. This means that receipts and payments are unlikely to be confused.
Combined computer and manual cash books	The manual cash book reflects transactions generated by the computer system (for instance cheque payments from the purchase ledger), and also transactions initiated outside the computer system ('one-off' events such as the purchase of capital assets). The manual transactions will also be entered on to the computer. When a bank reconciliation is due to take place, the first job might be to make sure that the computer bank account and the cash book balances agree.

7 Bank services and types of account

7.1 Competition

Competition is fierce in the financial services industry. Banks must now compete against other kinds of financial institutions, such as building societies. As a result, the **range of services** and **types of account** offered to both personal and business customers has expanded.

7.2 Types of account

All the banks and building societies offer different types of account. The majority fall into one of these categories.

- Current account
- Deposit account
- Savings account
- Loan account
- Mortgage

All these accounts may be offered on different terms by different institutions, but they all offer a trade-off between:

- Minimum/maximum investment
- Charges/level of interest receivable or payable
- Withdrawal with or without penalties
- Minimum/maximum investment period
- Security required
- Maximum payment period (for loans/mortgage)

With such a wide range of accounts on offer, people can find the account which most suits their needs. It is worth visiting your local bank and building society offices and reading their literature on all the different accounts they offer. (This covers knowledge and understanding point 3 and will be useful for your portfolio.)

7.3 Business accounts

The majority of businesses will only run a **current account**. Deposit accounts are also available as **business** current accounts will **not usually** pay interest if the balance is in credit.

If a business has excess cash for a certain period of time, then it may put the money on **short term deposit on the money market** to earn some interest.

There may be restrictions on withdrawing money at short notice from deposit accounts.

7.4 Foreign exchange and related services

Compared to a personal customer, a business customer will have a very different requirement for foreign exchange services from a bank. Some of the services for both importers and exporters are highly specialised and we will not consider them in too much detail. The main services supplied will be:

- Foreign exchange
- Handling payments from buyers to suppliers
- The provision of finance
- The provision of information to exporters

7.5 Other services

Banks offer other services to business clients; the main ones are listed here.

Name of service	Nature of service
Safe custody services	Valuables, including deeds or share certificates, can be held in the vaults of the bank.
Insurance services	These might include insuring the business's buildings.
Business finance services	(a) **Discounting** and **factoring** involves administering the client's debts. (b) **Leasing** and **hire purchase** are forms of rental which help clients to buy large assets.
Home banking	Customers can control their banking needs from their own home or office by being connected directly to the bank's computer: (a) Using a television and telephone link (b) Using a computer This service is very useful for those who are either housebound or need constant access to their accounts but have no time to contact their bank personally.
CHAPS	This stands for **Clearing House Automated Payment System**. It was introduced to allow the clearing banks to transmit high value, guaranteed, sterling payments for same day settlement. This can only be done by computer. Security procedures are rigorous.
Pensions	Most banks now offer advice on pensions, for both directors and employees.

Key learning points

- A **bank reconciliation** is a comparison between the bank balance recorded in the books of a business and the balance appearing on the bank statement.

- The comparison may reveal **errors** or **omissions** in the records of the business, which should be corrected by appropriate adjustments in the cash book.

- Once the cash book has been corrected it should be possible to reconcile its balance with the bank statement balance by taking account of **timing differences**: payments made and cheques received which are recorded in the cash book but have not yet appeared on the bank statement.

- Banks offer a **wide range of services**, only some of which are relevant to the business customer.

PART A   REVISE BOOKKEEPING AND BALANCE BANK TRANSACTIONS

Quick quiz

1   What are the three main reasons why a business's cash book balance might differ from the balance on a bank statement?

2   What is a bank reconciliation?

   A   Resolving a dispute between the bank and its customer
   B   Comparing the bank statement with the sales ledger
   C   Comparing the balance on the cash book with the bank statement balance
   D   Comparing the cash book with the control accounts in the main ledger

3   What is a bank statement?

4   Cheque numbers are shown on the bank statement to aid _____. *Complete the blank.*

5   What are the two parts of a bank reconciliation statement?

6   Business bank accounts usually pay interest. True or false?

Answers to quick quiz

1   Reasons for disagreement are: errors; bank charges or interest; timing differences (for amounts to clear).

2   **C**. A bank reconciliation compares the balance of cash in the business's records to the balance held by the bank.

3   A bank statement is a document sent by a bank to its customers, itemising transactions over a certain period.

4   Cheque numbers are shown on the bank statement to aid **identification** (the amount only would not be enough).

5   (a) The adjustment of the cash book balance.
    (b) The reconciliation of the cash book balance to the bank statement.

6   False. Business bank accounts do not usually pay interest, but it depends on the individual business's arrangement with the bank.

3: BANK RECONCILIATIONS

Activity checklist

This checklist shows which performance criteria, range statement or knowledge and understanding point is covered by each activity in this chapter. Tick off each activity as you complete it.

Activity

3.1	☐	This activity deals with range statement 3.1.1 primary documentation: bank statement
3.2	☐	This activity deals with performance criteria 3.1.A and 3.1.B
3.3	☐	This activity deals with performance criteria 3.1.C and 3.1.D
3.4	☐	This activity deals with performance criteria 3.1.A, 3.1.B, 3.1.C and 3.1.D
3.5	☐	This activity deals with performance criteria 3.1.A, 3.1.B, 3.1.C and 3.1.D, as well as range statement 3.1.1 primary documentation: standing order and direct debit schedules.

PART A REVISE BOOKKEEPING AND BALANCE BANK TRANSACTIONS

PART B

Control accounts

chapter 4

Sales ledger control account

Contents

1. The problem
2. The solution
3. Sales ledger control account
4. Posting to the sales ledger control account
5. Bad debts
6. Comprehensive example: accounting for debtors
7. Purpose of the sales ledger control account
8. Sales ledger control account reconciliation

Performance criteria

- 3.2.A Make and record authorised adjustments
- 3.2.B Total relevant accounts in the main ledger
- 3.2.C Reconcile control accounts with the totals of the balance in the subsidiary ledger
- 3.2.E Identify discrepancies arising from the reconciliation of control accounts and either resolve or refer to the appropriate person

Range statement

- 3.2.2. Adjustments: to correct errors; to write off bad debts
- 3.2.3   Control accounts; sales ledger; manual; computerised
- 3.2.4   Discrepancies; manual sales ledger control account not agreeing with subsidiary ledger

Knowledge and understanding

- 12 Relationship between the accounting system and the ledger
- 17 Reconciling control accounts with memorandum accounts

1 The problem

In Chapter 2 we saw that:

(a) Sales invoices and cash received are logged in a **day book** or onto some equivalent listing or computer file which serves a similar purpose

(b) Each invoice and cash receipt is posted **singly** to an appropriate personal account in the sales ledger

But these personal accounts are for memorandum purposes only and do not form a part of the double entry system.

To extract the value of total sales for the period from the individual sales ledger accounts would be very time-consuming.

2 The solution

To record these transactions in the **double entry system** we do not need to deal with each invoice singly. Instead, the day books can be totalled at convenient intervals (eg daily, weekly or monthly) and these total amounts are recorded in the main ledger. For sales invoices, this means an accounting entry is made as follows.

DEBIT	Sales ledger control account (SLCA)	£1,175	
CREDIT	Sales account(s)		£1,000
	VAT account		£175

This should be revision from Units 1 and 2.

3 Sales ledger control account

3.1 Control accounts

A control account is an (impersonal) ledger account which appears in the main ledger. The sales ledger control account (SLCA) records the total amounts owing to the business from its customers (debtors). The balance on the SLCA should be equal to the total of all the individual debtor balances in the sales ledger.

3.2 Control accounts and personal accounts

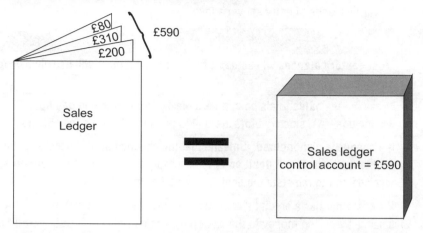

For example, if a business has three debtors, A Ashton who owes £80, B Bolton who owes £310 and C Collins who owes £200, the balances on the various accounts would be:

Sales ledger (personal accounts)

	£
A Ashton	80
B Bolton	310
C Collins	200
	590

All of these balances would be debit balances.

Main ledger: sales ledger control account   590

4 Posting to the sales ledger control account

This should be revision from your studies for Unit 1 and 2. The SLCA deals with the asset of debtors.

Typical entries in a sales ledger control account are shown in the example below. The reference 'Jnl' in this example indicates that this particular transaction is first **entered** in the **journal** before **posting** to the **control account** and other accounts indicated. The reference SDB is the sales day book, SRDB is the sales returns day book and CB is the cash book. We will deal with journals in Chapter 7.

SALES LEDGER CONTROL ACCOUNT

		£			£
Debit balances	b/d	7,000	Credit balances		200
Sales	SDB	52,390	Cash received	CB	52,250
Dishonoured cheques	Jnl	1,000	Discounts allowed	CB	1,250
Cash paid to clear			Returns inwards from		
credit balances	CB	110	debtors	SRDB	800
Credit balances	c/d	120	Bad debts	Jnl	300
			Debit balances	c/d	5,820
		60,620			60,620
Debit balances	b/d	5,820	Credit balances	b/d	120

PART B CONTROL ACCOUNTS

Bad debts are dealt with in Section 5 of this chapter.

Note some points about the various kinds of entry shown above.

Debit entries	Points to note
Debit balances b/d	Most **debtor balances** will be **debit balances**: customers will usually owe money to the business.
Sales	These are the **sales** totals posted periodically from the **sales day book**. The amounts recorded will include VAT, since debtors are due to pay the VAT to us (see Section 2 of this chapter).
Dishonoured cheques	If a cheque is dishonoured, it means that the cheque has 'bounced' and the amount will not be paid to the business. A **debit entry** is necessary to 'reverse' the recording of the cheque received and to reinstate the debt. The **credit entry** is to cash.
Cash paid by us to clear credit balances	If a customer has a credit balance, **we owe money** to that customer, and we may clear the balance by paying money to the customer. The entry is **debit** SLCA; **credit** cash.
Credit balances c/d	Any closing credit balances are carried down.

Credit entries	Points to note
Credit balances b/d	**Credit balances** in the sales ledger control account can arise, for example, if goods which have already been paid for are **returned**, or if a customer has **overpaid**. Such balances will be unusual.
Cash received	**Cash received from debtors** will be posted **debit** cash; **credit** SLCA.
Discounts allowed	**Cash discounts allowed** may be recorded in a memorandum column in the cash book. They form a part of the amounts invoiced to customers, which we are 'allowing' them not to pay. A credit entry is needed to cancel that part of amounts invoiced. **Debit** discounts allowed: **credit** SLCA
Returns inwards	**Credit notes** for returns inwards must be posted from the **sales returns day book**. **Debit** sales (or sales returns if recorded separately); **credit** SLCA.
Bad debts	Bad debts written off need to be **cancelled** from the control account. **Debit** bad debts; **credit** SLCA.
Debit balances c/d	The bulk of sales ledger balances to carry forward will be debit balances.

Activity 4.1

Prepare a specimen sales ledger control account in T account form. Show clearly the information it would contain and the sources of this information.

Activity 4.2

Tick the items below which you would **not** expect to see as individual items in a sales ledger control account.

1. Credit balances on individual debtor accounts
2. Debit balances on individual debtor accounts
3. Cash sales
4. Sales on credit
5. Credit notes issued
6. Settlement discounts allowed
7. Trade discounts received
8. Cash receipts
9. Bad debts written off
10. Sales returns
11. Credit notes received

5 Bad debts

5.1 Bad debts

For some balances on the ledger, there may be little or no prospect of the business being paid.

- The customer is **bankrupt**
- The customer has gone **out of business**
- **Dishonesty** may be involved

For one reason or another, therefore, a business decides to give up expecting payment and to **write the debt off** as unlikely to be recovered. The company does not expect to get its money.

5.2 Bad debts written off: ledger accounting entries

For bad debts written off, there is a **bad debts account** in the main ledger. Bad debts are an expense to the company as it has provided goods for which the customer has not paid. The double-entry bookkeeping is fairly straightforward. When it is decided that a particular debt will not be paid, the customer becomes a bad debt. We therefore:

DEBIT	Bad debts account (expense)	£100	
CREDIT	SLCA		£100

A write off of any bad debt will need the authorisation of a senior official in the organisation.

Example: Bad debts written off

At 1 October 20X1 a business had total outstanding debtors of £8,600. During the year to 30 September 20X2:

(a) Credit sales amounted to £44,000.
(b) Payments from various debtors amounted to £49,000.
(c) Two debts, for £180 and £420 (both including VAT) were declared bad. These are to be written off.

We need to prepare the sales ledger control account and the bad debts account for the year.

Solution

SALES LEDGER CONTROL ACCOUNT

Date	Details	£	Date	Details	£
1.10.X1	Balance b/d	8,600		Cash	49,000
	Sales for the year	44,000	30.9.X2	Bad debts	180
			30.9.X2	Bad debts	420
			30.9.X2	Balance c/d	3,000
		52,600			52,600
	Balance b/d	3,000			

BAD DEBTS

Date	Details	£	Date	Details	£
30.9.X2	SLCA	180	30.9.X2	Balance c/d	600
30.9.X2	SLCA	420			
		600			600
	Balance b/d	600			

In the sales ledger, personal accounts of the customers whose debts are bad will be **taken off the ledger**. The business should then take steps to ensure that it does not sell goods to those customers again.

The balance on the bad debts account will be charged to the profit and loss account.

5.3 Bad debts and VAT

A business can claim relief from VAT on bad debts which:

- Are **at least six months old** (from the time of supply)
- Which have been **written off** in the accounts of the business

VAT bad debt relief is accounted for as follows:

DEBIT	VAT account	£17.50	
	Bad debts	£100.00	
CREDIT	SLCA		£117.50

Example: Bad debts and VAT

If both the debts written off in the example above were inclusive of VAT, the accounts would look as follows:

SALES LEGER CONTROL ACCOUNT – no change

BAD DEBTS

Date	Details	£	Date	Details	£
30.9.X2	SLCA	153.20	30.9.X2	Balance	510.65
30.9.X2	SLCA	357.45			
		510.65			510.65

VAT ACCOUNT (part)

Date	Details	£	Date	Details	£
30.9.X2	SLCA	26.80			
30.9.X2	SLCA	62.55			

5.4 Provision for doubtful debts: ledger accounting entries

A provision for doubtful debts is rather different from a bad debt written off. A business might know from past experience that, say, 2% of debtors balances are unlikely to be collected. It would then be considered prudent to make a **general provision of 2% of total debtor balances.**

It may be that no particular customers are regarded as suspect and so it is not possible to write off any individual customer balances as bad debts.

The procedure is, then, to leave the sales ledger control account completely untouched, but to open up a provision account by the following entries:

DEBIT	Doubtful debts account (expense)	£250	
CREDIT	Provision for doubtful debts		£250

When giving a figure for debtors, the credit balance on the provision account is deducted from the debit balance on total debtors.

In **subsequent** years, adjustments may be needed to the amount of the provision. The procedure to be followed then is as follows.

Step 1   Calculate the new provision required.

Step 2   Compare it with the existing balance on the provision account (ie the balance b/f from the previous accounting period).

Step 3   Calculate the increase or decrease required.

    (i)   If a higher provision is required now

DEBIT	Doubtful debts account (expense)	£X	
CREDIT	Provision for doubtful debts		£X

with the amount of the increase. The credit to the provision account reduces an asset (debtors)

(ii) If a lower provision is needed now than before

DEBIT   Provision for doubtful debts   £X
CREDIT Doubtful debts account (expense)   £X

with the amount of the decrease. The debit to the provision account increases debtors.

Example: Provision for doubtful debts

John Seager has total debtor balances outstanding at 31 December 20X3 of £28,000. He believes that about 1% of these balances will not be paid and wishes to make an appropriate provision. Before now, he has not made any provision for doubtful debts at all.

On 31 December 20X4 his debtor balances amount to £40,000. His experience during the year has convinced him that a provision of 5% should be made.

What accounting entries should John make on 31 December 20X3 and 31 December 20X4, and what will be his net figure for debtors at those dates?

Solution

At 31 December 20X3

Provision required = 1% × £28,000
              = £280

John will make the following entries.

DEBIT   Doubtful debts account   £280
CREDIT Provision for doubtful debts   £280

The net debtors figure will be:

	£
Sales ledger balances	28,000
Less provision for doubtful debts	280
	27,720

At 31 December 20X4

Following the procedure described above, John will calculate:

	£
Provision required now (5% × £40,000)	2,000
Existing provision	(280)
Additional provision required	1,720

DEBIT   Doubtful debts account   £1,720
CREDIT Provision for doubtful debts   £1,720

The provision account will appear as follows.

PROVISION FOR DOUBTFUL DEBTS

Date	Details	£	Date	Details	£
20X3			20X3		
31 Dec	Balance c/d	280	31 Dec	Doubtful debts account	280
20X4			20X4		
31 Dec	Balance c/d	2,000	1 Jan	Balance b/d	280
			31 Dec	Doubtful debts account	1,720
		2,000			2,000
			20X5		
			1 Jan	Balance b/d	2,000

Net debtors will be:

	£
Sales ledger balances/SLCA	40,000
Less provision for doubtful debts	2,000
	38,000

5.4.1 Doubtful debts and VAT

Because it is a general provision, the provision for doubtful debts has no effect whatsoever on VAT.

Activity 4.3

Gavin is a wholesaler and the following information relates to his accounting year ending 30 September 20X2.

(a) Goods are sold on credit terms, but some cash sales are also transacted.

(b) At 1 October 20X1 Gavin's trade debtors amounted to £30,000 against which he had set aside a provision for doubtful debts of 5%.

(c) On 15 January 20X2 Gavin was informed that Fall Ltd had gone into liquidation, owing him £2,000. This debt was outstanding from the previous year.

(d) Cash sales during the year totalled £46,800, whilst credit sales amounted to £187,800.

(e) £182,500 was received from trade debtors.

(f) Settlement discounts allowed to credit customers were £5,300.

(g) Apart from Fall Ltd's bad debt, other certain bad debts amounted to £3,500.

(h) Gavin intends to retain the provision for doubtful debts account at 5% of outstanding trade debtors as at the end of the year, and the necessary entry is to be made.

Task

Enter the above transactions in Gavin's ledger accounts, balance off the accounts and bring down the balances as at 1 October 20X2. (There is no need to balance off the cash and bank and profit and loss accounts.)

6 Comprehensive example: Accounting for debtors: Revision from Unit 1

This is a good point at which to go through the steps of how transactions involving debtors are **accounted for** in a comprehensive illustrative example. Code numbers are shown in the accounts to illustrate the cross-referencing that is needed and in the example code numbers begin with either:

(a) SDB, referring to the sales day book; or

(b) SL, referring to a particular account in the sales ledger; or

(c) GL, referring to a particular account in the general ledger(sometimes referred to by AAT as 'main ledger'); or

(d) CB, referring to the cash book.

Note. This activity does not test bad and doubtful debts.

At 1 July 20X7, the Software Design Company had no debtors at all. During July, the following transactions affecting credit sales and customers occurred. All sales figures are gross; VAT on sales is charged at 17.5%.

- July 3 Invoiced A Ashton for the sale on credit of hardware goods: £100.
- July 11 Invoiced B Bolton for the sale on credit of electrical goods: £150.
- July 15 Invoiced C Collins for the sale on credit of hardware goods: £250.
- July 17 Invoiced D Derby for the sale on credit of hardware goods: £400. Goods invoiced at £120 were returned for full credit on the next day.
- July 10 Received payment from A Ashton of £100, in settlement of his debt in full.
- July 18 Received a payment of £80 from B Bolton.
- July 28 Received a payment of £120 from C Collins.
- July 29 Received a payment of £280 from D Derby.

Cash sales in July amounted to £2,502, all including VAT. £976 was for hardware goods, the balance for electrical.

Account numbers are as follows.

SL4   Personal account A Ashton
SL 9   Personal account B Bolton
SL 13 Personal account C Collins
SL 21 Personal account D Derby
GL6   Sales ledger control account
GL21   Sales – hardware
GL22   Sales – electrical
GL1   Cash account
GL2   VAT account

We will begin by making entries in the sales day book and cash book and then carry those entries forward into the individual sales ledger accounts and the main (general) ledger accounts.

Solution

The recording entries, suitably dated, would be as follows.

SALES DAY BOOK

Date 20X7	Name		Gross total £	VAT £	Net total £	Hardware £	Electrical £
July 3	A Ashton	SL4 Dr	100.00	14.89	85.11	85.11	
July 11	B Bolton	SL9 Dr	150.00	22.34	127.66		127.66
July 15	C Collins	SL13 Dr	250.00	37.23	212.77	212.77	
July 17	D Derby	SL21 Dr	400.00	59.57	340.43	340.43	
July 18	D Derby	SL21 Cr	(120.00)	(17.87)	(102.13)	(102.13)	
			780.00	116.16	663.84	536.18	127.66
			GL6 Dr	GL2 Cr		GL21 Cr	GL22 Cr

Note. The personal accounts in the sales ledger are debited on the day the invoices and credit notes are sent out. The double entry in the main ledger accounts might be made at the end of each day, week or month; here it is made at the end of the month, by posting from the sales day book as follows.

POSTING SUMMARY - 31/7/X7

		Debit £	Credit £
GL 6	SLCA	780.00	
GL21	Sales – hardware		536.18
GL22	Sales – electrical		127.66
GL2	VAT		116.16

CASH BOOK EXTRACT
RECEIPTS – JULY 20X7

Date 20X7	Name		Gross total £	VAT £	Net total £	Debtors £	Hardware £	Electrical £
July 10	A Ashton	SL4 Cr	100.00		100.00	100.00		
July 18	B Bolton	SL9 Cr	80.00		80.00	80.00		
July 28	C Collins	SL13 Cr	120.00		120.00	120.00		
July 29	D Derby	SL 21 Cr	280.00		280.00	280.00		
July	Cash sales		2,502.00	372.63	2,129.37		830.64	1,298.73
			3,082.00	372.63	2,709.37	580.00	830.64	1,298.73
			GL1 Dr	GL2 Cr		GL 6 Cr	GL21 Cr	GL22 Cr

As with the sales day book, a posting summary to the main ledger needs to be drawn up for the cash book.

PART B CONTROL ACCOUNTS

POSTING SUMMARY – 31/7/X7

		Debit £	Credit £
GL 1	Cash account	3,082.00	
GL 6	SLCA		580.00
GL 21	Sales – hardware		830.64
GL 22	Sales – electrical		1,298.73
GL 2	VAT		372.63

The personal accounts in the sales ledger are memorandum accounts, because they are not a part of the double entry system.

MEMORANDUM SALES LEDGER

A ASHTON A/c no: SL4

Date 20X7	Narrative		£	Date 20X7	Narrative		£
July 3	Sales	SDB	100.00	July 10	Cash	CB	100.00
			100.00				100.00

B BOLTON A/c no: SL9

Date 20X7	Narrative		£	Date 20X7	Narrative		£
July 11	Sales	SDB	150.00	July 18	Cash	CB	80.00
				July 31	Balance b/d		70.00
			150.00				150.00
Aug 1	Balance b/d		70.00				

C COLLINS A/c no: SL13

Date 20X7	Narrative		£	Date 20X7	Narrative		£
July 15	Sales	SDB	250.00	July 28	Cash	CB	120.00
				July 31	Balance c/d		130.00
			250.00				250.00
Aug 1	Balance b/d		130.00				

D DERBY A/c no: SL21

Date 20X7	Narrative		£	Date 20X7	Narrative		£
July 17	Sales	SDB	400.00	July 18	Returns	SDB	120.00
				July 29	Cash	CB	280.00
			400.00				400.00

In the main ledger, the accounting entries can be made from the books of prime entry to the ledger accounts, in this example at the end of the month. Note that in the main ledger we are posting the totals from the sales day book and cash book.

4: SALES LEDGER CONTROL ACCOUNT

MAIN LEDGER (EXTRACT)

SALES LEDGER CONTROL ACCOUNT — A/c no: GL6

Date 20X7	Narrative		£	Date 20X7	Narrative		£
July 31	Sales	SDB	780.00	July 31	Cash	CB	580.00
					Balance c/d		200.00
			780.00				780.00
Aug 1	Balance b/d		200.00				

Note. At 31 July the closing balance on the sales ledger control account (£200) is the same as the total of the individual balances on the personal accounts in the sales ledger (£0 + £70 + £130 + £0).

VAT — A/c no: GL 2

Date 20X7	Narrative		£	Date 20X7	Narrative		£
				July 31	SLCA	SDB	116.16
				July 31	Cash	CB	372.63

CASH ACCOUNT — A/c no: GL1

Date 20X7	Narrative		£	Date	Narrative		£
July 31	Cash received	CB	3,082.00				

SALES – HARDWARE — A/c no: GL21

Date	Narrative		£	Date 20X7	Narrative		£
				July 31	SLCA	SDB	536.18
				July 31	Cash	CB	830.64

SALES – ELECTRICAL — A/c no: GL22

Date	Narrative		£	Date 20X7	Narrative		£
				July 31	SLCA	SDB	127.66
				July 31	Cash	CB	1,298.73

PART B CONTROL ACCOUNTS

7 Purpose of the sales ledger control account

There are a number of reasons for having a sales ledger control account, mainly to do with the usefulness of **reconciling the control account to the list of memorandum sales ledger balances**.

Purpose	Details
To check the accuracy of entries made in the personal accounts	Comparing the balance on the sales ledger control account with the total of individual balances on the sales ledger personal accounts means we can identify the fact that errors have been made.
To **trace errors**	By using the sales ledger control account, a comparison with the individual balances in the sales ledger can be made for **every week** or **day** of the month, and the error found much more quickly than if a control account like this did not exist.
To provide an **internal check**	The person posting entries to the sales ledger control account will act as a check on a different person whose job it is to post entries to the sales ledger accounts.
To provide a **debtors balance quickly**	This is useful when producing a trial balance.

Activity 4.4

Your supervisor informs you that the following information for the year ended 31 May 20X7 comes from the accounting records of Supernova Ltd.

	£
Sales ledger control account as at 1 June 20X6	
Debit balance	12,404.86
Credit balance	322.94
Credit sales	96,464.41
Goods returned from trade debtors	1,142.92
Payments received from trade debtors	94,648.71*
Discounts allowed to trade debtors	3,311.47**

* This figures includes cheques totalling £192.00 which were dishonoured before 31 May 20X7, the debts in respect of which remained outstanding at 31 May 20X7. The only sales ledger account with a credit balance at 31 May 20X7 was that of ENR Ltd with a balance of £337.75.

** The discounts are all settlement discounts, taken against invoice values.

You are told that, after the preparation of the sales ledger control account for the year ended 31 May 20X7 from the information given above, the following accounting errors were discovered.

(i)   In July 20X6, a debt due of £77.00 from PAL Ltd had been written off as bad. Whilst the correct entries have been made in PAL Ltd's personal account, no reference to the debt being written off has been made in the sales ledger control account.

(ii)   Cash sales of £3,440.00 in November 20X6 have been included in the payments received from trade debtors of £94,648.71.

(iii) The sales day book for January 20X7 had been undercast by £427.80.

(iv) Credit sales £96,464.41 includes goods costing £3,711.86 returned to suppliers by Supernova Ltd.

(v) No entries have been made in the personal accounts for goods returned from trade debtors of £1,142.92.

(vi) The debit side of FTR Ltd's personal account has been overcast by £71.66.

Tasks

(a) Prepare the sales ledger control account for the year ended 31 May 20X7 as it would have been *before* the various accounting errors outlined above were discovered.

(b) Prepare a computation of the amount arising from the sales ledger to be shown as trade debtors as at 31 May 20X7.

Tutorial note. Think carefully whether all the errors listed affect the control account.

8 Sales ledger control account reconciliation

8.1 Manual systems

The sales ledger control account should be **balanced regularly** (at least monthly), and the balance on the account **agreed to the sum of the individual debtors balances** extracted from the sales ledger.

In practice, more often than not the balance on the control account does not agree with the sum of balances extracted, for one or more of the following reasons.

Reason for disagreement	How to correct
Miscast of the total in the book of prime entry (adding up incorrectly).	The main ledger debit and credit postings will balance, but the sales ledger control account balance will not agree with the sum of individual balances extracted from the (memorandum) sales ledger. A journal entry must then be made in the main ledger to correct the sales ledger control account and the corresponding sales account.
A **transposition error** in **posting** an individual's transaction from the book of prime entry to the memorandum ledger.	For example the sale to C Collins of £250 might be posted to his account as £520. The **sum of balances** extracted from the memorandum ledger **must be corrected**. No double entry would be required to do this, only alter the figure in C Collins' account.
Omission of a transaction from the sales ledger control account or the memorandum account, but not both.	A single entry will correct an omission from the memorandum account in the sales ledger. Where a transaction is missing from the sales ledger control account, then the double entry will have to be checked and corrected.
The **sum of balances** extracted from the sales ledger may be **incorrectly extracted** or **miscast**.	Correct the total of the balances.

PART B CONTROL ACCOUNTS

Reconciling the sales ledger control account balance with the sum of the balances extracted from the (memorandum) sales ledger is an important procedure. It should be performed **regularly** so that any errors are revealed and appropriate action can be taken. The reconciliation should be done in five steps.

Step 1 Balance the accounts in the memorandum ledger, and review for errors.

Step 2 Correct the total of the balances extracted from the memorandum ledger.

	£	£
Sales ledger total		
Original total extracted		15,320
Add: difference arising from transposition error (£95 written as £59)		36
		15,356
Less: Credit balance of £60 extracted as a debit balance (£60 × 2)	120	
Overcast of list of balances	90	
		(210)
		15,146

Step 3 Balance the sales ledger control account, and review for errors.

Step 4 Adjust or post the sales ledger control account with correcting entries.

Step 5 Prepare a statement showing how the corrected sales ledger agrees to the corrected sales ledger control account.

SALES LEDGER CONTROL ACCOUNT

	£		£
Balance before adjustments	15,091	Returns inwards: individual posting omitted from control a/c	45
Undercast of total invoices issued in sales day book	100	Balance c/d (now in agreement with the corrected total of individual balances above)	15,146
	15,191		15,191
Balance b/d	15,146		

Once the five steps are completed, the total sales ledger balances should equal the sales ledger control account balance.

The sales ledger control account reconciliation will be carried out by the **sales ledger clerk** and reviewed and approved by a **senior member of staff**.

Activity 4.5

(a) You are an employee of Ultrabrite Ltd and have been asked to help prepare the end of year accounts for the period ended 30 November 20X7 by agreeing the figure for total debtors.

The following figures, relating to the financial year, have been obtained from the books of prime entry.

	£
Purchases for the year	361,947
Sales	472,185
Returns inwards	41,226
Returns outwards	16,979
Bad debts written off	1,914
Discounts allowed	2,672
Discounts received	1,864
Cheques paid to creditors	342,791
Cheques received from debtors	429,811
Customer cheques dishonoured	626

You discover that at the close of business on 30 November 20X6 the total of the debtors amounted to £50,241.

Task

Prepare Ultrabrite Ltd's sales ledger control account for the year ended 30 November 20X7.

(b) To give you some assistance, your rather inexperienced colleague, Peter Johnson, has attempted to extract and total the individual balances in the sales ledger. He provides you with the following listing which he has prepared.

	£
Bury plc	7,500
P Fox & Son (Swindon) Ltd	2,000
Frank Wendlebury & Co Ltd	4,297
D Richardson & Co Ltd	6,847
Ultra Ltd	783
Lawrenson Ltd	3,765
Walkers plc	4,091
P Fox & Son (Swindon) Ltd	2,000
Whitchurch Ltd	8,112
Ron Bradbury & Co Ltd	5,910
Anderson Ltd	1,442
	46,347

Subsequent to the drawing up of the list, the following errors have so far been found.

(i) A sales invoice for £267 sent to Whitchurch Ltd had been correctly entered in the day book but had not then been posted to the account for Whitchurch Ltd in the sales ledger.

(ii) One of the errors made by Peter Johnson (you suspect that his list may contain others) was to omit the £2,435 balance of Rectofon Ltd from the list.

(iii) A credit note for £95 sent to Bury plc had been correctly entered in the day book but was entered in the account in the sales ledger as £75.

Task

Prepare a statement reconciling the £46,347 total provided by Peter Johnson with the balance of your own sales ledger control account.

Tutorial note. Review Peter Johnson's list very carefully and check the casting.

8.2 Integrated accounting systems

In an **integrated system**, postings to the sales ledger are carried out automatically in the same way as the corresponding posting to the sales ledger control account in the main ledger.

- (a) Differences between the sales ledger control account and the total of the individual sales ledger accounts might still arise, however. This is because, in any accounting system, adjustments may be made to accounts by the different method of using **the journal**.
- (b) There will still then be a need to perform a sales ledger control account reconciliation.

In a computerised accounting system, different parts of the system (for example, the main ledger, the sales ledger and the purchase ledger) may be 'integrated'.

In a **non-integrated system**, the different operations involved are not combined.

- (a) A posting must be made to the sales ledger **and** a posting must also be made to the sales ledger control account in the main ledger.
- (b) This gives rise to the need for day books, which list and produce summary totals of transactions for posting in summarised form to the sales ledger control account.
- (c) A non-integrated system of ledgers may be either computer-based or manual.

The AAT have advised that all skills testing and exams will be based on a **non-integrated** system.

Key learning points

- A control account is an account which keeps a total record for a collective item (for example debtors) which in reality consists of many individual items (for example individual debtors). It is an impersonal account maintained in the main ledger.

- The sales ledger control account is a record of the total of the balances owed by customers. Postings are made from the sales and sales returns day books, the cash book and the journal, in order to maintain this record.

- Some debts may not be collectable and are written off as **bad debts**.

- If a proportion of debtor balances are unlikely to be collected, a **provision for doubtful debts** may be needed.

- The sales ledger control account serves a number of purposes.

    - Reconciling the control account provides a check on the accuracy of entries made in the personal sales ledger accounts, and helps with the tracing of any errors which may have occurred.

    - A reconciliation also provides an internal check on employees' work.

    - The sales ledger control account gives a convenient total debtors balance when the time comes to produce a trial balance or a balance sheet.

- The balance on the sales ledger control account should be reconciled regularly with the sum of the memorandum sales ledger account balances so that any necessary action can be taken.

Quick quiz

1. What does the balance on the sales ledger control account represent?
2. A dishonoured cheque is a credit entry in the sales ledger control account. True or false?
3. How might a credit balance arise in the sales ledger control account?
4. Why might the balance on the sales ledger control account not agree with the total of the individual debtors' balances?
5. When setting up a provision for doubtful debts, the VAT should be written off. True or false?

Answers to quick quiz

1. The total amount due to the business from its debtors.
2. False. Cash received is a credit entry, therefore a dishonoured cheque must be a debit.
3. A customer may return goods or overpay his balance.
4. (i) There may be a transposition error in posting an individual's transaction from the book of prime entry to the memorandum ledger.
   (ii) The day book could be miscast.
   (iii) A transaction may be omitted from the control account or the memorandum account.
   (iv) The total may be incorrectly extracted.
5. False. It is a general provision and does not affect VAT.

Activity checklist

This checklist shows which performance criteria, range statement or knowledge and understanding point is covered by each activity in this chapter. Tick off each activity as you complete it.

Activity

4.1		This activity deals with range statement 3.2.3 control accounts: sales ledger.
4.2		This activity deals with range statement 3.2.3 control accounts: sales ledger.
4.3		This activity deals with performance criteria 3.2.A and 3.2.B.
4.4		This activity deals with performance criteria 3.2.A and 3.2.B.
4.5		This activity deals with performance criteria 3.2.A, 3.2.B, 3.2.C and 3.2.E

chapter 5

Purchase ledger control account

Contents

1. The problem
2. The solution
3. Purpose of the purchase ledger control account
4. Posting to the purchase ledger control account
5. Purchase ledger control account reconciliation

Performance criteria
- 3.2.A Make and record authorised adjustments
- 3.2.B Total relevant accounts in the main ledger
- 3.2.C Reconcile control accounts with the totals of the balances in the subsidiary ledger
- 3.2.E Identify discrepancies arising from the reconciliation of control accounts and either resolve or refer to the appropriate person

Range statement
- 3.2.2 Adjustments to correct errors
- 3.2.3 Control accounts: purchase ledger; manual; computerised
- 3.2.4 Discrepancies: manual purchases ledger control account not agreeing with subsidiary ledger

Knowledge and understanding
- 12 Relationship between the accounting system and the ledger
- 13 Reconciling control accounts with memorandum accounts

PART B   CONTROL ACCOUNTS

1 The problem

As with the sales ledger, the memorandum purchase ledger is not part of the double entry system.

How do we record purchases in the main ledger?

2 Solution

The answer is by means of the purchase ledger control account, which you have already met in your studies for Units 1 and 2.

DEBIT	Purchases/expense accounts	£1,000	
	VAT account	£175	
CREDIT	Purchase ledger control account (PLCA)		£1,175

Now that you have seen how the sales ledger control account works (in Chapter 4), you should find the purchase ledger control account fairly straightforward.

3 Purpose of the purchase ledger control account

3.1 What is the purchase ledger control account?

The two control accounts which you will meet most often are the control accounts for the sales ledger and for the purchase ledger.

The balance on the sales ledger control account is the **total amount due to the business at that time from its debtors**.

Therefore the balance on the purchase ledger control account at any time is the **total amount owed by the business at that time to its creditors**.

The purchase ledger control account records all of the transactions involving the trade creditors of the business.

The purchase ledger control account, and the reconciliation from the PLCA to the purchase ledger, provide:

- A check on the **accuracy of entries** in the individual personal accounts
- Help in **locating errors**
- A form of **internal check**
- A total trade creditors balance for when a **trial balance** or balance sheet needs to be prepared

3.2 How the control account works

It works very much like the sales ledger control account.

Step 1   The **purchase day book** records the individual purchase invoices which a business receives. There may also be a separate purchase returns day book for credit notes received.

Step 2   Each invoice and credit note is recorded individually in the appropriate personal account in the **purchase ledger** for the supplier.

Step 3   The personal accounts for creditors are, usually, **memorandum accounts** and do not form part of the double entry system.

Step 4   The total purchase invoice and credit note transactions shown in the day books can be posted to the main ledger using **double entry**.

Activity 5.1

Which one of the following statements describes the relationship between the **purchase ledger control account** and the purchase **ledger**?

A   The **purchase ledger control account** is where the corresponding debit side of credit entries to the **purchase ledger** are posted.

B   The **purchase ledger control account** is where invoices from customers for whom you have not set up an account in the **purchase ledger** are posted.

C   The **purchase ledger** is a memorandum list of invoices and related transactions analysed by supplier. The **purchase ledger control account** is the total of amounts owed to all suppliers.

D   The **purchase ledger** forms part of the double entry. The **purchase ledger control account** is a memorandum control total used for internal checking purposes.

4 Posting to the purchase ledger control account

This section should be revision from your studies for Units 1 and 2.

Typical entries in the purchase ledger control account (PLCA) are shown in the example below. The references PDB and PRDB are to the purchase day book and purchase returns day book respectively.

PURCHASE LEDGER CONTROL ACCOUNT

		£			£
Opening debit balances	b/d	70	Opening credit balances	b/d	8,300
Cash paid	CB	29,840	Purchases and other expenses	PDB	31,000
Discounts received	CB	30	Cash received clearing debit balances	CB	20
Returns outwards	PRDB	60	Closing debit balances	c/d	80
Closing credit balances	c/d	9,400			
		39,400			39,400
Debit balances	b/d	80	Credit balances	b/d	9,400

Let's consider these entries in more detail.

Debit entries – reducing the liability	Explanation
Opening debit balances	This is unusual, perhaps an overpayment to a creditor, or a deposit made before a supplier has sent an invoice.
Cash paid	**Debit** PLCA; **credit** cash.
Discounts received	The debit is the difference between the full amount invoiced by suppliers and the discounted amount which we paid. **Debit** PLCA; **credit** discounts received.
Returns outwards	These are returns of goods to suppliers recorded as credit notes received. **Debit** PLCA; **credit** purchases.
Closing credit balances	Represent the **total** of the creditors carried down.

Credit entries – increasing the liability	Explanation
Opening credit balances	Represent total creditors brought down (disregarding any debit balances).
Purchases and other expenses	The amounts invoiced by suppliers. **Debit** purchases; **credit** PLCA.
Cash received clearing debit balances	An unusual item. **Debit** cash; **credit** PLCA.
Closing debit balances	Carried down separately from credit balances.

Example: Control accounts

On examining the books of Steps Ltd, you discover that on 1 October 20X1 the purchase ledger balances were £6,235 credit and £105 debit.

For the year ended 30 September 20X2 the following details are available.

	£
Sales	63,728
Purchases	39,974
Cash received from debtors	55,212
Cash paid to creditors	37,307
Discount received	1,475
Discount allowed	2,328
Returns inwards	1,002
Returns outwards	535
Bad debts written off	326
Cash received in respect of debit balances in purchase ledger	105
Amount due from customer as shown by sales ledger, offset against amount due to the same firm as shown by purchase ledger (settlement by contra)	434

On 30 September 20X2 there were no debit balances in the purchase ledger.

We need to write up the purchase ledger control account recording the above transactions and bringing down balances at 30 September 20X2 (note that assessments will often include extra information not needed in the solution).

Solution

PURCHASE LEDGER CONTROL ACCOUNT

		£			£
20X1			20X1		
Oct 1	Balances b/d	105	Oct 1	Balances b/d	6,235
20X2			20X2		
Sept 30	Cash paid to creditors	37,307	Sept 30	Purchases	39,974
	Discount received	1,475		Cash	105
	Returns outwards	535			
	Transfer SLCA	434			
	Balances c/d	6,458			
		46,314			46,314

PART B CONTROL ACCOUNTS

5 Purchase ledger control account reconciliation

5.1 Manual systems

There are good reasons for performing this reconciliation.

(a) The account should be **balanced regularly.**

(b) The balance on the account should be agreed with the sum of the individual suppliers balances extracted from the purchase ledger.

As with the sales ledger control account, this routine will be carried out on a monthly basis in many businesses.

Items in the reconciliation are likely to arise from similar occurrences to those already identified in the case of the sales ledger control account discussed in Chapter 4.

Error	Affects
• Miscast of purchase day book or cash book	PLCA
• Transposition error in entry from day book to purchase ledger	Purchase ledger balances
• Missing entries in *either* purchase ledger *or* control account	*Either* purchase ledger *or* control account
• Miscast of total purchase ledger balances	Purchase ledger balances
• Miscast of PLCA	PLCA

The reconciliation of the purchase ledger control account should be carried out in five steps.

Step 1 Balance the accounts in the subsidiary ledger, and review for errors.

Step 2 Correct the total of the balances extracted from the subsidiary purchase ledger.

Step 3 Balance the purchase ledger control account, and review for errors.

Step 4 Adjust or post the necessary correcting entries to the control account.

Step 5 Prepare a statement showing how the corrected purchase ledger agrees to the corrected control account.

In the example below, it is necessary to write up the account for the year and then to prepare the **control account reconciliation statement.**

Example: Control account reconciliation

Minster plc at present makes use of a manual system of accounting consisting of a main ledger, a sales ledger and a purchase ledger together with books of prime entry. The various accounts within the ledgers are drawn up on ledger cards which are updated by hand from the books of prime entry when relevant transactions take place. The decision has now been taken to use a control account in the main ledger to help keep a check on the purchase ledger and the following figures relating to the financial year ended 31 October 20X1 have been extracted from the books of prime entry.

	£
Credit purchases	132,485
Cash purchases	18,917
Credit notes received from credit suppliers	2,361
Discounts received from credit suppliers	4,153
Cheques paid to credit suppliers	124,426
Balances in the sales ledger set off against balances in the purchase ledger	542

On 1 November 20X0 the total of the creditors was £28,603.

The purchase ledger accounts have been totalled at £28,185 as at 31 October 20X1.

Subsequent to the totalling procedure, the following matters are discovered.

(a) Whilst the totalling was taking place, the chief accountant was reviewing the account of Peterbury Ltd, a supplier, and the ledger card was on his desk. The balance of the account at 31 October was £1,836.

(b) A credit note for £387 issued by John Danbury Ltd, a credit supplier, was correctly entered in the day book but had not then been posted to John Danbury Ltd's account in the ledger.

(c) An invoice for £1,204 issued by Hartley Ltd, a credit supplier, was correctly entered in the day book and was then entered in Hardy Ltd's account in the purchase ledger.

(d) An invoice for £898 relating to a credit purchase from Intergram plc, although correctly entered in the day book, was posted to the supplier's account in the ledger as £889.

(e) A discount for £37 allowed to Minster plc by the credit supplier K Barden Ltd, had been correctly entered in the cash book but was then omitted from the company's account in the ledger.

Tasks

(a) Prepare a statement reconciling the original total of the purchase ledger accounts with the balance of your purchase ledger control account.

(b) Prepare Minster plc's purchase ledger control account for the year ended 31 October 20X1.

Solution

Steps 1, 2 and 5

		£	£
Balance as per listing of creditors accounts			28,185
Add:	Peterbury Ltd ledger card omitted	1,836	
	Posting error (Intergram plc)	9	
			1,845
			30,030
Less:	Credit note not posted (John Danbury Ltd)	387	
	Discount received (K Barden Ltd)	37	
			424
Balance as per PLCA			29,606

PART B CONTROL ACCOUNTS

Note. Item (c), the invoice from Hartley Ltd, although entered in the wrong personal account, is included in the purchase ledger listing and so does not affect the total.

Steps 3 and 4

PURCHASE LEDGER CONTROL ACCOUNT

	£		£
Credit notes received	2,361	Balance b/d	28,603
Discounts received	4,153	Purchases	132,485
Bank	124,426		
Contra sales ledger	542		
Balance c/d	29,606		
	161,088		161,088

Activity 5.2

(a) Which, if any, of the following could you see in a reconciliation of the purchase ledger control account with the purchase ledger list of balances?

    (i)   Mispostings of cash payments to suppliers
    (ii)   Casting errors
    (iii) Transposition errors

(b) Which of the following would you not expect to see reflected in a purchase ledger control account?

    (i)   Dividend payments
    (ii)   Invoices received, in summary
    (iii) Drawings
    (iv) Cheque payments
    (v)   Contras
    (vi) Returns to suppliers
    (vii) Debit notes to suppliers
    (viii) Discounts received

(c) You would never see a debit balance on a purchase ledger account.

	Tick
True	☐
False	☐

5.2 Integrated accounting systems

When we looked at the sales ledger control account in Chapter 4 we noted that, in a computerised system, different parts of the accounting system may be **'integrated'** together. Similar points apply to the purchase ledger as well.

Activity 5.3

A computerised accounting system contains three modules:

(a) Main ledger
(b) Purchase ledger
(c) Sales ledger

The system is an **integrated** one. This means that postings to the **main ledger** are made **automatically** from the sales and purchase ledgers.

In this situation, indicate whether the following statement is TRUE or FALSE.

		Tick
The purchase ledger control account total will *always* agree with the sum of the balances on the individual creditor accounts in the purchase ledger, and no disagreement is ever possible	True	☐
	False	☐

Activity 5.4

You are employed by Wallace & Grommet, a partnership. You have ascertained that as at 31 July 20X7 the purchase ledger control account balance of £57,997.34 does not agree with the total of the balances extracted from the purchase ledger of £54,842.40.

On investigation, some errors come to light.

(a) An account with a balance of £8,300.00 had been omitted from the purchase ledger balances.
(b) Purchases of £7,449.60 for June had not been credited to the purchase ledger control account.
(c) RNH Ltd's account in the purchase ledger had been undercast by £620.40.
(d) A van bought on credit for £6,400.00 had been credited to the purchase ledger control account.
(e) Returns outwards of £1,424.50 had been omitted from the purchase ledger control account.
(f) A cheque for £5,000.00 payable to SPL Ltd had not been debited to its account in the purchase ledger.
(g) Discounts received of £740.36 had been entered twice in the purchase ledger control account.
(h) A contra arrangement of £400.00 with a trade debtor had not been set off in the purchase ledger.

Tutorial note. With item (f), think carefully whether you are adding or deducting.

Task

Set out the necessary adjustments to:

(a) The schedule of balances as extracted from the purchase ledger
(b) The balance in the purchase ledger control account

5.3 And finally ...

Look back to the diagram in Section 3 of Chapter 2. Now you know about control accounts, it should all fall into place!

PART B CONTROL ACCOUNTS

Key learning points

- The purchase ledger control account (PLCA) records the total of the balances owed to credit suppliers. This record is prepared from postings from the purchase and purchase returns day books, the cash book and the journal.

- The PLCA, when reconciled to the purchase ledger, acts as a check on the accuracy of individual suppliers' purchase accounts in the purchase ledger, as well as acting as a form of internal check. If a trial balance or balance sheet is needed, a total trade creditors balance can be extracted from the account.

- The balance on the PLCA should be reconciled regularly with the sum of the subsidiary purchase ledger account balances.

Quick quiz

1. What does the balance on the purchase ledger control account represent?
2. Name two uses of a purchase ledger control account.
3. Discounts received from suppliers are credited to the purchase ledger control account. True or false?
4. What is the double entry for cash received to clear a debit balance on the purchase ledger control account?

    A   Debit cash; credit PLCA
    B   Debit PLCA; credit cash
    C   Debit PLCA; credit SLCA
    D   Credit PLCA; debit SLCA

5. The purchase day book is miscast. Would this affect the purchase ledger control account or the purchase ledger?
6. An invoice has been incorrectly entered in the purchase day book. Would this give rise to a difference between the purchase ledger control account and the total of purchase ledger balances?

Answers to quick quiz

1. The total amount owed by the business to its creditors.
2. (i) Provides means of checking accuracy of entries in the personal accounts.
   (ii) Provides a total creditors figure for the balance sheet.
3. False. They are debited.
4. A   DEBIT   Cash
       CREDIT   Purchase ledger control account
5. The purchase ledger control account.
6. No. Both would be incorrect.

PART B CONTROL ACCOUNTS

Activity checklist

This checklist shows which performance criteria, range statement or knowledge and understanding point is covered by each activity in this chapter. Tick off each activity as you complete it.

Activity

5.1 ☐ This activity deals with knowledge and understanding point 12: relationship between the accounting system and the ledger.

5.2 ☐ This activity deals with performance criteria 3.2.C.

5.3 ☐ This activity deals with range statement 3.2.3 control accounts: purchase ledger; computerised.

5.4 ☐ This activity deals with performance criteria 3.2.A, 3.2.B, 3.2.C and 3.2.E.

chapter 6

Other control accounts

Contents

1   The problem
2   The solution
3   Other control accounts

Performance criteria

3.2.A Make and record authorised adjustments
3.2.B Total relevant accounts in the main ledger
3.2.D Reconcile petty cash control account with cash in hand and subsidiary record
3.2.E Identify discrepancies arising from the reconciliation of control accounts and either resolve or refer to the appropriate person

Range statement

3.2.2 Adjustments: to correct errors
3.2.3 Control accounts: non-trade debtors
3.2.4 Discrepancies: cash in hand not agreeing with subsidiary record and control account.

Knowledge and understanding

13 Petty cash procedures: imprest and non imprest methods; analysis
15 Inter-relationship of accounts – double entry system
19 Relevant understanding of the organisation's accounting systems and administrative systems and procedures

1 The problem

The most common control accounts are for the purchase ledger and the sales ledger.

However other items need to be controlled as well.

- Wages and salaries
- Cash in hand
- Cash at bank
- Stocks
- Sundry debtors

2 The solution

The wages and salaries control account was dealt with in detail in Units 1 and 2.

The stock control account will form part of your Unit 5 studies.

The other items form part of your Unit 3 studies.

- Cash in hand (petty cash: Units 1 and 2 and this chapter)
- Cash at bank (bank reconciliation – see Chapter 3)
- Sundry debtors (this chapter)

3 Other control accounts

3.1 Petty cash

You have covered petty cash payments and receipts in your studies for Units 1 and 2. A **petty cash control account** may be used with the petty cash book. In this case, the subsidiary account is the petty cash book.

A petty cash control account might look like this.

PETTY CASH CONTROL ACCOUNT

Date 20X1	Details	£	Date 20X1	Details	£
6 June	Balance b/d	100.00	12 June	Petty cash book (Note)	76.42
12 June	Bank	76.42	12 June	Balance c/d	100.00
		176.42			176.42
13 June	Balance b/d	100.00			

Note. £76.42 is the total of the analysis columns for the week. A transfer of £76.42 from the bank account is needed to restore the imprest amount to £100.

The cash control account forms **part of the double entry**. It should be agreed to the petty cash book (the subsidiary account) and the cash in hand at regular intervals. Any discrepancies need to be investigated and either resolved or referred to your supervisor.

To make sure you have understood the cash control account, try this activity.

Activity 6.1

A petty cash control account is kept in the main ledger of Astbury Ltd. The petty cash book is the subsidiary account. Astbury Ltd do not operate an imprest system. At the beginning of August there is a balance brought forward of £214.

During August £196 was spent from petty cash, and at the end of the month £200 was put into the petty cash box from the bank. The cash in hand at the end of the month is £212.00.

Task

Enter these transactions into the petty cash control account below, showing clearly the balance carried down. Identify any discrepancy to cash in hand.

PETTY CASH CONTROL ACCOUNT

Date 20X1	Details	£	Date 20X1	Details	£

Activity 6.2

Following the events in Activity 6.1, you discover that an IOU for £2 was not included in the petty cash count of £212. Also a payment of £4 out of petty cash (supported by a valid petty cash voucher) had been omitted form the petty cash book and control account. Resolve the discrepancy found in Activity 6.1.

3.2 Non-trade debtors

The sales ledger control account only deals with trade debtors.

There could also be amounts owed to the business from non-trade debtors.

- Amounts owed for sale of fixed assets.
- Rents receivable from letting part of the factory or office premises.
- Recovery of incorrect payments

These non-trade debtors can be kept track of by means of a non-trade debtors control account. It is a convenient way of bringing all non-trade debtor balances together.

Example: Non trade debtors

Macon Ltd lets part of its office premises to Chardonnay Ltd at a rent of £2,000 pa, payable quarterly in advance. At 1 January 20X5 Chardonnay Ltd owed £500 rent due on 31 December 20X4 and also £1,500 for second-hand office furniture bought from Macon Ltd. What is the balance on the non-trade debtors control account at 1 January 20X5?

Solution

NON TRADE DEBTORS CONTROL ACCOUNT (NTDC)

	£		£
Rent receivable	500	Balance c/d	2,000
Sales of fixed assets	1,500		
	2,000		2,000
Balance b/f	2,000		

The other side of the entries will be as follows:

RENT RECEIVABLE

	£		£
Rent for year (P&L a/c)	2,000	Cash (3 × £500)	500
		NTDC	500
	2,000		2,000

SALE OF FIXED ASSETS

	£		£
Fixed assets disposal	1,500	NTDC	1,500

6: OTHER CONTROL ACCOUNTS

Key learning points

- ☑ **Petty cash** can be controlled by use of a control account and cash counts.
- ☑ Sundry **non-trade debtors** can be collected into one convenient total by means of a control account.

Quick quiz

1 A petty cash control account is not needed if an imprest system is used. True or false?
2 _____ debtors can be kept track of by using a control account. *Complete the blank.*

Answers to quick quiz

1 False. Even under an imprest system, checks need to be made that: cash in hand + IOUs + vouchers held = imprest amount.
2 **Non-trade** debtors can be kept track of by using a control account.

Activity checklist

This checklist shows which performance criteria, range statement or knowledge and understanding point is covered by each activity in this chapter. Tick off each activity as you complete it.

Activity

6.1 ☐ This activity deals with performance criteria 3.2.B and 3.2.D.

6.2 ☐ This activity deals with performance criteria 3.2.A and 3.2.E.

PART C

Initial trial balance

chapter 7

The correction of errors

Contents

1 The problem
2 The solution
3 Types of error in accounting
4 The correction of errors: journal entries
5 The correction of errors: suspense accounts

Performance criteria

3.2.A Make and record authorised adjustments

Range statement

3.2.1 Record: manual journal; computerised journal
3.2.2 Adjustments: to correct errors
3.3.3 Rectify imbalances in an manual accounting system by: adjusting errors; creating a suspense account

Knowledge and understanding

11 Identification of different types of errors
16 Use of journals

PART C INITIAL TRIAL BALANCE

1 The problem

Using control accounts, we have identified errors in the records. How do we document the corrections needed?

2 The solution

As with all accounting entries, we need documentation. In Chapter 2 the journal was mentioned as a book of prime entry.

The **journal** is a way of recording entries that do not go through the other books of prime entry e.g.
- Writing off bad debts (see Chapter 4)
- Setting up provision for doubtful debts (see Chapter 4)
- Correcting errors (this Chapter)

3 Types of error in accounting

You have already learned about errors which arise in the context of the cash book or the sales and purchase ledgers and their control accounts. Here we deal with errors that may be corrected by means of the **journal** or a **suspense account**.

It is not possible to draw up a complete list of all the errors which might be made by bookkeepers and accountants. If you tried, it is likely someone would commit a completely new error that you had not thought of.

However, it is possible to describe five **types of error** which cover most of the errors which can occur.

- Errors of **transposition**
- Errors of **omission**
- Errors of **principle**
- Errors of **commission**
- **Compensating** errors

Once an error has been detected, it needs to be put right.

If the error **involves a double entry** in the ledger accounts, then it is corrected using a **journal entry**.

When the error **breaks the rule of double entry**, then it is corrected by the use of a **suspense account** as well as a journal entry.

3.1 Errors of transposition

Transposition is when two digits are accidentally recorded the wrong way round.

Example: Transposition

A sale is recorded in the sales account as £11,279, but it has been incorrectly recorded in the sales ledger control account as £11,729. The error is the transposition of the **7** and the **2**. The consequence is that the debit will not be equal to the credit.

You can often detect a transposition error by checking whether the difference between debits and credits can be divided exactly by 9. For example, £11,729 − £11,279 = £450; £450 ÷ 9 = 50. (This only works, if transposition is the *only* problem!)

3.2 Errors of omission

An **error of omission** means failing to record a transaction at all, or making a debit or credit entry, but not the corresponding double entry.

Examples: Omission

If a business receives an invoice from a supplier for £1,350, the transaction might be omitted from the books entirely. As a result, both the total debits and the total credits of the business will be out by £1,350.

If a business receives an invoice from a supplier for £820, the purchase ledger control account might be credited, but the debit entry in the purchases account might be omitted. In this case, the total credits would not equal total debits (because total debits are £820 less than they ought to be).

3.3 Errors of principle

An **error of principle** involves making a double entry in the belief that the transaction is being entered in the correct accounts, but subsequently finding out that the accounting entry breaks the 'rules' of an accounting principle or concept.

Examples: Principle

Repairs to a machine costing £300 should be treated as revenue expenditure, and debited to a repairs account. If the repair costs are added to the cost of the fixed asset (capital expenditure) an error of principle has occurred. Although total debits equal total credits, the repairs account is £300 less than it should be and the cost of the fixed asset is £300 greater than it should be.

A proprietor sometimes takes cash for his personal use and during a certain year these drawings amount to £1,400. The bookkeeper reduces cash sales by £1,400 so that the cash book balances. This is an error of principle, and the result of it is the drawings account is understated by £1,400, and so is the total value of sales in the sales account.

3.1 Errors of commission

Errors of commission are where the bookkeeper makes a mistake in carrying out his or her task of recording transactions in the accounts.

Examples: Commission

Putting a debit entry or a credit entry in the wrong account. If telephone expenses of £342 are debited to the electricity expenses account, an error of commission has occurred. Although total debits and total credits balance, telephone expenses are understated by £342 and electricity expenses are overstated by £342.

Errors of casting (adding up). The total daily credit sales in the sales day book of a business should add up to £79,925, but are incorrectly added up as £79,325. The total sales in the sales day book are then used to credit total sales and debit sales ledger control account in the main ledger, so that total debits and total credits are still equal, although incorrect.

3.2 Compensating errors

Compensating errors are, coincidentally, equal and opposite to one another.

Example: Compensating errors

Two transposition errors of £360 might occur in extracting ledger balances, one on each side of the double entry. In the administration expenses account, £3,158 is written instead of £3,518, while in the sundry income account, £6,483 is written instead of £6,843. The debits and the credits are each £360 too low. Consequently, compensating errors hide the fact that there are errors.

4 The correction of errors: journal entries

Journal entries were covered in Units 1 and 2, so this will be familiar to you.

4.1 Journals

Date	Code	Debit £	Credit £
Account to be debited		X	
Account to be credited			X
(Narrative to explain the transaction)			

The journal requires the debit and credit entries to be equal. You will notice that we have used the journal format to show double entry postings earlier in this text.

Assessors often ask you to 'journalise' a transaction (ie to show the postings in the form of a journal entry), even where there are no errors and journals are not normally used. This is because journals show that you understand the double entry postings involved.

4.2 Using journals to correct errors

£200 is misposted to the gas account instead of to the rent account. A journal entry is made to correct the misposting error as follows.

1 May 20X7

DEBIT	Rent account	£200	
CREDIT	Gas account		£200

To correct a misposting of £200 between the gas account and the rent account.

If total debits were equal to total credits before the journal, then they will still be equal after the journal is posted.

Suppose total debits were originally £100,000 but total credits were £99,520. If the same correcting journal is put through, total debits will remain £100,000 and total credits will remain £99,520. Total debits were different by £480 *before* the journal, and they are still different by £480 *after* the journal.

This means that journals can only be used to correct errors which require both a credit and (an equal) debit adjustment.

Example: Journal entries

Write out the journal entries which would correct these errors. Ignore VAT.

(a) A business receives an invoice for £1,350 from a supplier which was omitted from the books entirely.

(b) Repairs worth £300 were incorrectly debited to the fixed asset (machinery) account instead of the repairs account.

(c) The bookkeeper of a business reduces cash sales by £1,400 because he was not sure what the £1,400 represented. In fact, it was drawings.

(d) Telephone expenses of £342 are incorrectly debited to the electricity account.

(e) A page in the sales day book has been added up to £79,325 instead of £79,925.

Solution

(a)
	DEBIT	Purchases	£1,350	
	CREDIT	PLCA		£1,350

A transaction previously omitted.

(b)
	DEBIT	Repairs account	£300	
	CREDIT	Fixed asset (machinery) a/c		£300

The correction of an error of principle: repairs costs incorrectly added to fixed asset costs

(c) DEBIT   Drawings   £1,400
    CREDIT   Sales   £1,400

An error of principle, in which sales were reduced to compensate for cash drawings not accounted for.

(d) DEBIT   Telephone expenses   £342
    CREDIT   Electricity expenses   £342

Correction of an error of commission; telephone expenses wrongly charged to the electricity account

(e) DEBIT   SLCA   £600
    CREDIT   Sales   £600

The correction of a casting error in the sales day book
(£79,925 – £79,325 = £600)

4.1 Computerised journals

Errors can be made on computerised systems just as easily as on manual ones. Computerised journals have the same format and use as manual ones.

5 The correction of errors: suspense accounts

5.1 What is a suspense account?

A suspense account is a **temporary** account which can be opened for a number of reasons. The most common reasons are as follows.

(a) A trial balance is drawn up which **does not balance,** ie total debits do not equal total credits (see Chapter 8).

(b) The bookkeeper knows where to post the credit side of a transaction, but **does not know where to post the debit (or vice versa)**. A cash payment might be made and must obviously be credited to cash. The bookkeeper may not know what the payment is for, and so will not know which account to debit.

In both these cases, the procedure is as follows:

Step 1   A temporary suspense account is opened up.

Step 2   Identify the problem and decide how to resolve it.

Step 3   Post the correcting entries using the journal.

5.2 Use of suspense account: when the trial balance does not balance

An error occurs which results in an **imbalance** between total debits and total credits in the ledger accounts. An accountant draws up a trial balance and finds that, for some reason total debits exceed total credits by £207. (The trial balance is a list of account balances. It will be covered more fully in Chapter 8.)

7: THE CORRECTION OF ERRORS

Step 1 He knows that there is an error somewhere, but for the time being he opens a suspense account and enters a credit of £207 in it. This serves two purposes.

(a) The accountant will not forget that there is an error to be sorted out.

(b) Now that there is a credit of £207 in the suspense account, the total debits equal total credits.

Step 2 He finds that he had accidentally failed to make a credit of £207 to purchases.

Step 3 The journal entry would be:

DEBIT   Suspense a/c   £207
CREDIT   Purchases   £207

To close off suspense a/c and correct error

When an error results in total debits not being equal to total credits, the first step an accountant makes is to open up a **suspense account**. Three more examples are given below.

Example: Transposition error

The bookkeeper of Remico made a transposition error when entering an amount for sales in the sales account. Instead of entering the correct amount of £49,287.90 he entered £49,827.90, transposing the **2** and **8**. The debtors were posted correctly, and so when total debits and credits on the ledger accounts were compared, it was found that credits exceeded debits by £(49,827.90 – 49,287.90) = £540.

Solution

The initial step is to equalise the total debits and credits by posting a debit of £540 to a suspense account. When the cause of the error is discovered, the double entry to correct it should be logged in the journal as:

DEBIT   Sales   £540
CREDIT   Suspense a/c   £540

To close off suspense a/c and correct transposition error

Example: Error of omission

When Reckless Records paid the monthly salary cheques to its office staff, the payment of £21,372 was correctly entered in the cash account, but the bookkeeper omitted to debit the office salaries account. So the total debit and credit balances on the ledger accounts were not equal, and total credits exceeded total debits by £21,372.

Solution

The initial step in correcting the situation is to debit £21,372 to a suspense account, to equalise the total debits and total credits.

When the cause of the error is discovered, the double entry to correct it should be logged in the journal as:

DEBIT	Office salaries account	£21,372	
CREDIT	Suspense account		£21,372

To close off suspense account and correct error of omission

Example: Error of commission

A credit customer pays £1,220 of the £1,500 he owes to Polypaint Ltd, but Polypaint's bookkeeper has debited £1,220 on the sales ledger control account in the main ledger by mistake instead of crediting the payment received.

Solution

The total debit balances in Polypaint's ledger accounts now exceed the total credits by 2 × £1,220 = £2,440. The initial step would be to make a credit entry of £2,440 in a suspense account. When the cause of the error is discovered, it should be corrected as follows.

DEBIT	Suspense account	£2,440	
CREDIT	SLCA		£2,440

To close off suspense account and correct error of commission

In the sales ledger control account in the main ledger, the correction would appear as follows (assuming that this customer is the only customer for clarity).

SALES LEDGER CONTROL ACCOUNT

	£		£
Balance b/d	1,500	Suspense account: error corrected	2,440
Payment incorrectly debited	1,220	Balance c/d	280
	2,720		2,720

The balance carried forward of £280 represents the original debt (£1,500) less the payment received (£1,220).

5.3 Use of suspense account: not knowing where to post a transaction

The second use of suspense accounts is when a bookkeeper **does not know in which account to post one side of a transaction**. Until this is sorted out, the entry can be recorded in a suspense account. An example is when cash is received through the post from a source which cannot be determined. Another example is to credit proceeds on disposal of fixed assets to the suspense account instead of working out the profit or loss on disposal.

Example: Not knowing where to post a transaction

Conway received a cheque in the post for £350. The name on the cheque is B Down, but the staff have no idea who this is, nor why he should be sending £350. The bookkeeper opens a suspense account, so that the double entry for the transaction is:

DEBIT	Cash	£350
CREDIT	Suspense account	£350

It turns out that the cheque was for a debt owed by Bob's Boutique and paid out of the proprietor's personal bank account. The suspense account can now be cleared.

DEBIT	Suspense account	£350
CREDIT	SLCA	£350

(and the correct entry will also be put through the sales ledger account for Bob's Boutique).

5.4 Suspense accounts might contain several items

If more than one error or unidentifiable posting to a ledger account arises during an accounting period, they will all be **merged together** in the same suspense account. Indeed, until the causes of the errors are discovered, the bookkeepers are unlikely to know exactly how many errors there are.

Activity 7.1

You are assisting the accountant of Ranchurch Ltd in preparing the accounts for the year ended 31 December 20X7. You draw up a trial balance and you notice that the credit side is greater than the debit side by £5,607.82. You enter this difference in a suspense account.

On investigation, the following errors and omissions are found to have occurred.

(a) An invoice for £1,327.40 for general insurance has been posted to cash but not to the ledger account.

(b) A customer went into liquidation just before the year end, owing Ranchurch £428.52. The amount was taken off the sales ledger control account but the corresponding entry to expense the bad debt has not been made.

(c) A cheque paid for purchases has been posted to the purchases account as £5,296.38, when the cheque was made out for £5,926.38.

(d) A van was purchased during the year for £1,610.95, but this amount was credited to the motor vehicles account.

Task

Set up a suspense account and show the entries to clear it.

Tutorial note. As total credits exceed total debits, you are missing a debit of £5,607.82.

Activity 7.2

Using the information in Activity 7.1, set out the journal needed to clear the suspense account.

5.5 Suspense accounts are temporary

A suspense account can only be **temporary**. Postings to a suspense account are only made when the bookkeeper doesn't know yet what to do, or when an error has occurred.

Mysteries must be solved, and errors must be corrected. Under no circumstances should there still be a suspense account when it comes to preparing the final accounts.

The suspense account **must be cleared** and all the correcting entries made before the final accounts are drawn up.

7: THE CORRECTION OF ERRORS

Key learning points

- ☑ There are five **types of error**.
    - Errors of transposition
    - Errors of omission
    - Errors of principle
    - Errors of commission
    - Compensating errors

- ☑ Errors which leave total debits and total credits on the ledger accounts in balance can be corrected by using **journal entries**. Otherwise, a suspense account has to be opened first (and a journal entry used later to record the correction of the error, clearing the suspense account in the process).

- ☑ **Suspense accounts**, as well as being used to correct some errors, are also opened when it is not known immediately where to post an amount. When the mystery is solved, the suspense account is closed and the amount correctly posted using a journal entry.

- ☑ **Suspense accounts are only temporary**. None should exist when it comes to drawing up the financial statements at the end of the accounting period.

Quick quiz

1. What are the five main types of error which might occur in accounting?
2. The two common errors of commission are putting a debit or credit in the _____ account and errors of _____ (adding up). *Complete the blanks.*
3. What is a suspense account?
4. Suspense accounts are temporary. True or false?

Answers to quick quiz

1. Errors of transposition, omission, principle, commission and compensating errors.
2. The two common errors of commission are putting a debit entry or a credit entry in the **wrong** account and errors of **casting** (adding up).
3. A suspense account is an account showing a balance equal to the difference between total debits and total credits.
4. True. Suspense accounts must be cleared before the final accounts are drawn up.

Activity checklist

This checklist shows which performance criteria, range statement or knowledge and understanding point is covered by each activity in this chapter. Tick off each activity as you complete it.

Activity

7.1	☐	This activity deals with performance criteria 3.2.A and range statement 3.3.3 creating a suspense account.
7.2	☐	This activity deals with performance criteria 3.2.A and range statement 3.2.1 manual journal.

chapter 8

From ledger accounts to initial trial balance

Contents

1 The problem
2 The solution
3 The initial trial balance
4 Computerised systems

Performance criteria
3.3.A Prepare the draft initial trial balance in line with the organisation's policies and procedures
3.3.B Identify discrepancies in the balancing process
3.3.C Identify reasons for imbalance and rectify them
3.2.D Balance the trial balance

Range statement
3.3.1 Trial balance: manual; computerised
3.3.2 Discrepancies in a manual accounting system: incorrect double entries; missing entries; wrong calculations
3.3.3 Rectify imbalances in a manual accounting system by: adjusting errors; creating a suspense account.

PART C   INITIAL TRIAL BALANCE

Knowledge and understanding

5	Double entry bookkeeping, including balancing accounts
8	Operation of manual accounting systems
9	Operation of computerised accounting systems, including output
15	Inter-relationship of accounts – double entry system
16	Use of journals
18	Function and form of the trial balance

1 The problem

So far we have concentrated on keeping the books of account. How do we get from the ledgers to the accounts?

2 The solution

This chapter takes you from the ledger accounts to the trial balance, which is the stage before the final accounts.

When you have worked through it, you will really feel that you are getting somewhere.

3 The initial trial balance

3.1 What is a trial balance?

There is no foolproof method for making sure that all entries have been posted to the correct ledger account, but a technique which shows up the more obvious mistakes is to prepare a **trial balance** (or list of account balances).

A **trial balance** is a list of ledger balances shown in debit and credit columns.

3.2 Collecting together the ledger accounts

Before you draw up a trial balance, you must have a **collection of ledger accounts**. These are the ledger accounts of Shabnum Rashid, a sole trader.

CASH

	£		£
Capital: Shabnum Rashid	10,000	Rent	4,200
Bank loan	3,000	Shop fittings	3,600
Sales	14,000	PLCA	7,000
SLCA	3,300	Bank loan interest	130
		Other expenses	2,200
		Drawings	1,800
			18,930
		Balancing figure: the amount of cash left over after payments have been made	11,370
	30,300		30,300
Balance b/d	11,370		

CAPITAL (SHABNUM RASHID)

	£		£
		Cash	10,000

BANK LOAN

	£		£
		Cash	3,000

PURCHASES

	£		£
PLCA	7,000		

PLCA

	£		£
Cash	7,000	Purchases	7,000

RENT

	£		£
Cash	4,200		

SHOP FITTINGS

	£		£
Cash	3,600		

SALES

	£		£
		Cash	14,000
Balance b/d	17,300	SLCA	3,300
	17,300		17,300
		Balance b/d	17,300

SLCA

	£		£
Sales	3,300	Cash	3,300

BANK LOAN INTEREST

	£		£
Cash	130		

OTHER EXPENSES

	£		£
Cash	2,200		

DRAWINGS ACCOUNT

	£		£
Cash	1,800		

The first step is to **'balance' each account**.

3.3 Balancing ledger accounts

This has already been covered above but, as it is needed for knowledge and understanding point 5 and often features in the exam for Unit 3, we will go over it again.

At the end of an accounting period, a balance is struck on each account in turn. This means that all the **debits** on the account are totalled and so are all the **credits**.

- If the **total debits exceed the total credits** the account has a **debit balance.**
- If the **total credits exceed the total debits** then the account has a **credit balance**.

Let's see how this works with Shabnum Rashid's cash account, which is shown on page 119.

Step 1	**Calculate a total** for **both sides** of **each ledger account.**
	Dr £30,300, Cr £18,930
Step 2	**Deduct** the **lower** total **from** the **higher** total.
	£(30,300 – 18,930) = £11,370
Step 3	**Insert the result of Step 2 as the balance c/d** on the side of the account with the lower total. Here it will go on the credit side, because the total credits on the account are less than the total debits.
Step 4	**Check** that the **totals on both sides** of the account are **now the same.**
	Dr £30,300, Cr £(18,930 + 11,370) = £30,300
Step 5	**Insert the amount of the balance c/d as the new balance b/d on the other side of the account.**
	The new balance b/d is the balance on the account. The balance b/d on the cash account is £11,370 Dr. ie £11,370 cash at bank.

In our simple example, there is very little balancing to do.

(a) Both the purchase ledger control account and the sales ledger control account balance off to zero.
(b) The cash account has a debit balance (the new balance b/d) of £11,370 (see above).
(c) The total on the sales account is £17,300, which is a credit balance.

The other accounts have only one entry each, so there is no totalling to do, but each account must still be balanced off.

3.4 Collecting the balances on the ledger accounts

If the basic principle of double entry has been correctly applied throughout the period, the **credit balances will equal the debit balances** in total. This is illustrated by collecting together the balances on Shabnum Rashid's accounts.

	Debit £	Credit £
Cash	11,370	
Capital		10,000
Bank loan		3,000
Purchases	7,000	
PLCA	–	–
Rent	4,200	
Shop fittings	3,600	
Sales		17,300
SLCA	–	–
Bank loan interest	130	
Other expenses	2,200	
Drawings	1,800	
	30,300	30,300

The order of listing the various accounts listed in the **trial balance** does not matter. It is just a method used to test the accuracy of the double entry bookkeeping.

3.5 What if the trial balance shows unequal debit and credit balances?

If the trial balance does not **balance** there must be an **error in recording of transactions in the accounts**. A trial **balance** will **not** disclose the following types of errors.

Type 1 The **complete omission** of a transaction, because neither a debit nor a credit is made.

Type 2 A posting to the correct side of the ledger, but to a **wrong account** (also called errors of commission).

Type 3 **Compensating errors** (eg debit error of £100 is cancelled by credit £100 error elsewhere).

Type 4 **Errors of principle** (eg cash received from debtors being debited to the sales ledger control account and credited to cash instead of the other way round).

If the trial balance does not balance, the difference goes to a suspense account (see Chapter 7).

PART C INITIAL TRIAL BALANCE

Example: Trial balance

As at the end of 29 November 20X1, your business High & Mighty has the following balances on its ledger accounts.

Accounts	Balance £
Bank loan	15,000
Cash	13,080
Capital	11,000
Rent	2,000
Purchase ledger control account (PLCA)	14,370
Purchases	16,200
Sales	18,900
Sundry creditors	2,310
Sales ledger control account (SLCA)	13,800
Bank loan interest	1,000
Other expenses	12,500
Vehicles	2,000

During 30 November the business made the following transactions.

(a) Bought materials for £1,400, half for cash and half on credit
(b) Made £1,610 sales, £1,050 of which were for credit
(c) Paid wages to shop assistants of £300 in cash

You are required to draw up a trial balance showing the balances as at the end of 30 November 20X1.

Solution

Step 1   Put the opening balances into a trial balance, so decide which are debit and which are credit balances.

Account	Debit £	Credit £
Bank loan		15,000
Cash	13,080	
Capital		11,000
Rent	2,000	
PLCA		14,370
Purchases	16,200	
Sales		18,900
Sundry creditors		2,310
SLCA	13,800	
Bank loan interest	1,000	
Other expenses	12,500	
Vehicles	2,000	
	60,580	61,580
Suspense account	1,000	-
	61,580	61,580

8: FROM LEDGER ACCOUNTS TO INITIAL TRIAL BALANCE

Step 2 Take account of the effects of the three transactions which took place on 30 November 20X1.

			£	£
(a)	DEBIT	Purchases	1,400	
	CREDIT	Cash		700
		PLCA		700
(b)	DEBIT	Cash	560	
		SLCA	1,050	
	CREDIT	Sales		1,610
(c)	DEBIT	Other expenses	300	
	CREDIT	Cash		300

Note. Wages would normally be in a separate account, but in this example they are just included in 'other expenses'.

Step 3 Amend the trial balance for these entries.

HIGH & MIGHTY: TRIAL BALANCE AT 30 NOVEMBER 20X1

	29/11/20X1		Transactions		30/11/20X1	
	DR	CR	DR	CR	DR	CR
Bank loan		15,000				15,000
Cash	13,080		(b) 560	1,000 (a)(c)	12,640	
Capital		11,000				11,000
Rent	2,000				2,000	
PLCA		14,370		700 (a)		15,070
Purchases	16,200		(a) 1,400		17,600	
Sales		18,900		1,610 (b)		20,510
Sundry creditors		2,310				2,310
SLCA	13,800		(b) 1,050		14,850	
Bank loan interest	1,000				1,000	
Other expenses	12,500		(c) 300		12,800	
Vehicles	2,000				2,000	
Suspense account	1,000				1,000	
	61,580	61,580	3,310	3,310	63,890	63,890

Step 4 Identify the error(s) and clear the suspense account.

You discover that a vehicle was purchased for £3,000. The cash paid was correctly entered, but the entry to the vehicles account was debit £2,000. A journal is posted to clear the suspense account.

SUSPENSE ACCOUNT

	£		£
Balance b/d	1,000	Vehicles (Journal)	1,000

PART C INITIAL TRIAL BALANCE

VEHICLES

	£		£
Balance b/d	2,000	Balance c/d	3,000
Suspense (Journal)	1,000		
	3,000		3,000

Step 5 Revise the trial balance.

Trial balance at 30 November 20X1

Account	Debit £	Credit £
Bank loan		15,000
Cash	12,640	
Capital		11,000
Rent	2,000	
PLCA		15,070
Purchases	17,600	
Sales		20,510
Sundry creditors		2,310
SLCA	14,850	
Bank loan interest	1,000	
Other expenses	12,800	
Vehicles	3,000	
	63,890	63,890

Activity 8.1

Bailey Hughes started trading as a wholesale bookseller on 1 June 20X7 with capital of £10,000 with which he opened a bank account for his business.

During June the following transactions took place.

June	1	Bought warehouse shelving for cash from Warehouse Fitters Ltd for £3,500
	2	Purchased books on credit from Ransome House for £820
	4	Sold books on credit to Waterhouses for £1,200
	9	Purchased books on credit from Big, White for £450
	11	Sold books on credit to Books & Co for £740
	13	Paid cash sales of £310 from the warehouse shop intact into the bank
	16	Received cheque from Waterhouses in settlement of their account
	17	Purchased books on credit from RUP Ltd for £1,000
	18	Sold books on credit to R S Jones for £500
	19	Sent cheque to Ransome House in settlement of their account
	20	Paid rent of £300 by cheque
	21	Paid delivery expenses of £75 by cheque
	24	Received £350 from Books & Co on account
	30	Drew cheques for personal expenses of £270 and assistant's wages £400
	30	Settled the account of Big, White
	30	Received a mystery cheque for £500, post the other side of the entry to suspense

8: FROM LEDGER ACCOUNTS TO INITIAL TRIAL BALANCE

Tasks

(a) Record the foregoing in appropriate books of original entry.
(b) Post the entries to the ledger accounts.
(c) Balance the ledger accounts where necessary.
(d) Extract a trial balance at 30 June 20X7
(e) The cheque for £500 turned out to be from RS Jones. Clear the suspense account.

Helping hand. This is a long question which will be good practice for your exam. In (a) you need to record the entries in the cash book, the sales day book and the purchase day book. In (b) you will post to the following ledger accounts: cash, sales, purchases, debtors, creditors, (SLCA and PLCA), capital, fixtures and fittings, rent, delivery expenses, drawings, wages and suspense.

4 Computerised systems

So far we have looked at the way an accounting system is organised. You should note that all of the books of prime entry and the ledgers may be either **hand-written books** or **computer records.** Most businesses use computers, ranging from one **PC** to huge **mainframe computer systems**.

All computer activity can be divided into three processes.

Areas	Activity
Input	Entering data from original documents
Processing	Entering up books and ledgers and generally sorting the input information
Output	Producing any report desired by the managers of the business, including financial statements

Activity 8.2

Your friend Lou Dight believes that computerised accounting systems are more trouble than they are worth because 'you never know what is going on inside that funny box'.

Task

Explain briefly why computers might be useful in accounting.

4.1 Batch processing and control totals

Batch processing: similar transactions are gathered into batches, then sorted and processed by the computer.

Inputting individual invoices into a computer for processing (**transaction processing**), is time consuming and expensive. Invoices can be gathered into a **batch** and **input and processed all together**. Batches can vary in size, depending on the type and volume of transactions and on any limit imposed by the system on batch sizes.

Control totals are used to ensure there are no errors when the batch is input. They are used to ensure the total value of transactions input is the same as that previously calculated.

Say a batch of 30 sales invoices has a manually calculated total value of £42,378.47. When the batch is input, the computer adds up the total value of the invoices and produces a total of £42,378.47. The control totals agree, therefore no further action is required.

If the control total does **not agree,** then checks have to be carried out until the difference is found. An invoice might not have been entered or the manual total incorrectly calculated.

Key learning points

- Balances on ledger accounts can be collected on a trial balance. The debit and credit balances should be equal.
- Any imbalance on the trial balance should be posted to a **suspense account**.
- The suspense account is **temporary**. It must be **cleared** before final accounts are prepared.
- Computer accounting systems perform the same tasks as manual accounting systems, but they can cope with greater volumes of transactions and process them at a faster rate.

PART C   INITIAL TRIAL BALANCE

Quick quiz

1   What is the other name for a trial balance?
2   If the total debits in an account exceed the total credits, will there be a debit or credit balance on the account?
3   What types of error will not be discovered by drawing up a trial balance?
4   A suspense account on a trial balance can be ignored. True or false?
5   What are the advantages of batch processing?

Answers to quick quiz

1   The trial balance is also sometimes called the 'list of account balances'.
2   There will be a debit balance on the account.
3   There are four types, summarised as: complete omission; posted to wrong account; compensating errors; errors of principle.
4   False. The reason for the imbalance must be investigated and the suspense account cleared.
5   Batch processing is faster than transaction processing and checks on input can be made using control totals.

Activity checklist

This checklist shows which performance criteria, range statement or knowledge and understanding point is covered by each activity in this chapter. Tick off each activity as you complete it.

Activity

8.1   ☐   This activity deals with performance criteria 3.3.A, 3.3.B, 3.3.C and 3.3.D.

8.2   ☐   This activity deals with knowledge and understanding point 9: operation of computerised accounting systems, including output.

PART D

Filing

chapter 9

Filing

Contents

1 Introduction
2 Information storage
3 Classifying, indexing and cross-referencing information
4 Storing documents securely

Performance criteria

3.2.F Ensure documentation is stored securely and in line with the organisation's confidentiality requirements

Knowledge and understanding

21 Organisational procedures for filing source information

1 Introduction

So far we have talked a lot about processing documents and the accounting system. In this chapter we will look at ways of storing the information which we are going to use.

2 Information storage

We are now going to look at the characteristics of a **filing system**, and at how files are organised and stored. This chapter should help you to deal with files in practice:

- Getting hold of them
- Finding documents within them
- Putting new documents into them

2.1 The features of an information storage system

Information for business users takes many forms. Whatever form documents and recorded information take, if they are to be of any use they must be maintained so that:

(a) **Authorised people** (and only authorised people) can get to the information they require quickly and easily

(b) Information can be **added to, updated and removed** as necessary

(c) Information is **safe from fire, loss or handling damage** for as long as it is required (but not necessarily for ever)

(d) Accessibility, flexibility and security are achieved as **cheaply** as possible

2.2 Files

A **file** is a collection of data records with similar characteristics.

Here are some examples of files.

(a) A sales ledger
(b) A purchase ledger
(c) A cash book
(d) Stock records
(e) The nominal ledger
(f) A price list
(g) A collection of letters, memos and other papers all relating to the same matter, usually kept within a single folder

We will be talking mainly about **paper files** or **manual files** in this chapter; you should bear in mind, however, that **electronic files** can be created and used in a computer system as well.

Files of data may be temporary, permanent, active, and non-active.

(a) **Master files** and **reference files** are usually **permanent**, which means that they are never thrown away or scrapped. They will be **updated** from time to time, and so the information on the file might change, but the file itself will continue to exist. The data in a master file will not change very often.

(b) A **temporary file** is one that is eventually scrapped. Many **transaction files** are held for a very short time, until the transaction records have been processed, but are then thrown away. Other transaction files are permanent (for example a cash book) or are held for a considerable length of time before being scrapped.

(c) An **active file** is one that is frequently used. For example, sales invoice files relating to the current financial year, or correspondence files relating to current customers and suppliers.

(d) A **non-active file** is one that is no longer used on a day-to-day basis. For example, files that contain information relating to customers and suppliers who are no longer current, and purchase invoices relating to previous financial periods.

Apart from basic records which group items of information about personnel, sales or stock etc, there are huge amounts of information passing through organisations needing to be kept track of. Consider the following examples.

- Letters, memos, faxes, emails
- Notes of phone calls and meetings
- Reports
- Advertising material and press cuttings
- Mailing lists
- Important/routine addresses and phone numbers
- Machinery documents such as guarantees or service logs
- Legal documents such as contracts, property deeds or insurance policies

2.3 Characteristics of a filing system

A 'good' file should possess some or all of the following characteristics.

(a) It should **contain all the information** you might want to look up.

(b) It should allow you to **find particular information easily**.

(c) It needs to be of a **convenient size**.

(d) It needs to have **room for expansion**.

(e) The file should be **stored close to you** and/or should be easy to get to when it is needed.

(f) The method used for storage should be **strong and secure** so that the file will not get damaged and information will not get lost.

A **filing system** for an entire organisation is not really much different. It should:

(a) **Contain all the information** that users might want

(b) Be classified and indexed in such as way as to make it **easy to find information** quickly

(c) Be **suited to the people who will use it**

(d) Be **reliable and secure**

(e) Be **flexible** enough to allow for expansion

(f) Be **cost-effective** to install and maintain. There is no point spending more to hold information on file than the information is actually worth

(g) Allow users to **retrieve information quickly**

Activity 9.1

Your organisation has just received the following letter. List the details that are likely to be used when deciding where it should be filed. What other department would you send a copy of the letter to?

SANDIMANS LTD

72 High Street, Epsom
Surrey EP12 4AB

Your reference: Z/0335/MJD
Our reference: BRC/1249/871

Mr G Latchmore
Purchasing Department
Lightfoot & Co
7 West Broughton St
LONDON W12 9LM

4 May 20X6

Dear Mr Latchmore

Stationery supplies

I refer to your letter of 11 April 20X6.

I am afraid that we are still unable to trace receipt of your payment of £473.20 in settlement of our invoice number 147829. I should be grateful if you would look into this and issue a fresh cheque if necessary.

Your sincerely

Mandy Sands

Mandy Sands

So, with all of this information floating around, how are we going to locate a particular item of information? We need to make sure that our information is held in an organised fashion, and that we have procedures in place so we can find what we are looking for quickly and easily.

3 Classifying, indexing and cross-referencing information

3.1 Classifying information

Information has to be filed in such a way that its **users know where it is and how to retrieve it** when it is needed. This means having different files for different types of information, and then **holding each file in a particular order**. Information in an individual file might be divided into categories and then held in a particular order within each category.

Classification is the process of grouping related items of information together into categories that reflect the relationship between them.

There are various ways in which information can be grouped together, or **classified**.

- (a) By **name** (for example correspondence relating to a particular person or company).
- (b) By **geography** (for example all documents relating to a particular country, area or city).
- (c) By **subject matter** (for example all documents relating to a particular contract, transaction or type of problem).
- (d) By **date** (for example all invoices for a certain month or year).
- (e) By **department** (for example profits or costs for each department or employees of each department).

Once broad classifications are established, the material can be **put into a sequence** which will make individual items easier to retrieve. Again there are various systems for arranging files.

- (a) **Alphabetical order** - for example customers listed in name order.
- (b) **Numerical order** - for example invoices listed in numerical order of invoice numbers.
- (c) **Alpha-numerical** (A1, A2, A3, B1, B2 and so on).
- (d) **Chronological order** - for example letters within a subject file listed by the date they were written.

These ways of subdividing and arranging data in a logical way within suitable categories make it possible to store, find and also **index** or **cross-reference** information efficiently.

Let us have a look at some of these systems for arranging information.

3.2 Alphabetical classification

The most common means of classification is **alphabetical**. In an alphabetical name system, items are filed according to the first and then each following letter of a person's or company's name (for example in the phone book). This sounds simple enough, and indeed it is most of the time, but there are some rules which must be followed.

PART D FILING

Surnames. The system works by surname. The hyphen is ignored in double-barrelled names. When surnames are the same, initials or first names are taken into account. All of this is illustrated below.

Dawson
Ullyott
Vivian
Watkins
Williams
Williamson
Winters, Douglas
Winters, George

Initials. Names made up of initials may come before whole-word names.

PBAB Parties Ltd
Party Time Ltd

Prefixes are included as part of the surname.

De Beauvoir
Le Bon
McVitee
Von Richthofen

Mc, Mac etc are all treated as if they were Mac, so:

McGraw
MacLaverty

and St is usually treated as Saint, so:

St Angela's Convent
Saint George's Chapel.

Titles and common words. Words such as 'Mr', 'Mrs', 'Sir', 'The', 'A' are ignored for filing purposes (or most names would be under M or T!) while departments, ministries, offices, local authorities and so on are filed under the key part of their name:

Stanwick, B (Mrs)	Bromley, London Borough of
Stock Exchange (The)	Fair Trading, Department of
Trend, N U (Prof)	Foreign Office
Finance, Ministry of	

Businesses with names like 'Phillip Smith Ltd', 'Frank Tilsley & Son, are sometimes listed under the first letter of the surname (as usual) but perhaps more often under the first letter of the whole name (P and F in the examples given).

Numbers which appear as names may also count as if they were spelled out as words:

84 Charing Cross Road (under 'E' for Eighty)
2001: A Space Odyssey (under 'T' for Two)
3i plc (under 'T' for Three).

You will find things arranged differently in some cases. Rules do vary from system to system. **Get to know the ones you have to work with in your organisation.**

The **alphabetical name system** is used, for example, in files of clients or customers, students, employees or members and also for index cards and cross-referencing (which we will come to later). It is simple to use and easily expandable: there is a 'right' place for files, so they can simply be taken out or slotted in as necessary.

3.3 Numerical classification

Numerical sequence is natural where standard documents are concerned. Invoices, for example, are numbered. So, if an invoice needs to be checked, its number need only be established (quoted by the enquirer, or looked up in the customer account) and it can be easily found. This is known as a **numerical-sequential** system.

Numerical classification is very **flexible**. Unlike the alphabetical method, you do not have to decide how much filing space to allocate to each letter, wasting space if you are too generous and having to shuffle the whole system along if you are too 'mean'. With numerical order, you simply give a new file the next number and position in the system.

On the other hand, numbers may not be very meaningful in isolation. A strict **alphabetical index** also has to be kept, and also a **numerical file list** or **accession register**, in order to establish the file number to look for. It also means that there is little room for subdivisions for easier identification and retrieval, although blocks of numbers can be allotted to different departments, say.

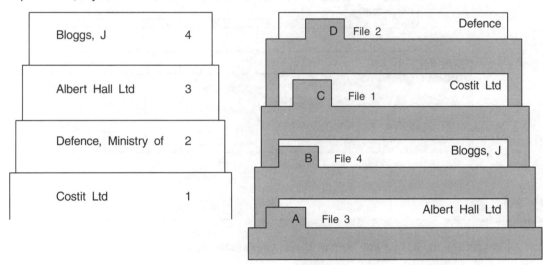

3.4 Alpha-numeric classification

In an **alpha-numeric system**, files are given a reference consisting of **letters** and **numbers**. For example a letter received from Mr Blotson about the purchase of a flat in Mayfair might be given the reference BLO/8745/99/1.

(a) The system uses the first three letters of the correspondent's name and a number to distinguish him from anybody else called Blotson and/or to indicate that the subject matter is domestic property. The number 99 indicates that this correspondence began in 1999.

(b) The 1 shows that it is the first file which has anything to do with this subject. If Mr Blotson's property deal fell through but he then found another flat, the correspondence relating to this would be kept in the separate but related file BLO/8745/99/2.

A system like this is most useful where there is a very large volume of correspondence on different but related topics. The Civil Service, for example, uses a system along these lines.

3.5 Other classifications

Using any of the above systems, bear in mind that you could group your files in any logical way. Common examples include:

(a) **Subject classification**, where all material relating to a particular subject (client, contract, project, product and so on) is kept together. (You just need to title your subjects thoughtfully, otherwise you end up with a lot of 'miscellaneous' items that do not fit your subject categories)

(b) **Geographical classification**, which is useful for sales, import/export and similar activities that may be organised by region or territory

Here is an example of geographical files, sub-classified by subject, in alphabetical order.

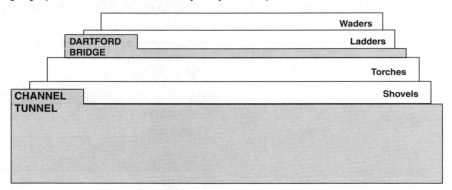

Activity 9.2

Listed below are details of thirty people who have written to your organisation.

	Name and address	Account	Date
1	Cottrell J, 5 Heathview Avenue, Bromley	–	2.6.96
2	Holden R, 27 Exning Road, Bexley	–	13.7.95
3	Williams J, 29 Gray Gardens, Dartford	100276	5.4.97
4	Bidwell D, 176 High Road, Dartford	–	16.5.98
5	Bexley J, 25 Romney Road, Orpington	400452	17.5.95
6	Maclean T, 1 Pitt Road, Orpington	400721	7.12.98
7	54321 Discos, 107 Warren Road, Bexley	300924	19.4.99
8	Dr J Crown, 20 Wimfred Street, Woolwich	–	1.1.96

	Name and address	Account	Date
9	Locke D, 22 Davis Street, Crayford	–	14.8.98
10	Sainton E, 15 Filmwell Close, Bromley	200516	3.5.99
11	Argent-Smith M, 17a Waterson Road, Bexley	–	7.8.99
12	Britton T, 81 Ward Avenue, Crayford	–	27.8.97
13	McLaughlin D, 80 Brookhill Road, Orpington	200435	4.3.97
14	Williams J A, 148 Godstow Road, Woolwich	–	6.6.99
15	O'Grady E, 40 Holborne Road, Sidcup	300989	4.4.94
16	Saint Francis Pet Shop, 14 Glenesh Road, Dartford	–	7.9.97
17	Emly P, 8 Faraday Avenue, Orpington	–	18.4.99
18	Harry Holden Ltd, 5 Clare Way, Bexley	100284	9.7.97
19	BRJ Plumbing, 132 Lodge Lane, Crayford	200223	25.11.98
20	Gisling B, 18 Dickens Avenue, Woolwich	–	6.3.99
21	Argentson S, 20 Porson Court, Dartford	400542	5.2.95
22	Kelsey L C, 58 Cudham Lane, Bromley	–	8.1.98
23	ILD Services Ltd, 4 Cobden Road, Orpington	200221	3.2.99
24	Van Saintby A, 69 Brookhill Close, Bromley	400693	5.2.99
25	Williams, John, 10 Buff Close, Dartford	–	2.12.98
26	Page W, 11 Leewood Place, Crayford	400442	9.7.96
27	Harrison P, Robinwood Drive, Dartford	101301	16.4.98
28	Briton N, 3 Chalet Close, Bexley	–	7.2.95
29	Richmond A, 9 Denham Close, Crayford	–	4.1.99
30	St Olave's Church, Church Way, Bromley	400371	21.2.98

Tasks

(a) Referring to the documents by number (1-30), in what order would they appear if they were filed in date order?

(b) Rearrange the names in alphabetical order, noting the reference number in brackets after the name.

(c) In what order would those correspondents with accounts appear if they were filed in account number order?

(d) Again referring to the documents by number, identify another sensible way of classifying them, and arrange them in this order.

Tutorial note. Use coloured highlighter pens!

PART D FILING

4 Storing documents securely

4.1 Environment

It is vital that material containing information is stored in an appropriate location and that its condition does not deteriorate.

Documents containing information may be classified and indexed so that they are easily accessible, but unless they can be kept in **good condition**, with **economy of storage space and cost**, they will not fulfil our requirements for an effective and efficient filing system.

4.2 Keeping documents in good condition

Paper can very easily get screwed up, torn, stained, or otherwise damaged. This can result in its contents becoming difficult to read or even getting lost. For example tearing off the edge of a misaligned print-out could easily result in the final column of figures being thrown away.

Punching holes in a document so that it can be placed in some form of ring binder also needs to be carefully done so that vital numbers or words are not affected. A sensible way of achieving this is shown below.

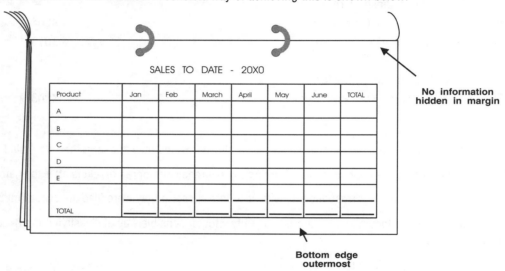

If **a file is too 'fat'** there is every likelihood that pages will get torn, fall out and get lost because of the difficulty of opening the file and keeping it open at the right page. If you need to be violent with a file it is not serving its purpose; you will be less inclined to consult the file and you run the risk of damaging its contents.

Obviously it is better not to let files get too fat in the first place, but if it is too late the best solution is to move some of the documents into a second volume. This may involve re-indexing the file or changing its title and altering any cross-references that have been made in the file itself or in other files.

Liquid and paper are not good friends: don't leave your coffee cup or your glass of water in places where you or somebody else is liable to knock them over.

4.3 Location

Most documents containing information will have to be placed in **folders** or **binders** before they can be housed in filing cabinets or other forms of storage. These come in a suitable range of sizes (for small pieces of paper or large computer printouts) and materials.

Plastic folders or **paper envelope (manila) folders** are the most common and cheapest methods. For larger volumes of information, there are **lever arch files** and **box files**. If information is to be kept for a long time but not referred to very frequently, then box files are useful. If they are to be referred to and updated more often, ring binders or lever arch files would provide security (there would be no loose bits of paper flying about) and accessibility.

4.4 Storage equipment

The following items of equipment are commonly used to store information.

- In-trays
- Pigeon-holes
- Filing cabinets
- Safes

An **in-tray** is a tray which lies horizontally, and is used to capture incoming documentation. If you have your own in-tray at work, you will know that it is best to sort through new information on a regular basis! When sorting through an in-tray it is usual to group documents which are **ready for filing, awaiting action**, or **for distribution**.

The main purpose of an in-tray is therefore **temporary storage** of information.

A **pigeon-hole** is very similar to an in-tray, but incoming documents are held in an upright, rather than a horizontal, position. In general, any incoming mail which is marked for your attention is placed in the first instance in your pigeon-hole. It is therefore also used as a **temporary store** for information.

Files containing information may be stored in an assortment of **filing cabinets**. The two main types of filing cabinet are **vertical suspension** and **lateral suspension**. The type of cabinet used will depend upon the space available in the office for such equipment, and the type of information to be stored.

4.5 Safes

A **safe** is a strong lockable cabinet which is used to store confidential or valuable information.

Most offices have some means of storing confidential or sensitive information. Safes normally have a **combination code** which must be entered correctly before they can be opened, and this code is normally known by one or two senior members of staff only.

Activity 9.3

Have a look around your office at work and look for examples of the different types of equipment that are used for storing and retrieving information.

4.6 Microfilm and microfiche

Microfilming is a particularly convenient means of information storage for saving space. Documents are photographed into a very much reduced ('micro') form. Microfilms are readable, but not to the unassisted naked eye, and a magnifying reading device (with a viewing screen) is needed by users. **Microfilm** is itself a **continuous strip** with images in frames along its length (like a photographic negative).

Micro film

Micro fiche

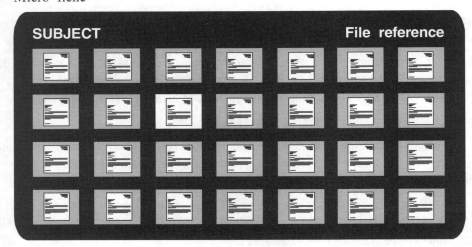

Microfiche is another method of storing information, but consists of **separate sheets of film**, rather than being a continuous strip like microfilm is. Microfiche is read by placing the fiche between two glass plates and moving a pointer (which is attached to the lens) across a grid. If you have never used a microfiche reader, see whether your local library has one, and have a practice.

Microfilm and microfiche need **special devices** in order to be read, updated or corrected. (If your organisation has 'computer aided retrieval' readers, see if you can get some coaching and practice on one.) However, they do offer very space-saving, durable and secure information storage.

4.7 File security and confidentiality

If files are **confidential** or **secret**, they will be '**classified**', which means that access will be limited to authorised people. A list of classified files will be required and a policy must be drawn up stipulating **conditions of access** (for example who keeps the keys to the security cabinet, and whether files may be copied or taken out of the filing room) and specifying who has clearance to consult classified material.

Circumstances in which files may become classified include the following.

(a) Where they contain **information of a personal nature**, for example personnel files, files about customers' credit status or (in a solicitor's office, say) details of a client's domestic circumstances.

(b) Where they contain **product or service information** which may be exploited by a competitor, like designs or marketing programmes.

(c) Where they contain **information concerning legal or financial deals**, the outcome of which could be affected by public knowledge of the details (for example when companies are considering merging or one is trying to take over another).

You can probably think of information which is '**sensitive**' in your organisation in that it could be misused to the organisation's disadvantage if it got into the wrong hands. If you are working on a 'classified' file, or if you have any reason to think documents in your possession may be of a sensitive nature, take care.

(a) Do not leave them lying around on your desk. **Put them away out of sight** when you are not using them, and lock them up if you have to leave your desk.

(b) Do not forget to **lock up secure cabinets** when you have finished with them, and return the keys to the authorised holder.

(c) **Do not send out copies** of potentially confidential material without checking with a superior that it is safe to do so.

(d) Do not leave confidential documents in the photocopier!

(e) **Respect the privacy of others**, just as you would expect them to respect yours.

Activity 9.4

Your manager is out of the office. He has phoned in and asked you to find a letter which is 'somewhere' on his desk and fax through a copy to him.

As you are searching for the letter you notice the following documents.

1 An electricity bill for £372.97 addressed to D Glover (your manager) at his home address.
2 A letter from a building society asking for a reference for one of your firm's clients.
3 A report entitled 'Potential Merger - Initial considerations'.
4 A mass of figures with your organisation's name at the head and the title 'Draft Budget'.
5 A staff appraisal report about you.
6 A thick sheaf of correspondence - the top sheet is signed 'Love, Nancy'.
7 A letter from P Glover asking for details about your organisation's services.
8 A *very* strongly worded letter of complaint from a Mrs Paribus.
9 A series of cuttings about your organisation from a trade journal.
10 A list of your organisation's directors with their addresses, telephone numbers and ages noted alongside.

Tasks

(a) Identify which, if any, of these documents you think should be filed away confidentially. Give reasons.
(b) Suppose that the letter that you had to fax was document 8 above. What would you do?

Key learning points

- Information is generally held on **files**. **Filing** is an integral part of creating information.
- A file is a collection of data records with similar characteristics. Files of data may be **temporary**, **permanent**, **active or non-active**.
- Characteristics of a **'good' file** are as follows.
  - It should contain all the information you may need
  - The information should be found easily
  - It should be of a convenient size
  - It should be capable of expansion
  - It should be easily accessible
  - It should be stored under suitable conditions so that it won't get damaged or lose its information
- An **index** is something which makes it easier to locate information or records.
- **Cross-referencing** information is commonly carried out when items of information could be filed in more than one place, or could be needed in connection with more than one enquiry.
- The three main systems for **classifying information** are **alphabetical**, **numerical** and **alpha-numerical**.

Quick quiz

1. A file is a collection of _____ with similar characteristics. *Complete the blank*
2. List four systems used for arranging files.
3. What procedures might be followed when adding new information to a filing system?
4. How is information that is no longer needed on a regular basis dealt with?
5. What are classified files?

Note: Questions 3 and 4 are revision of material from Units 1 and 2.

Answers to quick quiz

1. A collection of **data records** with similar characteristics.
2. Alphabetical order, numerical order, alpha-numerical, chronological order.
3. Indicate that document is ready for filing, remove any paperclips and binders, place documents at random in a filing tray, determine a reference number for the document if it does not already have one, determine into which file the document is to be inserted, sort batches of documents and insert into appropriate place in appropriate files.
4.
    - Microfilmed or microfiched
    - Archived
    - Destroyed
5. Confidential or secret.

Activity checklist

This checklist shows which performance criteria, range statement or knowledge and understanding point is covered by each activity in this chapter. Tick off each activity as you complete it.

Activity

9.1	☐	This activity deals with knowledge and understanding point 21: organisational procedures for filing source information.
9.2	☐	This activity deals with performance criteria 3.2.F.
9.3	☐	This activity deals with knowledge and understanding point 21 with regard to your own organisation.
9.4	☐	This activity deals with performance criteria 3.2.F.

PART D FILING

PART E

Answers to Activities

Answers to activities

Chapter 1

Answer 1.1

Transaction	Dr £	Cr £
Owner puts £500 into the business	Cash £500	Capital £500
Cash sales of £1,000	Cash £1,000	Sales £1,000
Purchases of £2,500 made on credit	Purchases £2,500	Creditors £2,500
Credit sales made totalling £5,000	Debtors £5,000	Sales £5,000
£2,000 received from debtor	Cash £2,000	Debtors £2,000
Business expenses paid of £750	Expenses £750	Cash £750
Drawing made of £1,000	Drawings £1,000	Cash £1,000

Note. Instead of debtors, you may have used the Sales Ledger Control Account and instead of creditors, you may have used the Purchase Ledger Control Account. If so, well done. We will be looking at Control Accounts in more detail in Part B.

Answer 1.2

(a) A balance sheet is a statement of the assets, liabilities and capital of a business at a given moment in time. The balance sheet will usually show the position on the date which is the end of the **accounting period** of the business; an accounting period is usually one year.

(b) (i) **Fixed assets** are assets acquired for use within the business, rather than for selling to a customer. A fixed asset must have a 'life' in use of more than one year.

   (ii) **Current assets** are:

   - Items owned by the business with the intention of turning them into cash within one year
   - Cash, including money in the bank, owned by the business

(c) (i) **Current liabilities** are debts of the business that must be paid within a year. This will normally include the bank overdraft, as overdrafts are repayable on demand unless special terms are negotiated.

   (ii) **Long-term liabilities** are debts which are not payable until some time after one year from the accounting date.

Answer 1.3

Revenue expenditure is the purchase of goods and services that will:

(a) Be used fully in the accounting period in which they are purchased, and so be a cost or expense in the profit and loss account

(b) Result in a current asset as at the end of the accounting period (because the goods or services have not yet been used or sold)

Capital expenditure is the purchase or improvement of fixed assets. These assets will provide benefits to the business in more than one accounting period and are not acquired to be resold in the normal course of trade. The cost of purchasing fixed assets is not charged in full to the profit and loss account. Instead, the fixed asset is gradually depreciated in the profit and loss account over a number of accounting periods. (Depreciation is dealt with later in your studies, in Unit 5.)

Since revenue items and capital items are accounted for in different ways, the correct and consistent calculation of profit for any accounting period depends on the correct and consistent classification of items as revenue or capital.

Answer 1.4

Tutorial note. The profit of £14,000 in the profit and loss account should be the balancing figure in the balance sheet.

SPOCK ENTERPRISES
BALANCE SHEET AS AT 30 APRIL 20X7

	£	£
Fixed assets		
Freehold premises		87,500
Fixtures and fittings		14,000
Motor vehicles		15,750
		117,250
Current assets		
Stocks	28,000	
Debtors	875	
Cash	700	
	29,575	
Current liabilities		
Bank overdraft	3,500	
Creditors	3,150	
Tax payable	6,125	
	12,775	
Net current assets		16,800
Total assets less current liabilities		134,050
Long-term liabilities		
Loan		43,750
Net assets		90,300
Capital		
Capital as at 1 May 20X6		76,300
Profit for the year		14,000
Capital as at 30 April 20X7		90,300

SPOCK ENTERPRISES
TRADING, PROFIT AND LOSS ACCOUNT FOR THE YEAR ENDED 30 APRIL 20X7

	£	£
Sales		243,775
Cost of sales		152,425
Gross profit		91,350
Other income		3,500
		94,850
Selling and distribution expenses	25,725	
Administration expenses	25,900	
Finance expenses	29,225	
		80,850
Net profit		14,000

Answer 1.5

You would normally expect the following documents to be involved in such a transaction.

(a) A letter of enquiry
(b) A quotation
(c) An order or letter of acceptance
(d) An order acknowledgement
(e) A delivery note
(f) An invoice
(g) A warranty or guarantee for the work performed (normally for a specified period of time)

Answer 1.6

Tutorial note. A trade discount is used to calculate the price at which goods change hands. In this question the price of the goods was £3,000 less a £600 trade discount, giving £2,400. The cash discount is then calculated on this figure, ie 5% of £2,400 = £120.

	£
60 toasters @ £50 each	3,000
Less 20% trade discount	600
Trade price	2,400
Less: 5% settlement discount (if taken)	120
	2,280

(a) From the above, if payment is made within 14 days, the total Smith Electrical would pay is £2,280.

(b) If payment is not made within 14 days, Smith Electrical can not take advantage of the cash discount and so would pay £2,400.

Answer 1.7

(a)
	£
Net amount (25 × £10)	250.00
Discount (5% × £250)	(12.50)
Net amount after discount	237.50
VAT @ 17.5% on £237.50	41.56

(b)
	£
Net amount (5 × £10)	50.00
Discount (5% × £50)	(2.50)
Net amount after discount	47.50
VAT @ 17.5% on £47.50	8.31

Remember VAT is **always** charged on the discounted price, even if the discount is not taken. Therefore VAT on any credit note should also be based on the full discounted price.

Chapter 2

Answer 2.1

(a) Cash book
(b) Sales day book
(c) Purchase day book
(d) Cash book
(e) Sales returns day book
(f) Purchase returns day book
(g) Cash book

Answer 2.2

(a) The two sides of the transaction are:

   (i) Cash is received (debit cash account).
   (ii) Sales increase by £60 (**credit** sales account).

CASH ACCOUNT

		£			£
07.04.X7	Sales a/c	60			

SALES ACCOUNT

		£			£
			07.04.X7	Cash a/c	60

(b) The two sides of the transaction are:
 (i) Cash is paid (**credit** cash account).
 (ii) Rent expense increases by £4,500 (**debit** rent account).

CASH ACCOUNT

	£			£
		07.04.X7	Rent a/c	4,500

RENT ACCOUNT

		£		£
07.04.X7	Cash a/c	4,500		

(c) The two sides of the transaction are:
 (i) Cash is paid (credit cash account).
 (ii) Purchases increase by £3,000 (debit purchases account).

CASH ACCOUNT

	£			£
		07.04.X7	Purchases a/c	3,000

PURCHASES ACCOUNT

		£		£
07.04.X7	Cash a/c	3,000		

(d) The two sides of the transaction are:
 (i) Cash is paid (credit cash account).
 (ii) Assets – in this case, shelves - increase by £6,000 (debit shelves account).

CASH ACCOUNT

	£			£
		07.04.X7	Shelves a/c	6,000

SHELVES (ASSET) ACCOUNT

		£		£
07.04.X7	Cash a/c	6,000		

Tutorial note. If all four of these transactions related to the same business, the cash account of that business would end up looking as follows.

CASH ACCOUNT

		£			£
07.04.X7	Sales a/c	60	07.04.X7	Rent a/c	4,500
				Purchases a/c	3,000
				Shelves a/c	6,000

Answer 2.3

(a)	DEBIT	Machine (fixed asset)	£8,000	
	CREDIT	Creditors (A)		£8,000
(b)	DEBIT	Purchases	£500	
	CREDIT	Creditors (B)		£500
(c)	DEBIT	Debtors (C)	£1,200	
	CREDIT	Sales		£1,200
(d)	DEBIT	Creditors (D)	£300	
	CREDIT	Cash		£300
(e)	DEBIT	Cash	£180	
	CREDIT	Debtors (E)		£180
(f)	DEBIT	Wages expense	£4,000	
	CREDIT	Cash		£4,000
(g)	DEBIT	Rent expense	£700	
	CREDIT	Creditors (G)		£700
(h)	DEBIT	Creditors (G)	£700	
	CREDIT	Cash		£700
(i)	DEBIT	Insurance expense	£90	
	CREDIT	Cash		£90

Answer 2.4

	Original document	*Book of prime entry*	*Accounts in main ledger to be posted to*	
			Dr	Cr
(a)	Sales invoice	Sales day book	Debtors	Sales
(b)	Credit note	Sales returns day book	Sales/Returns inward	Debtors
(c)	Till rolls and/or sales invoices and receipts, bank paying-in book	Cash book	Cash	Sales

All these transactions would be entered into the double entry system by means of periodic postings from the books of prime entry to the main ledger.

Answer 2.5

	Main ledger		Subsidiary ledger	
	Dr	Cr	Dr	Cr
(a)	PLCA	Cash	PL – Jones	–
(b)	Purchases	PLCA	–	PL – Davis Wholesalers Ltd
(c)	PLCA	Purchases	PL – K Williams	–
(d)	Fixtures a/c	Cash	–	–
(e)	Fixtures a/c	Cash	–	–
(f)	Purchases	Cash	–	–
(g)	SLCA	Sales	SL – R Newman	–
(h)	Insurance a/c	Cash	–	–
(i)	SLCA	Cash	SL – J Baxter	–

SLCA = Sales ledger control account
PLCA = Purchase ledger control account
SL = Sales ledger
PL = Purchase ledger

Answer 2.6

(a) *Purchase of goods on credit*

    (i)   The supplier's invoice would be the original document.
    (ii)   The original entry would be made in the purchase day book.
    (iii) The entries made would be:

DEBIT   Purchases
CREDIT   Purchase ledger control account

(b) *Allowances to credit customers on the return of faulty goods*

    (i)   The usual documentation is a credit note.
    (ii)   The book of original entry would be the sales returns day book.
    (iii) The double entry would be:

DEBIT   Sales (or sales returns)
CREDIT   Sales ledger control account/individual debtor's account in the sales ledger

(c) *Petty cash reimbursement*

    (i)   The original documents for the data would be receipts and a petty cash voucher.
    (ii)   The transaction would be entered in the petty cash book.
    (iii) The double entry would be:

DEBIT   Entertaining expenses
CREDIT   Petty cash

Chapter 3

Answer 3.1

(a) **Sheet number 72.** The bank numbers each statement sheet issued for the account. Transactions from 1 March 20X7 onwards will be shown on statement number 73, and so on. Numbering the statements in this way allows the customer to check that none of its bank statements are missing.

(b) **Bank giro credit.** The bank giro credit system enables money to be paid in to any bank for the credit of a third party's account at another bank. Pronto Motors has paid in £162.40 for the credit of Gary Jones Trading's account at Southern Bank. A bank giro credit may take around two or three days for the banks to process.

(c) **£59.03 OD.** This shows that there is a debit balance (an overdraft) of £59.03 at the bank on 11 February 20X7. Gary Jones Trading is at that point a *debtor* of the bank; the bank is a *creditor* of Gary Jones Trading.

(d) **Direct debit.** Swingate Ltd must have authority (by means of a direct debit mandate signed on behalf of Gary Jones Trading Ltd) to take a direct debit from its account. This arrangement allows payments to be made to a third party without a cheque having to be sent.

(e) **Bank charges.** The bank may make various charges to cover its costs in providing bank services to the customer. The bank will be able to explain how its charges are calculated.

Answer 3.2

CASH BOOK

Receipts				Payments		
Date 20X7	Details		£	Date 20X7	Details	£
	Balance b/d		596.74	21 Feb	Swingate	121.00
23 Feb	Bord & Sons		194.60	28 Feb	Bank charges	15.40
				28 Feb	Balance c/d	654.94
			791.34			791.34

Answer 3.3

GARY JONES TRADING LIMITED
BANK RECONCILIATION STATEMENT AS AT 28 FEBRUARY 20X7

	£	£
Balance per bank statement		611.93
Add outstanding lodgement (Warleys Ltd)		342.50
		954.43
Less: unpresented cheques		
800124	207.05	
800125	92.44	
		(299.49)
Balance per cash book		654.94

Answer 3.4

(a) (i)

CASH BOOK

	£		£
Uncorrected balance b/d	24.13	Overdraft interest	24.88
Error in cash book	27.00	Balance c/d	26.25
	51.13		51.13

(ii) GEMFIX ENGINEERING LIMITED
BANK RECONCILIATION STATEMENT AS AT 31 OCTOBER 20X7

	£
Balance as per bank statement (overdrawn)	(142.50)
Less: unpresented cheques (total)	(121.25)
	(263.75)
Add: cheque paid in, not yet credited on bank statement	290.00
Balance as per cash book	26.25

(b) There are three reasons why bank reconciliation statements should be prepared regularly and on time.

(i) The company's records should be updated for items such as bank charges and dishonoured cheques so that managers are not working with an incorrect figure for the bank balance.

(ii) Errors should be identified and corrected as soon as possible, whether they are made by the company or by the bank.

(iii) Checks should be made on the time delay between cheques being written and their presentation for payment, and to check the time taken for cheques and cash paid in to be credited to the account. A better understanding of such timing differences will help managers to improve their cash planning.

Answer 3.5

(a)

CASH BOOK

Date 20X0	Details	Bank £	Date 20X0	Cheque No	Details	Bank £
1 Sept	Balance b/f	13,400	1 Sept	108300	J Hibbert	1,200
1 Sept	L Peters	400	5 Sept	108301	Cleanglass	470
28 Sept	John Smith	2,400	25 Sept	108302	Denham Insurers	630
29 Sept	KKG Ltd	144	29 Sept	108303	Kelvin Ltd	160
8 Sept	Zebra Sales	4,000			Salaries	9,024
30 Sept	Bristol Ltd	2,000			West Council	300
					Any Bank	400
					Bank charges	132
					Balance c/d	10,028
		22,344				22,344
	Balance b/d	10,028				

(b) BANK RECONCILIATION AT 30 SEPTEMBER 20X0

	£
Balance per bank statement	8,114
Less: unpresented cheque 108302	(630)
	7,484
Add: uncleared receipts (2,400 + 144)	2,544
Balance per cash book	10,028

Chapter 4

Answer 4.1

SALES LEDGER CONTROL ACCOUNT

		£			£
Debit balances b/d	(1)	X	Credit balances b/d	(1)	X
Sales	(2)	X	Cash receipts	(3)	X
Bank (refunds)	(3) or (5)	X	Credit notes	(4)	X
Bank (dishonoured cheques)	(3) or (5)	X	Bad debt expense	(5)	X
Credit balances c/d	(6)	X	Discount allowed*	(3)	X
			Debit balances c/d	(6)	X
		X			X

Sources of entries

(1) Brought down from previous period's control account once closed off.
(2) Sales day book.
(3) Cash book and petty cash book.
(4) Sales returns day book.
(5) Journal.
(6) Calculated and reconciled with sales ledger total of balances.

Tutorial note

* Discounts allowed reflects only cash or settlement discounts, not trade discounts.

** Individual entries to the account would be dated and would have references to the appropriate book of prime entry/journal. These details have been omitted for the purposes of clarity.

Answer 4.2

ITEMS **NOT** APPEARING IN THE SALES LEDGER CONTROL ACCOUNT

1 and 2 Credit and debit balances on individual debtor accounts

Individual debtors accounts do not appear in the sales ledger control account, although the transactions which give rise to them (sales, cash receipts etc) do. The sales ledger control account is a total account.

ANSWERS TO ACTIVITIES

3 Cash sales

The sales ledger control account deals with sales made on credit. Cash sales (*Debit* Cash; *Credit* Sales) have nothing to do with it.

7 Trade discounts received

These are discounts on what has been purchased, so have nothing to do with sales.

11 Credit notes received

These have the effect of reducing what *we* owe to other people, so they have nothing to do with the sales ledger control account.

ITEMS THAT **DO** APPEAR IN THE SALES LEDGER CONTROL ACCOUNT (You would **not** include these in your answer.)

4 Sales on credit

This should need no explaining.

5 Credit notes issued

A credit note can be issued to reduce the value of the debt. This might be the result of a sales return, or correction of an error. (Note that if separate records of sales returns are processed, credit notes would only be processed in respect of other items, so as to avoid any double counting.)

6 Settlement discounts allowed

A settlement discount is given to a debtor who pays early, and so reduces the value of the debt. If someone owes £100, but you say that you'll reduce the amount to £95 if they pay within 2 weeks, then you have given a settlement discount of £5. The whole of the original debt is cleared - of the £100 owed, your customer has paid £95, and you have basically written off £5 to the profit and loss account.

8 Cash receipts

These are payments from debtors. They reduce the debt.

9 Bad debts written off

Writing off a bad debt involves removing the debt from the sales ledger and making a corresponding entry to the sales ledger control account, and then the profit and loss account.

10 Sales returns

These arise when sold goods are returned and the return is accepted. The debtor no longer owes the money, so the debt is cancelled. Sales returns would be posted from the sales returns day book as a total, a method similar to the way in which total sales are posted from the sales day book.

Answer 4.3

SLCA

Date	Description	£	Date	Description	£
1.10.X1	Balance b/f (b)	30,000	15.1.X2	Bad debts-Fall Ltd (c)	2,000
30.9.X2	Sales (d)	187,800	30.9.X2	Cash (e)	182,500
				Discounts allowed (f)	5,300
				Bad debts (g)	3,500
				Balance c/d	24,500
		217,800			217,800
1.10.X2	Balance b/d	24,500			

SALES ACCOUNT

Date	Description	£	Date	Description	£
30.9.X2	Trading profit and loss account	234,600	30.9.X2	Cash (d)	46,800
				SLCA (d)	187,800
		234,600			234,600

BAD DEBTS ACCOUNT

Date	Description	£	Date	Description	£
15.1.X2	SLCA-Fall Ltd (c)	2,000	30.9.X2	Trading profit and loss account	5,500
30.9.X2	SLCA (g)	3,500			
		5,500			5,500

PROVISION FOR DOUBTFUL DEBTS ACCOUNT

Date	Description	£	Date	Description	£
30.9.X2	Balance c/d (h) 5% × £24,500	1,225	1.10.X1	Balance b/f (b) 5% × £30,000	1,500
	Profit and loss account reduction in provision	275			
		1,500			1,500
			1.10.X2	Balance b/d	1,225

DISCOUNTS ALLOWED ACCOUNT

Date	Description	£	Date	Description	£
30.9.X2	SLCA(f)	5,300	30.9.X2	Trading profit and loss account	5,300

CASH ACCOUNT (EXTRACT)

Date	Description	£			
30.9.X2	SLCA(e)	182,500			
	Sales(d)	46,800			

TRADING PROFIT AND LOSS (EXTRACT)

		£			£
30.9.X2	Bad debts	5,500	30.9.X2	Sales	234,600
	Discounts allowed	5,300		Provision for doubtful debts	275

Note. The £275 reduction in the provision for doubtful debts can also be credited to the bad debts account rather than directly to the trading, profit and loss account. In that case, the balance transferred to the trading, profit and loss account for bad debts would be £5,225.

Answer 4.4

(a)

UNADJUSTED SALES LEDGER CONTROL ACCOUNT

	£		£
Balance b/d	12,404.86	Balance b/d	322.94
Sales	96,464.41	Returns inwards	1,142.92
Bank: cheques dishonoured	192.00	Bank	94,648.71
Balance c/d	337.75	Discounts allowed	3,311.47
		Balance c/d	9,972.98
	109,399.02		109,399.02
Balance b/d	9,972.98	Balance b/d	337.75

(b)

ADJUSTED SALES LEDGER CONTROL ACCOUNT

	£		£
Unadjusted balance b/d	9,972.98	Unadjusted balance b/d	337.75
Sales: receipts from cash sales wrongly credited to debtors	3,440.00	Bad debt written off	77.00
Sales day book undercast	427.80	Returns outwards: returns to suppliers wrongly debited to debtors	3,711.86
Balance c/d	337.75	Balance c/d	10,051.92
	14,178.53		14,178.53
Balance b/d	10,051.92	Balance b/d	337.75

Supernova Ltd has debtors of £10,051.92. It also has a creditor of £337.75.

Errors (v) and (vi) relate to entries in **individual customer accounts** in the sales ledger and have no effect on the control account in the main ledger.

Answer 4.5

(a)

SALES LEDGER CONTROL

		£			£
1.12.X6	Balance b/d	50,241	20X7	Returns inwards	41,226
20X7	Sales	472,185		Bad debts written off	1,914
	Cheques dishonoured	626		Discounts allowed	2,672
				Cheques received	429,811
			30.11	Balance c/d	47,429
		523,052			523,052

PART E ANSWERS TO ACTIVITIES

(b)

		£	£
Balance per P Johnson			46,347
Add:	Whitchurch Ltd invoice, previously omitted from ledger	267	
	Rectofon Ltd balance, previously omitted from list	2,435	
	casting error in list total (£46,747, not £46,347)	400	
			3,102
			49,449
Less:	error on posting of Bury plc's credit note to ledger	20	
	P Fox & Son (Swindon) Ltd's balance included twice	2,000	
			2,020
Balance per sales ledger control account			47,429

Chapter 5

Answer 5.1

Answer C is correct.

Helping hand. Computerisation has meant that a number of different ways of processing creditors can be implemented. Some of these you might encounter in your work. Two examples are given below.

(a) A separate purchase ledger module is *not* maintained. There is no purchase ledger control account. Instead there is a separate account for every creditor in the main ledger.

(b) A separate purchase ledger module is maintained, but the role of the purchase day book is different in that each invoice is posted individually to the purchase ledger control account, VAT account, and purchase ledger account (ie the posting to the purchases ledger control account is not on a summary basis). The control account is still only a total account, however.

The use of the purchase day book and the purchase ledger, as separate from the main ledger to which summary postings are made, is merely for *convenience*.

Answer 5.2

(a) All of them.

    (i) Not all cash payments are to trade creditors, so a payment could be given a wrong main ledger account code.

    (ii) These could be found in a manual system, or could be caused by a fault in a computer program.

    (iii) Transposition errors could be caused if the purchase ledger, main ledger and purchase day book were separate, and there were manual postings.

(b) (i) Dividend payments and (iii) drawings do not relate in any way to trade purchase.

(c) FALSE. You might overpay a supplier, or pay before the goods have been received and invoiced, or pay the wrong supplier.

Answer 5.3

FALSE

In any accounting system, whether computerised or manual, accounts can be altered by use of the journal. It would be quite possible to make adjustments to the purchase ledger control account which, for whatever reason, are not reflected in the purchase ledger. So, while the purchase ledger updates the purchase ledger control account, there might be other differences.

It depends on which type of accounting system is used.

Answer 5.4

WALLACE AND GROMMET
RECONCILIATION OF PURCHASE LEDGER BALANCES WITH THE PURCHASE LEDGER CONTROL ACCOUNT
AS AT 31 JULY 20X7

			£	£
(a)	Balances according to purchase ledger			54,842.40
	Add:	Account omitted (a)	8,300.00	
		RNH's account undercast (c)	620.40	
				8,920.40
				63,762.80
	Deduct:	Cheque not debited to SPL's account (f)	5,000.00	
		Contra arrangement omitted (h)	400.00	
				5,400.00
	Amended balance as at 31 July 20X7			58,362.80

Tutorial note. The cheque for £5,000 is deducted. If it had been properly debited in the first place it would have **reduced** SPL's balance.

			£	£
(b)	Balance according to the purchase ledger control account			57,997.34
	Add:	Discounts received entered twice (g)	740.36	
		Purchases for June (b)	7,449.60	
				8,189.96
				66,187.30
	Deduct:	Vehicle erroneously entered as purchases (d)	6,400.00	
		Returns outward omitted from account (e)	1,424.50	
				7,824.50
	Amended balance as at 31 July 20X7			58,362.80

Chapter 6

Answer 6.1

PETTY CASH CONTROL

Date 20X1	Details	£	Date 20X1	Details	£
1 Aug	Balance b/f	214	31 Aug	Petty cash	196
31 Aug	Bank	200	31 Aug	Balance c/d	218
		414			414
1 Sept	Balance b/d	218			

RECONCILIATION

	£
Balance per petty cash control account	218
Cash in hand	212
Discrepancy (to be investigated)	£6

Answer 6.2

	£
Balance per petty cash control account (as above)	218
Less: payment omitted from the analysis	(4)
Balance of cash in hand per accounts	214
Cash in hand (as above)	212
IOU omitted	2
Balance of cash in hand	214

Chapter 7

Answer 7.1

SUSPENSE ACCOUNT

	£		£
Balance b/d	5,607.82	Insurance	1,327.40
		Bad debt expense	428.52
		Purchases (£5,926.38 – £5,296.38)	630.00
		Motor vehicles (£1,610.95 × 2)	3,221.90
	5,607.82		5,607.82

ANSWERS TO ACTIVITIES

Tutorial note. The van should be **debited** to the motor vehicles account, but it has been credited in error. Therefore we need **two debit** entries in the **motor vehicles account** – one to cancel the original posting and the second to complete the correct double entry. The two credit entries are to suspense.

Answer 7.2

		£	£
DEBIT	Insurance	1,327.40	
	Bad debt expense	428.52	
	Purchases	630.00	
	Motor vehicles	3,221.90	
CREDIT	Suspense account		5,607.82

Correction of errors and clearance of suspense account.

Chapter 8

Answer 8.1

(a) The relevant books of prime entry are the cash book, the sales day book and the purchase day book.

CASH BOOK (RECEIPTS)

Date June	Narrative	Total £	Capital £	Sales £	Debtors £	Suspense £
1	Capital	10,000	10,000			
13	Sales	310		310		
16	Waterhouses	1,200			1,200	
24	Books & Co	350			350	
30	Unknown receipt	500				500
		12,360	10,000	310	1,550	500

CASH BOOK (PAYMENTS)

Date June	Narrative	Total £	Fixtures and fittings £	Creditors £	Rent £	Delivery expenses £	Drawings £	Wages £
1	Warehouse Fittings Ltd	3,500	3,500					
19	Ransome House	820		820				
20	Rent	300			300			
21	Delivery expenses	75				75		
30	Drawings	270					270	
30	Wages	400						400
30	Big, White	450		450				
		5,815	3,500	1,270	300	75	270	400

PART E ANSWERS TO ACTIVITIES

SALES DAY BOOK

Date	Customer	Amount £
June		
4	Waterhouses	1,200
11	Books & Co	740
18	R S Jones	500
		2,440

PURCHASE DAY BOOK

Date	Supplier	Amount £
June		
2	Ransome House	820
9	Big, White	450
17	RUP Ltd	1,000
		2,270

(b) and (c)

The relevant ledger accounts are for cash, sales, purchases, creditors, debtors, capital, fixtures and fittings, rent, delivery expenses, drawings and wages.

CASH ACCOUNT

	£		£
June receipts	12,360	June payments	5,815
		Balance c/d	6,545
	12,360		12,360
Balance b/d	6,545		

SALES ACCOUNT

	£		£
		Cash	310
Balance c/d	2,750	SLCA	2,440
	2,750		2,750
		Balance b/d	2,750

PURCHASES ACCOUNT

	£		£
PLCA	2,270	Balance c/d	2,270
Balance b/d	2,270		

SLCA

	£		£
Sales	2,440	Cash	1,550
		Balance c/d	890
	2,440		2,440
Balance b/d	890		

PLCA

	£		£
Cash	1,270	Purchases	2,270
Balance c/d	1,000		
	2,270		2,270
		Balance b/d	1,000

CAPITAL ACCOUNT

	£		£
Balance c/d	10,000	Cash	10,000
		Balance b/d	10,000

FIXTURES AND FITTINGS ACCOUNT

	£		£
Cash	3,500	Balance c/d	3,500
Balance b/d	3,500		

RENT ACCOUNT

	£		£
Cash	300	Balance c/d	300
Balance b/d	300		

DELIVERY EXPENSES ACCOUNT

	£		£
Cash	75	Balance c/d	75
Balance b/d	75		

DRAWINGS ACCOUNT

	£		£
Cash	270	Balance c/d	270
Balance b/d	270		

WAGES ACCOUNT

	£		£
Cash	400	Balance c/d	400
Balance b/d	400		

SUSPENSE ACCOUNT

	£		£
Balance c/d	500	Cash	500
		Balance b/d	500

PART E ANSWERS TO ACTIVITIES

(d) TRIAL BALANCE AS AT 30 JUNE 20X7

Account	Dr £	Cr £
Cash	6,545	
Sales		2,750
Purchases	2,270	
Debtors	890	
Creditors		1,000
Capital		10,000
Fixtures and fittings	3,500	
Rent	300	
Delivery expenses	75	
Drawings	270	
Wages	400	
Suspense		500
	14,250	14,250

(e)

SUSPENSE ACCOUNT

	£		£
SLCA	500	Balance c/d	500

SLCA

	£		£
Balance b/d	890	Suspense	500
		Balance c/d	390
	890		890

Tutorial note. The examiner for Unit 3 has indicated that you will usually be given the suspense account figure (as in Activity 3.1) and then asked to clear it.

Answer 8.2

The main advantage of computerised accounting systems is that a large amount of data can be processed very quickly. A further advantage is that computerised systems are more accurate than manual systems.

Lou's comment that 'you never know what is going on in that funny box' might be better expressed as 'lack of audit trail'. If a mistake occurs somewhere in the system it is not always easy to identify where and how it happened.

Chapter 9

Answer 9.1

You should have noted the following details.

Our (Lightfoot & Co's) reference:	Z/0335/MJD
Department:	Purchasing
Supplier name:	Sandimans Ltd
Previous correspondence:	11 April 20X6
Present correspondence:	4 May 20X6
Subject:	Stationery (invoice 147829)

It is most unlikely that details like the geographical source of the letter or the name of its writer would be needed for filing purposes.

The accounts department should be sent a copy so that they can chase up the cheque that has not been received.

Answer 9.2

(a) The order would be: 15, 21, 28, 2, 8, 1, 18 and 26, 16, 13, 3, 12, 22, 30, 27, 4, 5, 9, 19, 25, 6, 29, 23, 24, 20, 17, 7, 10, 14, 11.

   Tutorial note. A good approach would have been to highlight all the documents of the same year in the same colour, thereby breaking down the task into more manageable portions.

(b) 54321 Discos (7)
   Argent-Smith M (11)
   Argentson S (21)
   Bexley J (5)
   Bidwell D (4)
   Briton N (28)
   Britton T (12)
   BRJ Plumbing (19)
   Cottrell J (1)
   Crown Dr J (8)
   Emly P (17)
   Gisling B (20)
   Harrison P (27)
   Harry Holden Ltd (18)
   Holden R (2)
   ILD Services Ltd (23)
   Kelsey L C (22)
   Locke D (9)
   McLaughlin D (13)
   Maclean T (6)
   O'Grady E (15)

PART E ANSWERS TO ACTIVITIES

>Page W (26)
>Richmond A (29)
>Saint Francis Pet Shop (16)
>Sainton E (10)
>St Olave's Church (30)
>Van Saintby A (24)
>Williams J (3)
>Williams J A (14)
>Williams John (25)

Tutorial note. Slight variations are possible, for example with the treatment of numbers and initials, depending upon the policy of the organisation.

(c) The order would be: 3, 18, 27, 23, 19, 13, 10, 7, 15, 30, 26, 5, 21, 24, 6.

(d) Geographical classification by towns gives the following results.

Bexley:	2, 7, 11, 18, 28
Bromley:	1, 10, 22, 24, 30
Crayford:	9, 12, 19, 26, 29
Dartford:	3, 4, 16, 21, 25, 27
Orpington:	5, 6, 13, 17, 23
Sidcup:	15
Woolwich:	8, 14, 20

Answer 9.3

You were asked for relevant examples from your own workplace.

Answer 9.4

(a) There is room for some flexibility in answers here - what follows is very much a suggestion.

1. The bill is not confidential if Mr Glover chooses not to keep it so. It is nothing to do with your organisation anyway.

2. Not confidential. The reference that was given might be, but this is not mentioned.

3. This is probably very confidential: public knowledge of merger proposals could affect the outcome of the negotiations.

4. This may or may not be confidential depending upon your own organisation's policy. The general view is that budgeting should be done with the involvement of staff, so we are inclined to say that this is not, on the face of it, a confidential document.

5. This is obviously a highly personal document: it should be filed away in your personnel file.

6. This is probably not confidential. The familiarity of the signature is most likely to be due to the length of time your manager and 'Nancy' have been dealing with each other. If not, your manager is not ashamed of it and what business is it of yours anyway?

ANSWERS TO ACTIVITIES

7   There is nothing confidential about this: the surname is irrelevant.

8   Mrs Paribus's letter is probably not particularly confidential although the nature of her complaint might make it so. To preserve the reputation of your organisation it might be better to shut it away in a file to stop cleaners, caterers or other external parties reading it.

9   This material is published: it is clearly not confidential.

10 There is no reason why personal details of directors should be confidential. If the list or an item on it had a heading or note such as 'Do not disclose to anyone below the level of Senior Manager', however, your manager should be ensuring that it does not fall into the wrong hands.

To summarise, documents 3 and 5 are definitely confidential, and documents 2, 7 and 9 are definitely not. The remainder may or may not be confidential depending on the circumstances, and whose point of view you are considering the matter from.

(b) The danger here is that your fax will be collected by someone other than your manager. Its contents seem as if they might be damaging to your organisation in the wrong hands. You should therefore ring your manager and discuss the problem with him. The best solution is probably for him to stand over the receiving fax machine until your fax is received.

PART E ANSWERS TO ACTIVITIES

PART F

Practice Activities

Practice activities are short activities directly related to the actual content of Parts A and D of this BPP Combined Text and Kit.

		Page	Answers to activities	Done
Chapter 1 Revision of basic bookkeeping				
1	Stock or asset	174	213	
2	Advice note	174	213	
3	Redecoration	174	213	
4	Remittance advice	174	213	
5	Business documentation	175	213	
Chapter 2 Recording, summarising and posting transactions				
6	Which ledger?	177	214	
7	Delivery van	177	214	
8	Classifying accounts	177	214	
9	Entries	177	214	
10	Whereabouts	178	214	
11	Main ledger entries	178	215	
Chapter 3 Bank reconciliations				
12	Standing orders	180	216	
13	Standing order mandate	180	216	
14	Journals	181	217	
15	Bank statement entries	181	217	
16	Banking cheques	181	217	
17	Update	182	218	
18	Compare	186	219	
19	Balance	184	220	
20	Reconciliation	186	221	
Chapter 4 Sales ledger control account				
21	Recording transaction	189	222	
22	Errors cause a difference	189	222	
23	Bad debt	189	222	
24	Set off	190	222	
25	Three reasons	190	222	
26	Sales ledger control account reconciliation	190	223	

		Page	Answers to activities	Done

Chapter 5 Purchase ledger control account

27	Balance of PLCA	193	224	☐
28	Another set off	193	224	☐
29	Transactions with suppliers	193	224	☐
30	More differences	194	224	☐
31	Purchase ledger control account reconciliation	194	225	☐
32	Creditors control account	195	225	☐

Chapter 6 Other control accounts

33	Cash control 1	198	226	☐
34	Cash control 2	199	226	☐
35	Cash control 3	199	226	☐
36	Non-trade debtors 1	200	227	☐
37	Non-trade debtors 2	201	227	☐
38	Wages control account	201	228	☐

Chapter 7 The correction of errors

39	Errors 1	204	229	☐
40	Errors 2	204	229	☐
41	Errors 3	204	229	☐
42	Journal entries	204	229	☐
43	Errors and the trial balance	205	230	☐

Chapter 8 From ledger accounts to initial trial balance

44	MEL Factors	207	231	☐
45	Comart Supplies	207	231	☐
46	Trial balance	207	231	☐

Chapter 9 Filing

47	Documents for trial balance	209	233	☐
48	Filing correspondence	209	233	☐
49	Filing documents	209	233	☐
50	Storage	209	233	☐
51	Unauthorised access	209	234	☐
52	Suppliers accounts	210	234	☐
53	Accounts personnel	210	234	☐

chapter 1

Revision of basic bookkeeping

Activity checklist

This checklist shows which performance criteria, range statement or knowledge and understanding point is covered by each activity in this chapter. Tick off each activity as you complete it.

Activity		
1	☐	This activity deals with knowledge and understanding point 7: capital and revenue expenditure.
2	☐	This activity deals with knowledge and understanding point 1: types of business transactions and the documents involved.
3	☐	This activity deals with knowledge and understanding point 7: capital and revenue expenditure.
4	☐	This activity deals with knowledge and understanding point 1: types of business transactions and the documents involved.
5	☐	This activity deals with knowledge and understanding point 1: types of business transactions and the documents involved.

PRACTICE ACTIVITIES

1 Stock or asset

Comart Supplies Ltd has recently purchased five computers. Would the purchase be regarded as capital expenditure or revenue expenditure if:

(a)   The computers are to be used for data processing by the company?

   Capital/Revenue

(b)   The computers are to be held as stock for sale to customers?

   Capital/Revenue

2 Advice note

An advice note is a document sent to a customer acknowledging that an order has been received.

True/False

3 Redecoration

Mary Chang has decided that some of the offices are looking rather shabby. She arranges for the walls to be redecorated and for the purchase of some new office furniture.

(a)   Is the cost of the redecoration capital or revenue expenditure?

   Capital/Revenue

(b)   Is the cost of the new office furniture capital or revenue expenditure?

   Capital/Revenue

4 Remittance advice

A remittance advice is a document sent by a supplier to a customer to advise the customer that goods ordered have been sent off to the customer.

True/False

5 Business documentation

What would be the appropriate document to be used in each of the following cases?

(a) MEL Motor Factors Ltd sends out a document to a credit customer on a monthly basis summarising the transactions that have taken place and showing the amount owed by the customer.

(b) MEL Motor Factors Ltd sends out a document to a credit customer in order to correct an error where the customer has been overcharged on an invoice.

(c) MEL Motor Factors Ltd wishes to buy certain goods from a supplier and sends a document requesting that those goods should be supplied.

PRACTICE ACTIVITIES

chapter 2

Recording, summarising and posting transactions

Activity checklist

This checklist shows which performance criteria, range statement or knowledge and understanding point is covered by each activity in this chapter. Tick off each activity as you complete it.

Activity

6		This activity deals with knowledge and understanding point 12: relationships between the accounting system and the ledger.
7		This activity deals with knowledge and understanding point 13: petty cash procedures.
8		This activity deals with knowledge and understanding point 19: relevant understanding of the organisation's accounting systems.
9		This activity deals with knowledge and understanding points 1: documentation, 2: general principles of VAT and 5: double entry book keeping
10		This activity deals with knowledge and understanding point 12: relationship between the accounting system and the ledger.
11		This activity deals with knowledge and understanding points 5: double entry bookkeeping and 2: general principles of VAT.

6 Which ledger?

Would the following accounts be found in the main ledger, the purchase or the sales ledger?

(a) Sales ledger control account
(b) Sales account
(c) Shop fitting repairs account
(d) Customer personal accounts

7 Delivery van

MEL Motor Factors is about to purchase a new delivery van costing £7,821.

(a) Would it normally be appropriate to make a purchase of this kind out of petty cash?
(b) Explain, briefly, the reason for your answer.

8 Classifying accounts

Classify the balance on each of the following main ledger accounts as an asset, a liability, an expense or revenue.

(a) Advertising
(b) Discount received
(c) Sales ledger control
(d) VAT (credit balance)
(e) Postage and stationery

9 Entries

The credit balance of £92 (including VAT @ 17.5%) on the debtor's account of Euro Hair Style Ltd on 1 March arose because of an overcharge on a sales invoice which was subsequently corrected. However, Euro Hair Style has paid the original amount shown on the invoice.

(a) What document would have been sent to Euro Hair Style when the overcharge was corrected?

(b) Show the entries in the main ledger accounts, including amounts, made when this document was issued.

Debit	£	Credit	£

PRACTICE ACTIVITIES

10 Whereabouts

Would the following accounts be found in the main ledger, the purchase ledger or the sales ledger?

(a) Exotic Blooms Ltd (a credit supplier) _____

(b) Salaries and wages _____

(c) Motor vehicles _____

11 Main ledger entries

What bookkeeping entries would be required in the **main ledger** to correct the following error?

A credit note for £160 plus £28 VAT issued to a customer has been treated as if it were a credit note received.

Debit	Amount £	Credit	Amount
....	....	....	....
....	....	....	....
....	....	....	....
....	....	....	....
....	....	....	....

PRACTICE ACTIVITIES

chapter 3

Bank reconciliations

Activity checklist

This checklist shows which performance criteria, range statement or knowledge and understanding point is covered by each activity in this chapter. Tick off each activity as you complete it.

Activity

12	☐	This activity deals with range statement 3.1.1 primary documentation: standing order and direct debit schedules; and performance criteria 3.1.A.
13	☐	This activity deals with range statement 3.1.1 primary documentation: standing order and direct debit schedules; and performance criteria 3.1.A.
14	☐	This activity deals with performance criteria 3.1.A.
15	☐	This activity deals with performance criteria 3.1.A.
16	☐	This activity deals with performance criteria 3.1.C and .1.D.
17	☐	This activity deals with performance criteria 3.1.A, 3.1.B and 3.1.C.
18	☐	This activity deals with performance criteria 3.1.A, 3.1.B and 3.1.C and 3.1.D.
19	☐	This activity deals with performance criteria 3.1.A, 3.1.B and 3.1.C and 3.1.D.
20	☐	This activity deals with performance criteria 3.1.C and 3.1.D.

PRACTICE ACTIVITIES

12 Standing orders

Today's date is 1 May 20X1 and you are currently checking the month end balances on the ledger accounts as at 30 April 20X1. You have in front of you the authorised standing order and direct debits schedule and note the following standing orders that have not yet been entered into the accounting records.

25th of each month	Standing order	District Council (council tax)	£140
28th of each month	Standing order	Friendly Insurance Company	£80
30th of each month	Standing order	Telephone Corporation	£125

What is the double entry for each of these standing orders?

13 Standing order mandate

Carpet King has purchased a new computer from Technology Ltd. The computer will be paid for with an interest free loan of £1,500, payable by equal monthly installments over one year.

(a) Complete the standing order mandate below.

STANDING ORDER MANDATE	
To: High Street Bank plc	Sort Code: 20-16-45
Please pay to: Central Bank plc Worthing Branch	Sort Code: 30-29-53 Account No: 47930194
Name of account to be credited:	Technology Ltd
The sum of £ _____	Amount in words: _____
Date of first payment: 1 August 20X3	Frequency of payment: _____
Date of last payment: _____	
Account details to be debited	
Account name: _____	Account No: 48720928
Signature: _____	

(b) What will be the accounting entries each month in the accounting records of Carpet King to record each installment payment? (Ignore VAT).

Dr _____ £ _____

Cr _____ £ _____

PRACTICE ACTIVITIES

14 Journals

When the bank statement is received by your business for the month ending 30 June 20X0 three items appear on the bank statement which are not in the cash book:

14 June	Bank giro credit receipt	Johnson & Co (a debtor)	£1,245
30 June	Direct debit	English Gas Co	£330
30 June	Bank charges		£40

Prepare journal entries for each of these amounts showing the double entry required in the main ledger and a brief narrative explaining the entries.

15 Bank statement entries

When looking at the bank statement for your business for the month of January 20X1 you note the following entries.

		Debit £	Credit £
14 January	CR Cheque paid in		156.50
20 January	DR Returned cheque	156.50	

What do these entries in the bank statement mean and what further action should be taken?

16 Banking cheques

Although Carpet King normally banks a customer's cheque on the day it is received, it cannot make withdrawals against that cheque for a few days.

Briefly give the reason for this delay.

_____

_____

_____

_____

PRACTICE ACTIVITIES

17 Update

Given below is the cash book for your business for the month of June 20X1.

CASH BOOK						
RECEIPTS			**PAYMENTS**			
Date	Detail	£	Date	Detail	Cheque no	£
1 June	Bal b/d	572	5 June	J Taylor	013647	334
8 June	Hardy & Co	493	16 June	K Filter	013648	127
12 June	T Roberts	525	22 June	B Gas	013649	200
18 June	D Smith	617	28 June	Wages	BACS	940
25 June	Garnet Bros	369	29 June	D Perez	013650	317

You are also given the bank statement for the same period.

CENTRAL BANK
43, Main Street
York
YK2 3PT

CHEQUE ACCOUNT   Lenten Trading   Account number 19785682

SHEET 0141

		Paid out £	Paid in £	Balance £
1 June	Opening balance			572
4 June	Bank giro credit - A Hammond		136	708
11 June	Cheque 013647	334		374
12 June	Credit		493	867
16 June	Credit		525	1,392
18 June	DD – Telephone Company	146		1,246
22 June	Credit		617	1,863
27 June	Cheque 013649	200		1,663
28 June	BACS	940		723
30 June	Bank interest		11	734

Tasks

(a) Check the bank statement and the cash book and update the cash book for any missing entries.
(b) Balance the amended cash book.
(c) Explain what the reason for cheque numbers 013648 and 013650 not appearing on the bank statement might be.

18 Compare

Given below is the cash book for your business for the month of February 20X1.

CASH BOOK						
RECEIPTS			**PAYMENTS**			
Date	Detail	£	Date	Detail	Cheque no	£
2 Feb	Davis & Co	183	1 Feb	Balance b/d		306
7 Feb	A Thomas	179	4 Feb	J L Pedro	000351	169
14 Feb	K Sinders	146	11 Feb	P Gecko	000352	104
21 Feb	H Harvey	162	15 Feb	F Dimpner	000353	217
27 Feb	A Watts	180	23 Feb	O Roup	000354	258

You are also given the bank statement for the month.

```
EASTERN BANK
20/24 Miles Square
Huddersfield
LD3 5FS

CHEQUE ACCOUNT           L Arnold              Account number 29785643
SHEET 0298
                                      Paid out      Paid in      Balance
                                         £            £             £
1 February   Opening balance                                      306     O/D
8 Feb        Credit                                   183         123     O/D
12 Feb       Credit                                   179          56
15 Feb       SO – Telephone                65
             000352                       104                     113     O/D
20 Feb       Credit                                   146          33
             000353                       217                     184     O/D
24 Feb       DD - Electricity              30                     214     O/D
26 Feb       Credit                                   162
             000351                       169                     221     O/D
28 Feb       Interest                      15                     236     O/D
```

PRACTICE ACTIVITIES

Tasks

(a) Compare the bank statement to the cash book and amend the cash book accordingly.

(b) Find the closing balance on the amended cash book and state whether this would be a debit or a credit balance in the trial balance.

(c) Prepare a bank reconciliation statement.

19 Balance

Given below is the cash book for your organisation for the month of January 20X1.

CASH BOOK					
RECEIPTS			**PAYMENTS**		
Date	*Detail*	£	*Date*	*Detail*	*Cheque no*	£
1 Jan	Balance b/d	1,035	2 Jan	O J Trading	02475	368
2 Jan	Filter Bros	115	4 Jan	K D Partners	02476	463
8 Jan	Headway Ltd	640	7 Jan	L T Engineers	02477	874
15 Jan	Letterhead Ltd	409	14 Jan	R Trent	02478	315
22 Jan	Leaden Partners	265	20 Jan	I Rain	02479	85
			25 Jan	TDC	SO	150
			28 Jan	Wages	02480	490

You are also given the bank statement for the month.

WESTERN BANK
Bank House
Leeds Road
Halifax
LD3 5FS

CHEQUE ACCOUNT   Frant & Co   Account number 43709436

SHEET 0276

		Paid out £	Paid in £	Balance £
1 Jan	Opening balance			1,035
6 Jan	CR		115	
	CH 02475	368		782
12 Jan	CR		640	
	CH 02477	784		638
19 Jan	CR		409	1,047
20 Jan	BGC – T Elliot		161	
	CH 02478	315		893
23 Jan	CH 02476	463		430
25 Jan	SO – TDC	150		280
28 Jan	CR		265	
	Charges	10		535

Tasks

(a) Compare the cash book to the bank statement and amend the cash book appropriately.
(b) Balance the amended cash book.
(c) Prepare a bank reconciliation statement.

PRACTICE ACTIVITIES

20 Reconciliation

On 27 June Carpet King received the following bank statement as at 20 June 20X3.

HIGH STREET BANK plc
56 Avenue Road, Henley, CV28 1BW

To: Carpet King   Account No: 48720928   Sort Code 20-16-45   20 June 20X3

STATEMENT OF ACCOUNT

Date 2003	Details	Paid out £	Paid in £	Balance £
2 June	Balance b/f			1,048D
6 June	Cheque No 107201	2,600		3,648D
10 June	Cheque No 107202	58		3,706D
13 June	Cheque No 107203	6,319		10,025D
16 June	Bank Giro Credit P Smithson		11,517	1,492C
18 June	Direct Debit BB Skip Hire	200		1,292C
19 June	Bank Giro Credit Parish Ltd		9,154	10,446C
19 June	Direct Debit Henley MBC	982		9,464C
20 June	Bank charges	156		9,308C

D = Debit   C = Credit

The cash book as at 27 June 20X3 is shown below.

CASH BOOK

Date 20X3	Details	Bank £	Date 20X3	Cheque No	Details	Bank £
16 June	P Smithson	11,517	1 June		Balance b/f 1,048	
19 June	Kay and Kay	4,025	2 June	107201	Ingram Ltd	2,600
20 June	PKK Ltd	1,507	6 June	107202	TTO Ltd	58
			9 June	107203	Carter & Company	6,319
			18 June	107204	Letts Ltd	1,400

Tasks

(a) Check the items on the bank statement against the items in the cash book.

(b) Update the cash book as needed.

(c) Total the cash book and clearly show the balance carried down at 27 June.

(d) Using the information on the previous page, prepare a bank reconciliation statement as at 27 June. The bank reconciliation statement should start with the balance as per the bank statement and reconcile to the balance as per the cash book.

Bank reconciliation statement as at 27 June 20X3

£

Balance per bank statement

Add

Less

Balance as per cash book

PRACTICE ACTIVITIES

chapter 4

Sales ledger control account

Activity checklist

This checklist shows which performance criteria, range statement or knowledge and understanding point is covered by each activity in this chapter. Tick off each activity as you complete it.

Activity

21		This activity deals with knowledge and understanding point 5: double entry bookkeeping, and point 2: general principles of VAT.
22		This activity deals with performance criteria 3.2.A.
23		This activity deals with performance criteria 3.2.A.
24		This activity deals with performance criteria 3.2.A.
25		This activity deals with knowledge and understanding points 11: errors and 17: reconciling control accounts with memorandum accounts.
26		This activity deals with performance criteria 3.2.B, 3.2.C and 3.2.E.

21 Recording transaction

Software has been sold on credit by Comart Computers Ltd to Softsell Ltd, a new small business which is not registered for VAT. The invoice issued shows the cost of the software as £160 plus £28 VAT giving a total of £188. In recording the transaction, which main ledger account(s) will be debited and which will be credited:

(a) In the books of Comart Computers Ltd?

Debit   Credit

....

....

(b) In the books of Softsell Ltd?

Debit   Credit

....

....

22 Errors cause a difference

Would the following errors cause a difference to occur between the balance of the sales ledger control account and the total of the balances in the sales ledger?

(a) The total column of the sales day book was overcast by £100.

Yes/No

(b) In error H Lambert's account in the sales ledger was debited with £175 instead of M Lambert's account.

Yes/No

(c) An invoice for £76 was recorded in the sales day book as £67.

Yes/No

23 Bad debt

Carpet King is planning to write off a bad debt of £1,000.

What will be the accounting entries needed in Carpet King's Main (General) Ledger to record this bad debt write off? (Ignore VAT.)

Dr _____   £ _____

Cr _____   £ _____

24 Set off

Gift Box is both a supplier to and a customer of Bloomers Ltd. It has been agreed that a debt of £75 owing to Gift Box is to be set off against the balance of £300 owed by Gift Box.

What entries would be required in the main ledger to record this set off?

Debit	Amount £	Credit	Amount £

25 Three reasons

List three reasons for maintaining a sales ledger control account.

26 Sales ledger control account reconciliation

Using the summary of activity shown below, complete the sales ledger control account showing clearly the balance carried down. Use the list of balances in the subsidiary (sales) ledger to reconcile this balance with the sales ledger control account. If there is an imbalance, make a note to your supervisor suggesting where the error might be.

SALES LEDGER CONTROL ACCOUNT

Date 20X0	Details	Amount £	Date 20X0	Details	Amount £

Details for reconciliation of the sales ledger control account

Summary of activity

	£
Opening balance at 1 August 20X0	182,806
Sales in August	82,250
Sales returns in August	2,352
Discounts allowed	100
Bank receipts from debtors	73,648

Balances in subsidiary (sales) ledger

	£
Tadman Ltd	29,142
Silvertown & Co	16,000
Talbot & Co	38,400
Hibbert Industries	46,036
Galactic Cleaners	30,034
Smith Ltd	(448)
Waldon & Co	28,896

RECONCILIATION OF SALES LEDGER CONTROL ACCOUNT WITH SUBSIDIARY (SALES) LEDGER AT 31 AUGUST 20X0

	£
Closing balance of sales ledger control account	
Total balance of accounts in subsidiary (sales) ledger	
Imbalance	

NOTE TO SUPERVISOR

PRACTICE ACTIVITIES

chapter 5

Purchase ledger control account

Activity checklist

This checklist shows which performance criteria, range statement or knowledge and understanding point is covered by each activity in this chapter. Tick off each activity as you complete it.

Activity

Activity		Description
27		This activity deals with performance criteria 3.2.A.
28		This activity deals with performance criteria 3.2.A and knowledge and understanding point 5: double entry bookkeeping.
29		This activity deals with knowledge and understanding point 5: double entry bookkeeping.
30		This activity deals with performance criteria 3.2.A.
31		This activity deals with performance criteria 3.2.A, 3.2.B, 3.2.C and 3.2.E.
32		This activity deals with performance criteria 3.2.A, 3.2.B, 3.2.C and 3.2.E.

27 Balance of PLCA

Would the following errors cause a difference to occur between the balance of the purchase ledger control account and the total of the balances in the purchase ledger?

(a) A suppliers account has been balanced incorrectly.

Yes/No

(b) An invoice for £37 has been entered into the purchases day book as £39.

Yes/No

(c) An invoice has, in error, been omitted from the purchases day book.

Yes/No

28 Another set off

Which account in the main ledger would you debit and which account in the main ledger would you credit in respect of the following.

(a) A set-off is to be made between Peter Allen's account in the sales ledger, which has a balance of £200, and his account in the purchase ledger, which has a balance of £450.

Debit   *Credit*

(b) The correction of an error where it has been found that an invoice for £36, received from Allied Brokers Ltd for insurance, has been entered in the various columns of the purchase day book as £63. (*Note.* Ignore VAT)

Debit   *Credit*

(c) The correction of an error where it has been discovered that the purchase of £10 of stationery has been debited to the purchases account.

Debit   *Credit*

29 Transactions with suppliers

Which main ledger account would be debited and which main ledger account credited in respect of each of the following transactions?

(a) Bought office furniture on credit from Crome Supplies Ltd.
(b) Credit note sent to Jean Crane & Co.
(c) Paid by cheque a credit account 'Alf Green & Sons' for last month's van repairs.

Account to be debited	*Account to be credited*
(a)	
(b)	
(c)	

30 More differences

Would each of the following cause a difference between the totals of the main ledger debit and credit account balances at 31 March?

(a) A purchase invoice for £36 from P Smith was entered into P Short's account in the purchase ledger.

Yes/No

(b) A purchase invoice for £96 was not entered in the purchase day book.

Yes/No

(c) The total column of the purchase day book was undercast by £20.

Yes/No

(d) A purchase invoice from Short & Long for £42 for the goods for resale was entered as £24 in the purchase day book.

Yes/No

31 Purchase ledger control account reconciliation

A list of subsidiary ledger balances is shown below, together with a summary of activity in the month of August 20X0. Prepare a purchase ledger control account as at 31 August 20X0, showing clearly the balance carried down. Reconcile this balance with the list of balances in the subsidiary (purchase) ledger. Comment on any imbalance.

Details for reconciliation of the purchase ledger control account

Summary of activity

	£
Opening balance at 1 August 20X0	67,200
Purchases in August	63,450
Purchases returns in August	1,880
Discounts received	200
Bank payments to creditors	68,310

PURCHASE LEDGER CONTROL ACCOUNT

Date	Details	Amount £	Date	Details	Amount £

Balances in subsidiary (purchases) ledger

	£
Donna Ltd	19,270
ABC Controls	14,100
Alex & John	11,750
S Rashid	9,400
XYZ Ltd	5,740

RECONCILIATION OF PURCHASE LEDGER CONTROL ACCOUNT WITH SUBSIDIARY (PURCHASES) LEDGER AT 31 AUGUST 20X0

	£
Closing balance of purchase ledger control account	
Total balance of accounts in subsidiary (purchases) ledger	_____
Imbalance	_____

32 Creditors control account

The following is a summary of transactions with suppliers during the month of June.

	£
Balance of creditors at 1 June 20X3	167,169
Goods purchased on credit	54,517
Money paid to creditors	74,851
Goods returned to suppliers	500
Discount received	50

PRACTICE ACTIVITIES

Tasks

(a) Prepare a creditors control account from the details shown above. Show clearly the balance carried down at 30 June 20X3.

CREDITORS CONTROL

Date	Details	Amount £	Date	Details	Amount £

The following closing balances were in the Subsidiary (Purchases) Ledger on 30 June.

	£
Bizet Flooring	105,297 Credit
Plush Carpets	15,330 Credit
Bradley and Bell	22,000 Credit
Home Makers	1,503 Credit
AMR Ltd	2,205 Credit

(b) Reconcile the balances shown above with the creditors control account balance you have calculated in part (a).

	£
Creditors control account balance as at 30 June 20X3	
Total of Subsidiary (purchases) Ledger accounts as at 30 June 20X3	_____
Difference	_____

(c) What may have caused the difference you calculated in part (b) above?

_____

_____

_____

PRACTICE ACTIVITIES

chapter 6

Other control accounts

Activity checklist

This checklist shows which performance criteria, range statement or knowledge and understanding point is covered by each activity in this chapter. Tick off each activity as you complete it.

Activity

33		This activity deals with performance criteria 3.2.D.
34		This activity deals with performance criteria 3.2.D.
35		This activity deals with performance criteria 3.2.D.
36		This activity deals with performance criteria 3.2.A, 3.2.B, 3.2.C and 3.2.E regarding non-trade debtors.
37		This activity deals with performance criteria 3.2.A, 3.2.B, 3.2.C and 3.2.E regarding non-trade debtors.
38		This activity deals with performance criteria 3.2.A, 3.2.B.

33 Cash control 1

A petty cash control account is kept in the main ledger of Coulthurst Ltd. The petty cash book is the subsidiary account. At the beginning of August there is a balance brought forward of £175.

During August £125 was spent from petty cash, and at the end of the month, £150 was put into the petty cash box from the bank.

Task

Enter these transactions into the petty cash control account below, showing clearly the balance carried down. What does this balance represent?

PETTY CASH CONTROL ACCOUNT

Date 20X1	Details	Amount £	Date 20X1	Details	Amount £

34 Cash control 2

A petty cash control account is kept in the main ledger of Wye Ltd. The petty cash book is the subsidiary account. At the beginning of June there is a balance brought forward of £150.

During June £100 was spent from petty cash, and at the end of the month, £200 was put into the petty cash box from the bank.

Tasks

(a) Enter these transactions into the petty cash control account below, showing clearly the balance carried down.

PETTY CASH CONTROL ACCOUNT

Date 20X1	Details	Amount £	Date 20X1	Details	Amount £

(b) If Wye Ltd operated an imprest system, what would be the payment from the bank at the end of the month if it was decided to increase the imprest to £200.

35 Cash control 3

A petty cash control account is kept in the main ledger of Fabien Ltd. The petty cash book is the subsidiary account. At the beginning of April there is a balance brought forward of £232.

During April £210 was spent from petty cash, and at the end of the month, there was £2 cash in hand.

Tasks

(a) Enter these transactions into the petty cash control account below, showing clearly the balance carried down.

(b) Carry out a petty cash reconciliation.

(c) If there was an IOU for £18 in the petty cash box plus an unrecorded voucher for £2, reconcile the petty cash balance at the end of April.

PETTY CASH CONTROL ACCOUNT

Date 20X1	Details	Amount £	Date 20X1	Details	Amount £

36 Non-trade debtors 1

At 1 April 20X1, the balance on the non-trade debtors control account was £2,500. During April, further debts were due of £2,000 and cash was received of £4,000.

Task

Write up the non-trade debtors control account and show the balance carried forward.

NON-TRADE DEBTORS CONTROL ACCOUNT

Date 20X1	Details	Amount £	Date 20X1	Details	Amount £

37 Non-trade debtors 2

Using the details in activity 31 above, write up the non-trade debtors control account for May 20X1.

(a) Further debts were incurred of £4,000.
(b) Cash received was £2,500.
(c) An amount of £2,000 included in (a), should be included in the sales ledger control account.

NON-TRADE DEBTORS CONTROL ACCOUNT

Date 20X1	Details	Amount £	Date 20X1	Details	Amount £

38 Wages control account

The following wages summary is for June 2003.

Wages Summary

	£
Gross wages	6,000
Net wages	4,200
Employer's NIC	670
Employees' NIC	600
Trade union fees	50
PAYE	1,150

Make the relevant entries to the wages control account and then total it.

PRACTICE ACTIVITIES

WAGES CONTROL ACCOUNT

Date 20X3	Details	Amount £	Date 20X3	Details	Amount £

chapter 7

The correction of errors

Activity checklist

This checklist shows which performance criteria, range statement or knowledge and understanding point is covered by each activity in this chapter. Tick off each activity as you complete it.

Activity

39	☐	This activity deals with performance criteria 3.3.C.
40	☐	This activity deals with performance criteria 3.3.C.
41	☐	This activity deals with performance criteria 3.3.C.
42	☐	This activity deals with performance criteria 3.3.B.
43	☐	This activity deals with performance criteria 3.3.B.

39 Errors 1

Show the journal to correct the following error. An invoice received from Smith's Electrics Ltd had been entered in the day book correctly but the VAT element of £14 had been omitted.

40 Errors 2

The total of £98 discounts allowed column in the cash book had been wrongly posted to discounts received. Show the correcting journal.

41 Errors 3

Your trial balance does not agree. Debit balances exceed credit balances by £61. You post £61 to a suspense account. Upon further investigation you discover the following errors:

- A debit of £34 to telephone expense had been entered as £43.
- A receipt of £52 from a customer had not been credited to the sales ledger control account.

Tasks

(a) Show the journals which you would prepare in order to now correct these errors.
(b) Draw up the suspense account and show how the balance will be cleared.

42 Journal entries

The following errors have been made in the Main (General) Ledger of Carpet King.

(a) £700 has been debited to the purchases returns account instead of to the purchases account.

(b) A payment to a trade supplier had been entered in the creditors control account and cash book as £1,650 instead of £1,560.

(c) An entry to record an insurance payment of £870 has been reversed, so it has been debited to the bank and credited to the insurance account.

Record the journal entries needed in the Main (General) Ledger to correct the errors shown above. You do not need to give dates or narratives.

THE JOURNAL

Details	Dr	Cr
	£	£

43 Errors and the trial balance

A purchase invoice has been incorrectly calculated by the supplier and the incorrect total entered in the accounting records of Carpet King. (Ignore VAT).

(a) Would this cause an imbalance in the trial balance?

Yes / No (Circle your answer)

(b) Briefly give the reason for your answer.

_____

_____

_____

_____

PRACTICE ACTIVITIES

chapter 8

From ledger accounts to initial trial balance

Activity checklist

This checklist shows which performance criteria, range statement or knowledge and understanding point is covered by each activity in this chapter. Tick off each activity as you complete it.

Activity

44		This activity deals with performance criteria 3.3.A.
45		This activity deals with performance criteria 3.3.A, 3.3.B, 3.3.C and 3.3.D.
46		This activity deals with performance criteria 3.3.D.

44 MEL Factors

MEL Factors has the following balances at 30 April 20X1.

	£
Sales	10,000
Purchases	5,000
Expenses	2,000
Capital	20,000
Sales ledger control account	2,000
Purchase ledger control account	1,500
Cash in bank and in hand	3,000
Fixed assets	19,500

Task

Prepare an initial trial balance.

45 Comart Supplies

Comart's initial trial balance shows debits totalling £12,000 and credits totalling £14,500.

Tasks

(a) How would you deal with this discrepancy?

(b) Subsequently you discover that the sales ledger control account omits sales of £3,000 and that the purchase ledger control account omits purchases of £500. Show the suspense account and the journal to clear it.

46 Trial Balance

At 31 December 20X1 the balances on your accounts are as follows:

	£
Cash at bank and in hand	25,275
Capital	14,000
Sales ledger control account	23,004
Purchase ledger control account	11,632
Purchases	71,157
Sales	127,325
Wages	30,129
Telephone	3,392
Rent	10,000
Bank loan	10,000

You discover that one of your sales invoices for £350 (no VAT) had been omitted from the sales day book. The sales account and sales ledger control account balances need to be adjusted for this.

Task

Prepare an initial trial balance.

PRACTICE ACTIVITIES

chapter 9

Filing

Activity checklist

This checklist shows which performance criteria, range statement or knowledge and understanding point is covered by each activity in this chapter. Tick off each activity as you complete it.

Activity		
47		This activity deals with performance criteria 3.2.F.
48		This activity deals with performance criteria 3.2.F.
49		This activity deals with performance criteria 3.2.F.
50		This activity deals with performance criteria 3.2.F.
51		This activity deals with performance criteria 3.2.F.
52		This activity deals with performance criteria 3.2.F.
53		This activity deals with performance criteria 3.2.F.

47 Documents for trial balance

When preparing a trial balance at the end of an accounting period there will be a number of documents and reconciliations that you will need to be able to find from the filing system. List the documents and reconciliations that you will need to access before completing the initial trial balance.

48 Filing correspondence

A small business has always filed its correspondence with customers and suppliers in date order. However, as the business has grown, the owner has found that it is harder to locate the correspondence required from the filing system.

Suggest a different method of filing that might make accessing the required correspondence easier.

49 Filing documents

All documents sent out and received by Carpet King are filed alphabetically.

Suggest ONE alternative way of filing each of the following documents, giving a different method for each.

(a) Sales invoices _____

(b) Purchase invoices _____

(c) Contracts _____

50 Storage

You are the bookkeeper in a small business and your office currently has no facility for storing the ledger accounts and other accounting records which you work on, including the wages book. These are all left on your desk when you are not in the office. You are to write a memo to the owner of the business expressing any concerns you may have about this system and suggesting ways of improving it. Today's date is 4 May 20X1.

51 Unauthorised access

Each employee at Carpet King has their own personal password which they have to enter into the computer to gain access to the accounting records.

Give TWO examples of what might happen if an unauthorised person gained access to the accounting records.

PRACTICE ACTIVITIES

52 Creditors accounts

The creditors accounts in the purchase ledger are filed in alphabetical order. In what order would the following creditors accounts be filed?

- Smithson Ltd
- Sonic Partners
- Skelton Engineers
- Snipe Associates
- Spartan & Co
- Souter Finance

53 Accounts personnel

A fairly large engineering business has the following accounts personnel.

- Chief accountant
- Cashier
- Petty cashier and bookkeeper
- Sales ledger clerk
- Purchase ledger clerk
- Wages clerk

With which of these personnel are you likely to find the following?

- Wages book
- Aged debtors analysis
- Purchase ledger
- Bank statement
- Petty cash book
- Credit limits for customers
- Standing order schedule

Answers to Practice Activities

Answers to practice activities

Chapter 1: Revision of basic bookkeeping

1 Stock or asset

(a) Capital
(b) Revenue

2 Advice note

False. An advice note is usually sent out with the delivery of goods to the customer.

3 Redecoration

(a) Revenue
(b) Capital

4 Remittance advice

False. A remittance advice is sent by a customer with their payment, detailing which invoices are being paid.

5 Business documentation

(a) Monthly statement of account
(b) Credit note
(c) Purchase order

Chapter 2: Recording, summarising and posting transactions

6 Which ledger?

(a) Main ledger
(b) Main ledger
(c) Main ledger
(d) Sales ledger

7 Delivery van

(a) No

(b) The amount of money kept in petty cash should be kept to a minimum to prevent fraud and theft. The amount would be far too large to keep in petty cash.

8 Classifying accounts

(a) Expense
(b) Revenue
(c) Asset
(d) Liability
(e) Expense

9 Entries

(a) A credit note

(b)

		£	£
DEBIT	Sales	78.30	
	VAT	13.70	
CREDIT	Sales ledger control account		92.00

10 Whereabouts

(a) Purchase ledger
(b) Main ledger
(c) Main ledger

11 Main ledger entries

		£	£
DEBIT	VAT	28	
DEBIT	Returns outward	160	
CREDIT	Purchase ledger control		188

Reversal of incorrect entry

		£	£
DEBIT	VAT	28	
DEBIT	Returns inward	160	
CREDIT	Sales ledger control		188

Posting correct entry

Chapter 3: Bank reconciliations

12 Standing orders

	£	£
District Council:		
DEBIT Council tax account	140	
CREDIT Bank account		140
Friendly Insurance Company:		
DEBIT Insurance account	80	
CREDIT Bank account		80
Telephone Corporation:		
DEBIT Telephone account	125	
CREDIT Bank account		125

13 Standing order mandate

(a)

STANDING ORDER MANDATE			
To:	High Street Bank plc	Sort code:	20-16-45
Please pay to:	Central Bank plc Worthing Branch	Sort code:	30-29-53
		Account No:	47930194
Name of account to be credited:	**Technology Limited**		
The sum of **£125** Amount in words	**One hundred and twenty five pounds**		
Date of first payment: **1 August 20X3**	Frequency of payment:		**monthly**
Date of last payment: **1 July 20X4**			
Account details to be debited			
Account name: **Carpet King**		Account No:	**48720928**
Signature	Lucy Chan		

(b)   DEBIT   Loan   £125
        CREDIT Bank   £125

14 Journals

		Dr £	Cr £
DEBIT	Bank account	1,245	
CREDIT	Sales ledger control account		1,245

Being bank giro credit from Johnson & Co

		Dr £	Cr £
DEBIT	Gas account	330	
CREDIT	Bank account		330

Being direct debit payment to English Gas Co

		Dr £	Cr £
DEBIT	Bank charges account	40	
CREDIT	Bank account		40

Being bank charges for the period

15 Bank statement entries

A cheque for £156.50 was received from a customer and paid into your bank account on 14 January. The cheque then went through the bank clearing system but the bank was unable to clear the cheque, either due to the fact that the cheque was not correctly drawn up or the drawee did not have sufficient funds in his account. Therefore, the cheque will have been returned to you marked 'refer to drawer'.

The cash book must be amended as it will currently show a receipt for £156.50. However, the money has not been received and therefore a credit entry is needed in the bank account (debit: sales ledger control account; credit: cash). The cheque should be returned to the customer with a request for a replacement cheque.

16 Banking cheques

The cheque will have to pass through the clearing system before the funds become available. This means that after the cheque is banked by Carpet King, it will be passed to the bank of the customer for payment.

17 Update

(a)/(b)

CASH BOOK						
RECEIPTS			**PAYMENTS**			
Date	Detail	£	Date	Detail	Cheque no	£
1 June	Balance b/d	572	5 June	J Taylor	013647	334
8 June	Hardy & Co	493	16 June	K Filter	013648	127
12 June	T Roberts	525	22 June	B Gas	013649	200
18 June	D Smith	617	28 June	Wages	BACS	940
25 June	Garnet Bros	369	29 June	D Perez	013650	317
4 June	A Hammond – BGC	136	18 June	Telephone DD		146
30 June	Bank interest	11	30 June	Balance c/d		659
		2,723				2,723

(c) Cheque number 013650 was not written until 29 June and therefore could not possibly reach the supplier, be paid into the supplier's bank account and work its way through the bank clearing system by 30 June.

Cheque number 013648 was written into the cash book on 16 June and therefore, theoretically, should have cleared through the banking system by the end of the month. However, there may have been a delay in sending the cheque out to the payee or the payee may have delayed in paying the cheque into his bank account, meaning that by 30 June the cheque has still not cleared.

18 Compare

(a)

CASH BOOK						
RECEIPTS			**PAYMENTS**			
Date	*Detail*	£	*Date*	*Detail*	*Cheque no*	£
2 Feb	Davis & Co	183	1 Feb	Balance b/d		306
7 Feb	A Thomas	179	4 Feb	J L Pedro	000351	169
14 Feb	K Sinders	146	11 Feb	P Gecko	000352	104
21 Feb	H Harvey	162	15 Feb	F Dimpner	000353	217
27 Feb	A Watts	180	23 Feb	O Roup	000354	258
			15 Feb	Telephone	SO	65
			24 Feb	Electricity	DD	30
28 Feb	Balance c/d	314	28 Feb	Interest		15
		1,164				1,164

(b) This is a debit balance carried down and so a credit balance brought down, representing an overdraft. This will appear in the trial balance as a credit balance.

BANK RECONCILIATION AS AT 28 FEBRUARY 20X1

	£
Balance per bank statement – overdrawn	(236)
Add: outstanding lodgement (A Watts)	180
	(56)
Less: outstanding cheque (000354)	(258)
Balance per amended cash book	(314)

19 Balance

(a)(b)

CASH BOOK						
RECEIPTS			**PAYMENTS**			
Date	Detail	£	Date	Detail	Cheque no	£
1 Jan	Balance b/d	1,035	2 Jan	O J Trading	02475	368
2 Jan	Filter Bros	115	4 Jan	K D Partners	02476	463
8 Jan	Headway Ltd	640	7 Jan	L T Engineers	02477	874
15 Jan	Letterhead Ltd	409	14 Jan	R Trent	02478	315
22 Jan	Leaden Partners	265	20 Jan	I Rain	02479	85
20 Jan	BGC - T Elliot	161	25 Jan	TDC	SO	150
31 Jan	Adjustment to cheque no 02477	90	28 Jan	Wages	02480	490
			28 Jan	Bank charges		10
31 Jan	Balance c/d	40				
		2,755				2,755

Tutorial note. Cheque 02477 has been recorded in the cash bank as £874 but the bank statement shows £784, the difference of £90 needs to be adjusted.

BANK RECONCILIATION STATEMENT AT 31 JANUARY 20X1

	£	£
Balance per bank statement		535
Less outstanding lodgements:		
02479	85	
02480	490	
		575
Balance per amended cash book (overdrawn)		(40)

20 Reconciliation

(a) – (c)

CASH BOOK

Date 20X3	Details	Amount £	Date 20X3	Chq no	Details	Amount £
16 June	P Smithson	11,517	1 June		Balance b/f	1,048
19 June	Kay and Kay	4,025	2 June	107201	Ingram Ltd	2,600
20 June	PKK Ltd	1,507	6 June	107202	TTO Ltd	58
19 June	Parish Ltd	9,154	9 June	107203	Carter & Company	6,319
			18 June	107204	Letts Ltd	1,400
			18 June		BB Skip Hire	200
			19 June		Henley MBC	982
			20 June		Bank charges	156
			27 June		Balance c/d	13,440
		26,203				26,203
28 June	Balance b/f	13,440				

(d) **Bank reconciliation statement as at 27 June 20X3**

	£
Balance per bank statement	9,308
Add : Kay and Kay receipt	4,025
PKK receipt	1,507
Less : Cheque 107204 – Letts Ltd	(1,400)
Balance as per cash book	13,440

Chapter 4: Sales ledger control account

21 Recording transaction

(a)   DEBIT   Sales ledger control a/c   £188
        CREDIT   Sales   £160
        CREDIT   VAT   £28

(b)   DEBIT   Purchases   £188
        CREDIT   Purchase ledger control a/c   £188

Tutorial note. Softsell is not registered for VAT and so cannot reclaim input VAT. The VAT, therefore, forms part of the cost of the purchase.

22 Errors cause a difference

(a) Yes
(b) No
(c) No. The same mistake would be processed in the sales ledger and the sales ledger control account.

23 Bad debt

DEBIT   Bad debts   £1,000
CREDIT   Debtors control account   £1,000

24 Set off

DEBIT   Purchase ledger control a/c   £75
CREDIT   Sales ledger control a/c   £75

25 Three reasons

(a) To aid in the prevention of fraud
(b) To assist in the location of errors
(c) To enable the total debtors figure to be known at any time

26 Sales ledger control account reconciliation

SALES LEDGER CONTROL ACCOUNT

Date 20X0	Details	Amount £	Date 20X0	Details	Amount £
1 August	Balance b/f	182,806	31 August	Sales returns	2,352
31 August	Sales	82,250	31 August	Discounts allowed	100
			31 August	Bank	73,648
			31 August	Balance c/d	188,956
		265,056			265,056
1 Sept	Balance b/d	188,956			

RECONCILIATION OF SALES LEDGER CONTROL ACCOUNT WITH SUBSIDIARY (SALES) LEDGER AT 31 AUGUST 20X0

	£
Closing balance of sales ledger control account	188,956
Total balance of accounts in subsidiary (sales) ledger	188,060
Imbalance	896

> **NOTE TO SUPERVISOR**
>
> There is an imbalance between the sales ledger control account and subsidiary (sales) ledger of £896. This may be for any number of reasons, but the most likely explanation is that the account of Smith Ltd has a credit balance of £448. Is this correct? If Smith Ltd should, in fact, be a debit balance, then the difference is 2 × £448, ie £896.

Chapter 5: Purchase ledger control account

27 Balance of PLCA

(a) Yes
(b) No, both the purchase ledger and the PLCA will record the same error.
(c) No

28 Another set off

(a) DEBIT   Purchase ledger control a/c   £200
    CREDIT   Sales ledger control a/c   £200

(b) DEBIT   Purchase ledger control a/c   £27
    CREDIT   Insurance expense   £27

Tutorial note. We have assumed that the day book has been posted already to the main ledger.

(c) DEBIT   Stationery   £10
    CREDIT   Purchases   £10

29 Transactions with suppliers

(a) DEBIT   Fixed assets
    CREDIT   Purchase ledger control account

(b) DEBIT   Sales returns
    CREDIT   Sales ledger control account

(c) DEBIT   Purchase ledger control account
    CREDIT   Bank

30 More differences

(a) No
(b) No
(c) Yes
(d) No

31 Purchase ledger control account reconciliation

PURCHASE LEDGER CONTROL ACCOUNT

Date 20X0	Details	Amount £	Date 20X0	Details	Amount £
31 Aug	Purchases returns	1,880	1 Aug	Balance b/f	67,200
31 Aug	Discounts received	200	31 Aug	Purchases	63,450
31 Aug	Bank	68,310			
31 Aug	Balance c/d	60,260			
		130,650			130,650
			1 Sept	Balance b/d	60,260

RECONCILIATION OF PURCHASE LEDGER CONTROL ACCOUNT WITH SUBSIDIARY (PURCHASES) LEDGER AT 31 AUGUST 20X0

	£
Closing balance of purchase ledger control account	60,260
Total balance of accounts in subsidiary (purchases) ledger	60,260
Imbalance	NIL

32 Creditors control account

(a)

CREDITORS CONTROL ACCOUNT

Date 20X3	Details	Amount £	Date 20X3	Details	Amount £
30 June	Bank	74,851	30 June	Balance b/f	167,169
30 June	Purchases return	500	30 June	Purchases	54,517
30 June	Discounts received	50			
30 June	Balance c/d	146,285			
		221,686			221,686
			1 July	Balance b/d	146,285

(b)

	£
Creditors control account balance as at 30 June 20X3	146,285
Total of Subsidiary (Purchases) Ledger accounts as at 30 June 20X3	146,335
Difference	50

(c) The discount received may not have been recorded in the Subsidiary (Purchases) Ledger.

Chapter 6: Other control accounts

33 Cash control 1

PETTY CASH CONTROL

Date 20X1	Details	Amount £	Date 20X1	Details	Amount £
1 Aug	Balance b/f	175	31 Aug	Petty cash	125
31 Aug	Bank	150	31 Aug	Balance c/d	200
		325			325
1 Sept	Balance b/d	200			

The control account balance b/d shows that there should be cash in hand of £200.

34 Cash control 2

(a) PETTY CASH CONTROL

Date 20X1	Details	Amount £	Date 20X1	Details	Amount £
1 Jun	Balance b/f	150	30 Jun	Petty cash	100
30 Jun	Bank	200	30 Jun	Balance c/d	250
		350			350
1 July	Balance b/d	250			

(b) £150. Current imprest is £150, spending in month was £100. Imprest is increased by £50 (£200 – £150), so reimbursement is £150 (£100 + £50).

35 Cash control 3

(a) PETTY CASH CONTROL

Date 20X1	Details	Amount £	Date 20X1	Details	Amount £
1 April	Balance b/f	232	30 Apr	Petty cash	210
			30 Apr	Balance c/d	22
		232			232
1 May	Balance b/d	22			

(b) PETTY CASH RECONCILIATION AT 30 APRIL 20X1

	£
Balance per petty cash control account	22
Cash in hand	2
Imbalance	20

(c)

		£
Cash in hand		2
Add: IOU	18	
Unrecorded voucher	2	
		20
Balance as petty cash control account		22

Tutorial note. As the voucher has not yet been recorded, it is added to cash in hand.

36 Non-trade debtors 1

NON-TRADE DEBTORS CONTROL ACCOUNT

Date 20X1	Details	Amount £	Date 20X1	Details	Amount £
1 April	Balance b/d	2,500	April	Cash book	4,000
April	Further debts	2,000	30 April	Balance c/d	500
		4,500			4,500
1 May	Balance b/d	500			

37 Non-trade debtors 2

NON-TRADE DEBTORS CONTROL ACCOUNT

Date 20X1	Details	Amount £	Date 20X1	Details	Amount £
1 May	Balance b/d	500	May	Cash book (b)	2,500
May	Further debts (a)	4,000	May	SLCA (c)	2,000
		4,500			4,500

38 Wages control account

WAGES CONTROL ACCOUNT

Date 20X3	Details	Amount £	Date 20X3	Details	Amount £
30 June	Net wages	4,200	30 June	Gross wages	6,000
30 June	Employers NIC	670	30 June	Employers NIC	670
30 June	Employees NIC	600			
30 June	Trade union fees	50			
30 June	PAYE	1,150			
		6,670			6,670

Chapter 7: The correction of errors

39 Errors 1

DEBIT	VAT	£14	
CREDIT	Purchase ledger control account		£14

To account for VAT omitted from the original posting

40 Errors 2

DEBIT	Discounts allowed	£98	
CREDIT	Discounts received		£98

To correct wrong posting

41 Errors 3

(a)
DEBIT	Suspense	£9	
CREDIT	Telephone		£9

To correct overstated telephone expense

DEBIT	Suspense	£52	
CREDIT	SLCA		£52

To post omitted customer receipt

(b)

SUSPENSE

		£		£
JNL	Credit to telephone	9	Difference on trial balance	61
JNL	Credit to SLCA	52		
		61		61

42 Journal entries

		Dr £	Cr £
(a)	Purchases	700	
	Purchases returns		700
(b)	Bank	90	
	Creditors control		90
(c)	Insurance	1,740	
	Bank		1,740

43 Errors and the trial balance

(a) No

(b) Because if the error had not been identified on receipt, the incorrect total would have been entered consistently in the accounting records, thus not causing an imbalance.

Chapter 8: From ledger accounts to initial trial balance

44 MEL factors

TRIAL BALANCE AS AT 30 APRIL 20X1

	DR £	CR £
Sales		10,000
Purchases	5,000	
Expenses	2,000	
Capital		20,000
Sales ledger control account	2,000	
Purchase ledger control account		1,500
Cash at bank and in hand	3,000	
Fixed assets	19,500	
	31,500	31,500

45 Comart supplies

(a) The difference is debit £2.500 and a suspense account needs to be set up for this amount.

(b)

SUSPENSE ACCOUNT

	£		£
Balance b/d	2,500	SLCA	3,000
PLCA	500		
	3,000		3,000

		£	£
DEBIT	Suspense account	500	
	Sales ledger control account	3,000	
CREDIT	Suspense account		3,000
	Purchase ledger control account		500

Entries to close suspense account

46 Trial balance

Begin by making an adjustment for the sales invoice. The journal will be:

DEBIT	Sales ledger control account	£350	
CREDIT	Sales		£350

Our amended balances for these two accounts will now be:

	DR £	CR £
Sales ledger control account (23,004 + 350)	23,354	
Sales (127,325 + 350)		127,675

TRIAL BALANCE AS AT 31 DECEMBER 20X1

	DR £	CR £
Cash at bank and in hand	25,275	
Capital		14,000
Sales ledger control account	23,354	
Purchase ledger control account		11,632
Purchases	71,157	
Sales		127,675
Wages	30,129	
Telephone	3,392	
Rent	10,000	
Bank loan		10,000
	163,307	163,307

Chapter 9: Filing

47 Documents for trial balance

- Cash book
- Bank reconciliation
- Petty cash book
- Reconciliation of petty cash vouchers and cash
- Sales ledger control account reconciliation
- Purchase ledger control account reconciliation
- Non trade debtors control account reconciliation

48 Filing correspondence

File in alphabetical order of the suppliers' and customers' names.

49 Filing documents

(a) By number
(b) By date
(c) By subject

Other relevant answers will be accepted.

50 Storage

MEMO

To: The owner
From: The bookkeeper
Date: 4 May 20X1
Subject: Confidentiality of ledgers

I am concerned about the confidentiality of the ledger and accounting documents which I work on, particularly the wages book, as I currently have nowhere to file these documents. When I am not in my office, including overnight, I have to leave the ledger and documents on my desk. This means that anyone in the building: employees, customers, visitors etc could, potentially, access the information contained in the documents.

I suggest that I should have a lockable filing cabinet which I can use to store the ledger and documents safely when I am not working on them.

51 Unauthorised access

Any two from:

- Confidential records may be viewed without authorisation
- Fraudulent entries may be made
- Data may be corrupted

52 Suppliers accounts

Skelton Engineers
Smithson Ltd
Snipe Associates
Sonic Partners
Souter Finance
Spartan & Co

53 Accounts personnel

- Wages book – wages clerk
- Aged debtors analysis – sales ledger clerk
- Purchase ledger accounts – purchase ledger clerk
- Bank statement – cashier
- Petty cash book – petty cashier
- Credit limits for customers – sales ledger clerk
- Standing order schedule – cashier

PART G

Full Skills based Assessments

FULL SKILLS BASED ASSESSMENT 1
HURRELL MARKETING

FOUNDATION STAGE – NVQ/SVQ2

Unit 3

Preparing Ledger Balances and an Initial Trial Balance

The purpose of this Full Skills Based Assessment is to give you an idea of what an AAT simulation looks like. It is not intended as a definitive guide to the tasks you may be required to perform.

The suggested time allowance for this Assessment is **three hours**. Up to 30 minutes extra time may be permitted in an AAT simulation. Breaks in assessment will be allowed in the AAT simulation, but it must normally be completed in one day.

Calculators may be used but no reference material is permitted.

DO NOT OPEN THIS PAPER UNTIL YOU ARE READY TO START
UNDER EXAM CONDITIONS

FULL SKILLS BASED ASSESSMENT 1

COVERAGE OF PERFORMANCE CRITERIA

All performance criteria in Unit 3 are covered by this full skills based assessment.

Element	PC Coverage
3.1	**Balance bank transactions**
	Record details from the relevant primary documentation in the cash book and ledger.
	Correctly calculate totals and balances of receipts and payments.
	Compare individual items on the bank statement and in the cash book for accuracy.
	Identify discrepancies and prepare a bank reconciliation statement.
3.2	**Prepare ledger balances and control accounts**
	Make and record authorised adjustments.
	Total relevant accounts in the main ledger.
	Reconcile control accounts with the total of the balance in the subsidiary ledger.
	Reconcile petty cash control account with cash in hand and subsidiary records.
	Identify discrepancies arising from the reconciliation of control accounts and either resolve or refer to the appropriate person.
	Ensure documentation is stored securely and in line with the organisation's confidentiality requirements.
3.3	**Draft an initial trial balance**
	Prepare the draft initial trial balance in line with the organisation's policies and procedures.
	Identify discrepancies in the balancing process.
	Identify reasons for imbalance and rectify them.
	Balance the trial balance.

Knowledge and understanding

Whilst some areas of knowledge and understanding can be inferred through performance, there will be gaps in evidence which should be plugged by other assessment methods, eg questioning.

Centres are reminded that there should be a mix of evidence across the unit, simulations cannot stand alone as evidence of competent performance, and the evidence in the portfolio should be mapped clearly to the student record.

INSTRUCTIONS

This simulation is designed to let you show your ability in preparing ledger balances and an initial trial balance.

This simulation is divided into 11 tasks. You are advised to look through the whole simulation first to gain a general appreciation of your tasks.

The situation is provided on page 240. The tasks to be completed are set out on pages 241 to 243.

Your answers should be set out in the answer booklet provided.

You are allowed **three hours** to complete your work.

A high level of accuracy is required. Check your work carefully.

Correcting fluid may be used but it should be used in moderation. Errors should be crossed out neatly and clearly. You should write in black ink, not pencil.

THE SITUATION

This simulation is concerned with Hurrell Marketing, a consultancy owned by Helen Hurrell which offers marketing services to a range of clients.

Your name is Pam Jones and you work for Hurrell Marketing as a finance assistant. You report to the finance controller, Dipak Malawi. There are 15 other members of staff at Hurrell Marketing, most of whom are paid by BACS on the third Monday of the month. Occasionally further salary BACS payments are made at the end of the month, if employees have joined in the month.

Today's date is 4 October 2005, and you are dealing with transactions in the month of September 2005.

All books of account are maintained manually. The petty cash book and cash book are part of the main ledger. The sales, purchases and rent receivable ledgers are subsidiary ledgers, each of which has a control account in the main ledger.

Bank account and cash book

A bank statement is received weekly. This is checked by reference to cash book entries, remittance advices, credit transfer details, and a schedule of direct debits and standing orders. Any entries appearing in the bank statement, but not in the cash book, are checked against supporting documentation and entered in the cash book if correct. Note that the only supporting documentation that is needed to record bank charges is the bank statement itself.

Sales and purchases

All sales and purchases are on credit terms and are subject to VAT at the standard rate.

Rent receivable

Hurrell Marketing owns its own premises and sublets half the floorspace to three different tenants, Ragoussi Science, Thompson Training and Farrar and Co. Each should pay £400 per month in arrears, on the last working day of the month.

1: HURRELL MARKETING

THE TASKS TO BE PERFORMED

Task 1

The petty cash book has been written up for the week ending 30 September 2005 on page 250 of the answer booklet. On the same page you will see a list of the notes and coins in the petty cash box at close of business on 30 September 2005, and a reconciliation schedule.

- Total the petty cash book and bring down a balance at close of business on 30 September 2005.
- Complete the reconciliation schedule on page 250 of the answer booklet, listing out clearly the amount of any discrepancy.
- Explain the cause of any discrepancy and the action required in the space provided on page 250 of the answer booklet.
- Post the petty cash book to the main ledger accounts as indicated in the petty cash book. The main ledger accounts, written up for the month of September 2005, are on pages 251-255 of the answer booklet.

Task 2

- Check the entries on the business bank statement for week ending 30 September 2005 on page 244 of this booklet. You will need to refer to the schedule of credit transfers, the schedule of standing orders and direct debits and the remittance advice on page 245 of this booklet, and to the cash book for the week ending 30 September on page 256 of the answer booklet. You can assume that there were no reconciling items on the previous bank reconciliation for the week ending 23 September 2005.
- Make further entries in the cash book where appropriate.
- Make a note beneath the cash book as to any item appearing on the bank statement and not in the cash book that you cannot enter as you have no supporting documentation.

Task 3

- Prepare a bank reconciliation statement as at 31 September 2005, clearly identifying all discrepancies between the cash book and the bank statement. Use page 257 of the answer booklet.

Task 4

- Total the cash book for the week ending 30 September 2005 and bring down a balance as at start of business on 1 October 2005.
- Post the cash book to the main ledger accounts as indicated in the cash book.

Task 5

Dipak Malawi has sent you an email on page 246 of this booklet.

- Prepare journal vouchers to make the required adjustments on page 257 of the answer booklet.
- Post the adjustments from the journal to the main ledger accounts, dating the entries 30 September 2005.

Task 6

- Total the list of sales ledger balances as at 30 September 2005 on page 258 of the answer booklet, and calculate the balance on the sales ledger control account.
- Prepare a sales ledger reconciliation on page 258 of the answer booklet, listing out clearly the amount of any discrepancy.
- Explain the cause of any discrepancy and the action required in the space provided on page 258 of the answer booklet.

Task 7

- Total the list of purchases ledger balances as at 30 September 2005 on page 258 of the answer booklet, and calculate the balance on the purchases ledger control account.
- Prepare a purchases ledger reconciliation on page 258 of the answer booklet, listing out clearly the amount of any discrepancy.
- Explain the cause of any discrepancy and the action required in the space provided on page 258 of the answer booklet.

Task 8

- Total the list of rent receivable balances as at 30 September 2005 on page 259 of the answer booklet, and calculate the balance on the rent receivable control account.
- Prepare a rent receivable reconciliation on page 259 of the answer booklet, listing out clearly the amount of any discrepancy.
- Explain the cause of any discrepancy and the action required in the space provided on page 259 of the answer booklet.

Task 9

- Total all accounts in the main ledger and bring down balances as at the start of business on 1 October 2005.
- Enter the main ledger balances, the cash book balance and the petty cash book balance at 30 September 2005 in the trial balance on page 260 of the answer booklet.
- Total the trial balance.
- Enter a suspense account to make the total debits and credits balance.

Task 10

Having informed Dipak Malawi of the suspense account balance and why it was opened you have now received the email on page 247 of this booklet.

- In the space provided beneath the trial balance, identify the reason for the suspense account.
- Prepare the journal referred to in the email, including appropriate narrative, using the journal voucher on page 257 of the answer booklet.

Task 11

Complete the schedule of queries on page 261 of the answer booklet that Dipak Malawi has passed to you for resolution.

FULL SKILLS BASED ASSESSMENT 1

Avalon Bank plc
1 Market Square, Salisbury, Wilts BS5 4XK

STATEMENT
50-64-73

Account: Hurrell Marketing

Statement no: 148

Account number: 3215654

Date	Details		Payments £	Receipts £	Balance £
2005					
26/9	Balance from previous sheet				6,473.21
27/9	Cash and cheques			10,675.63	
28/9	Cheque 456165		5,000.00		
28/9	Cheque 456167		26.34		
28/9	Salem District Council	DD	552.35		
28/9	Cheque 456169		720.30		
30/9	Ragoussi Science			400.00	
30/9	Farrar & Co			400.00	
30/9	Cash and cheques	CC		2,976.34	
30/9	Bank charges	CHGS	25.00		
30/9	TransPower plc	STO	158.00		
30/9	Salaries	BACS	1,678.60		
30/9	FIXA Insurance	DD	120.00		
30-Sept	MAX Marketing	BGC		6,687.02	
	Balance				19,331.61
			8,280.59	21,138.99	

Key	SO Standing order	CC Cash and/or cheques	CHGS Bank charges	DD Direct debit
	O/D Overdrawn	BGC Bank Giro Credit	BACS Automated clearing	

Avalon Bank plc
Sort code: 50-64-73
Schedule of credit transfers of net pay end September 2005

Customer name: Hurrell Marketing

Account number: 03215654

Due date for payments: 30 September 2005

Total value of payments: £1,678.60

Payee	Sort code	Account no	Amount £
Rachel Folwell	10-75-64	14657686	852.14
Simon Hammond	20-55-43	54987945	826.46

Helen Hurrell   27/9/05

Signature of customer ……………………………………….   Date ………………..

Schedule of standing orders and direct debits (extract)

Payee/reference	Amount	When payable
IXA Insurance Ltd	£120.00	Monthly
TransPower plc	£158.00	Monthly

REMITTANCE ADVICE		
MAX Marketing, Trenchant Way, Gosport, Hants PO8 5AS		
Supplier:	Hurrell Marketing	
Subsidiary (purchase) ledger code	465464	
Date	**Transaction reference**	**Amount £**
25/9/05	Invoice 5464448	6,687.02
30/9/05	Payment by BACS	-6,687.02

EMAIL	
To	dipak.malawi@hurrell_market.com
From	pam.jones@hurrell_market.com
CC	
Date	4 October 2005
Subject	Errors and bad debts

Pam

Thank you for pointing out the direct debit to Salem District Council that has appeared on our bank statement. I have looked into the matter and find that the bank has made an error here, which will be corrected on our next statement.

There are, however, some matters that I would like you to prepare journals for, if appropriate, to adjust the main ledger.

1   I notice that an amount of £5,000 was paid to Lennox Ltd on 26 September. On looking further into this I find that Lennox Ltd's invoice was recorded in the purchase day book in August, and £5,000 was analysed to purchases (there was no VAT). This actually relates to a fixed asset acquired. Please make the necessary adjustment.

2   I have had a letter to the effect that an amount of £739.76 due from Hamilton Trading as at 1 September will not be recoverable by us, as the customer has ceased to trade. Please make the necessary adjustment.

3   On looking at the postings from the purchases returns day book, I note that a credit note from Syrillian plc for £394.86 was correctly recorded in the day book but was posted to the wrong side of the ledger account for this supplier.

4   Rental income due of £1,200.

Thanks

Dipak

1: HURRELL MARKETING

EMAIL	
To	dipak.malawi@hurrell_market.com
From	pam.jones@hurrell_market.com
CC	
Date	4 October 2005
Subject	Errors and bad debts

Pam

Thank you for pointing out that you have had to create a suspense account in order to make the trial balance as at 30 September balance. I have looked through the main ledger and have spotted what I believe is the error at issue. On 19 September, when the bulk of the employees were paid, employer's NI of £1,046.98 was correctly debited to administration overheads but was also debited to the PAYE/NIC creditor account.

Please prepare a journal to correct the error and clear the suspense account.

Thanks

Dipak

FULL SKILLS BASED ASSESSMENT 1

HURRELL MARKETING

ANSWER BOOKLET

Unit 3

ANSWERS (Task 1)

Petty cash book

PCB 39

Receipts £	Date 2005	Details	Voucher	Total £	VAT £	Sundry expenses £
65.21	26/9	Balance b/f				
	27/9	Postage		7.20		7.20
	28/9	Stationery		18.95	2.82	16.13
	29/9	Postage		7.20		7.20
	30/9	Tea, coffee etc		10.58		10.58
		Totals				
		Balance c/d				

Notes and coins in the petty cash tin 30 September 2005

Value	Number	Total value £
£20	0	
£10	0	
£5	2	
£2	3	
£1	3	
50p	2	
20p	4	
10p	3	
5p	3	
2p	1	
1p	1	

Petty cash reconciliation

Date   30 September 2005

£

Balance per petty cash book

Total of notes and coins

Discrepancy (if any)

Explanation of discrepancy (if any)

Answers Tasks 1 and 4

ACCOUNT: Administration overheads

DEBIT			CREDIT		
Date	Details	Amount	Date	Details	Amount
2005		£	2005		£
29 Sept	Brought down	50,564.35			

ACCOUNT: Bad debts

DEBIT			CREDIT		
Date	Details	Amount	Date	Details	Amount
2005		£	2005		£
29 Sept	Brought down	900.20			

ACCOUNT: Capital

DEBIT			CREDIT		
Date	Details	Amount	Date	Details	Amount
2005		£	2005		£
			29 Sept	Brought down	160,000.00

Answers Tasks 1 and 4

ACCOUNT: Distribution costs

DEBIT			CREDIT		
Date 2005	Details	Amount £	Date 2005	Details	Amount £
29 Sept	Brought down	18,642.80			

ACCOUNT: Fixed assets

DEBIT			CREDIT		
Date 2005	Details	Amount £	Date 2005	Details	Amount £
29 Sept	Brought down	174,000.00			

ACCOUNT: PAYE/NIC creditor

DEBIT			CREDIT		
Date 2005	Details	Amount £	Date 2005	Details	Amount £
			29 Sept	Brought down	1,305.45

Answers Tasks 1 and 4

ACCOUNT: Purchases

DEBIT			CREDIT		
Date	Details	Amount	Date	Details	Amount
2005		£	2005		£
29 Sept	Brought down	88,491.46			

ACCOUNT: Purchases ledger control

DEBIT			CREDIT		
Date	Details	Amount	Date	Details	Amount
2005		£	2005		£
			29 Sept	Brought down	55,436.55

ACCOUNT: Rental income

DEBIT			CREDIT		
Date	Details	Amount	Date	Details	Amount
2005		£	2005		£
			29 Sept	Brought down	9,600.00

ACCOUNT: Rent receivable control

DEBIT			CREDIT		
Date	Details	Amount	Date	Details	Amount
2005		£	2005		£
29 Sept	Brought down	800.00			

ACCOUNT: Sales

DEBIT			CREDIT		
Date	Details	Amount	Date	Details	Amount
2005		£	2005		£
			29 Sept	Brought down	185,840.55

ACCOUNT: Sales ledger control

DEBIT			CREDIT		
Date	Details	Amount	Date	Details	Amount
2005		£	2005		£
29 Sept	Brought down	75,955.75			

Answers Tasks 1 and 4

ACCOUNT: Stock

DEBIT			CREDIT		
Date	Details	Amount	Date	Details	Amount
2005		£	2005		£
29 Sept	Brought down	3,269.40			

ACCOUNT: Sundry expenses

DEBIT			CREDIT		
Date	Details	Amount	Date	Details	Amount
2005		£	2005		£
29 Sept	Brought down	2,693.05			

ACCOUNT: VAT control

DEBIT			CREDIT		
Date	Details	Amount	Date	Details	Amount
2005		£	2005		£
			29 Sept	Brought down	3,985.05

ANSWERS (Tasks 2 and 4)

CASH BOOK

CB39

RECEIPTS					PAYMENTS						
Sales ledger £	Rent £	Total £	Date	Details	Cheque no	Total £	Purchase ledger £	Sundry expenses £	Admin overheads £	Distribution costs £
		2,879.34	01-Sep	Balance b/f						
35,231.82	800	36,031.82		TOTALS FOR MONTH TO DATE		32,437.95	7,256.31	2.00	20,192.07	4,987.57
10,675.63		10,675.63	26/9	Paget & Co						
			26/9	Lennox Ltd	456165	5,000.00	5,000.00			
			26/9	Syrillian plc	456166	6,142.01	6,142.01			
			26/9	T Vassell	456167	26.34		26.34		
			26/9	Rendle & Cooper	456168	324.68	324.68			
			26/9	Instis Ltd	456169	720.30	720.30			
2,976.34		2,976.34	29/9	WapWap plc						
4,212.05		4,212.05	30/9	Florin & Co						
			30/9	TransPower plc	STO	158.00	158.00			
			30/9	Salaries	BACS	1,678.60				1,678.60
			30/9	FIXA Insurance Ltd	DD	120.00	120.00			
	400.00	400.00	30/9	Ragoussi Science						
	400.00	400.00	30.9	Farrar & Co						
				Balance b/d						

Item not entered in cash book due to lack of supporting documentation

Action to be taken:

ANSWERS (Task 3)

Bank reconciliation at 30 September 2005

£

Balance per bank statement

_____

_____

Balance per cash book

ANSWERS (Tasks 5 and 10)

Journals

	DR £	CR £
1		
2		
3		
4		
5		

ANSWERS (Task 6)

Sales ledger balances as at 30 September 2005

Account code	Name of debtor	Amount owing as at 30 September 2005
		£
B673	Bristol plc	5,678.02
F039	Florin & Co	1,649.28
G182	Gwent Ltd	2,854.11
H004	Hamilton Trading	739.76
M893	MAX Marketing	6,687.02
P678	Paget & Co	1,640.38
W118	WapWap plc	2,108.00
Z365	Zebedee plc	1,503.34

Total of sales ledger balances _____

Difference (if any) _____

Explanation of difference and action required:

ANSWERS (Task 7)

Purchases ledger balances as at 30 September 2005

Account code	Name of creditor	Amount owed as at 30 September 2005
		£
A902	Armageddon plc	21456.26
D537	Drakes	2,879.64
I839	Instis Ltd	2,458.84
L012	Lennox Ltd	0.00
R643	Rendle & Cooper	5,872.00
S903	Syrillian plc	2,731.06
V555	Vodex plc	1,107.17

Total of purchase ledger balances _____

Difference (if any) _____

Explanation of difference and action required:

ANSWERS (Task 8)

Rent receivable ledger balances as at 30 September 2005

Name of tenant

	£
Ragoussi Science	0.00
Thompson Training	400.00
Farrar & Co	0.00
Total of rent receivable balances	
Total per control account	
Difference (if any)	

Explanation of difference and action required:

ANSWERS (Tasks 9 and 10)

Trial balance at 30 September 2005

Account name	Debit £	Credit £
Administration overheads		
Bad debts		
Cash book		
Capital		
Distribution costs		
Fixed assets		
PAYE/NIC liability		
Petty cash book		
Purchases		
Purchases ledger control		
Rental income		
Rent receivable control		
Sales		
Sales ledger control		
Stock		
Sundry expenses		
VAT control		
Suspense account		
Totals		

Reason for the suspense account:

ND

ANSWERS (Task 11)

To: Pam Jones
From: Dipak Malawi

Schedule of queries

I have been discussing various matters with Helen Hurrell recently, in connection with her plan to take on her brother as her business partner. Although he is very good at marketing, he has no practical finance or administration background and there are a number of basic issues about which he knows nothing. I have been putting together a checklist for him. Please complete the schedule below, for inclusion in the checklist.

1. When we make a sale to a customer we let them know the amount they have to pay by issuing an ---------------. This shows the amount that we will debit/credit* to sales, the amount we will debit/credit* to VAT, and the amount we will debit/credit* to their account in the sales ledger. If we agree with them that we have charged too much, we will issue them with a ----------------. (*Delete as applicable.)

2. An invoice from a supplier records how much we owe/are owed by* them, and is recorded by us in their account in the sales/purchases* ledger. Until we pay them this money the supplier is a debtor/creditor* of the business. (*Delete as applicable.)

3. The standard rate for VAT is ---------%. VAT appearing in the sales day book is called --------- tax. VAT appearing in the purchases day book is called ---------- tax. When there is a credit balance on the VAT control account this means that we owe/are owed* an amount of VAT to/by* HM Customs and Excise. (*Delete as applicable.)

4. Our bank is Avalon Bank plc, which supplies us with regular statements of account. If these show that we are overdrawn, this means that the bank is a debtor/creditor* of our business. When we write a cheque to a supplier, we are the ---------- of the cheque, the bank is the ------------ and the supplier is the -----------. The cheque will take -------- days to clear on our bank account, from the day that the supplier banks it.

5. Our cheques are printed by the bank with two vertical lines (a crossing) with the words 'Account payee' printed between them. This means that: -
   _____
   _____.

6. Both the sales ledger and the purchases ledger allocate account codes to each account they contain. Referring to the code numbers in the reconciliations for 30 September 2005, the coding system used is numeric/alphanumeric/alphabetical*. (*Delete as applicable.)

7. The maximum amount of cash our petty cash box is permitted to hold is £200. Every time the box is topped up, it is topped up to £200. This is called the --------------- amount.

8. We file our weekly bank statements with the relevant bank reconciliation. This is so that:
   _____
   _____

9. The deeds of our property and the lease agreements that we have with our three tenants are stored at our solicitor's offices. This is to ensure the ------------- and -------------------- of the documents.

10. In relation to our customers we should aim to keep the following matters confidential:
    1 _____
    2 _____

FULL SKILLS BASED ASSESSMENT 1

FULL SKILLS BASED ASSESSMENT 2
MARPLES COOKWARE

FOUNDATION STAGE – NVQ/SVQ2

Unit 3

Preparing Ledger Balances and an Initial Trial Balance

The purpose of this Full Skills Based Assessment is to give you an idea of what an AAT simulation looks like. It is not intended as a definitive guide to the tasks you may be required to perform.

The suggested time allowance for this Assessment is **three hours**. Up to 30 minutes extra time may be permitted in an AAT simulation. Breaks in assessment will be allowed in the AAT simulation, but it must normally be completed in one day.

Calculators may be used but no reference material is permitted.

**DO NOT OPEN THIS PAPER UNTIL YOU ARE READY TO START
UNDER EXAM CONDITIONS**

FULL SKILLS BASED ASSESSMENT 2

COVERAGE OF PERFORMANCE CRITERIA

The following performance criteria are covered in this simulation, except as indicated by an asterisk *.

Element	PC Coverage	
3.1	**Balance bank transactions**	
A	Record details from the relevant primary documentation in the cashbook and ledgers.	1
B	Correctly calculate totals and balances of receipts and payments	2
C	Compare individual items on the bank statement and in the cashbook for accuracy	1
D	Identify discrepancies and prepare a bank reconciliation statement.	3
3.2	**Prepare ledger balances and control accounts**	
A	Make and record authorised adjustments	4
B	Total relevant accounts in the main ledger	8
C	Reconcile control accounts with the totals of the balances in the subsidiary ledger	3, 5, 6, 7
D	Reconcile petty cash control account with cash in hand and subsidiary records	8
E	Identify discrepancies arising from the reconciliation of control accounts and either resolve or refer to the appropriate person	3, 5, 6, 7
F	Ensure documentation is stored securely and in line with the organisation's confidentiality requirements	*
3.3	**Draft an initial trial balance**	
A	Prepare the draft initial trial balance in line with the organisation's policies and procedures	9
B	Identify discrepancies in the balancing process	9
C	Identify reasons for imbalance and rectify them	10
D	Balance the trial balance	10

Knowledge and understanding

Whilst some areas of knowledge and understanding can be inferred through performance, there will be gaps in evidence which should be plugged by other assessment methods, eg questioning.

Centres are reminded that there should be a mix of evidence across the unit, simulations cannot stand alone as evidence of competent performance, and the evidence in the portfolio should be mapped clearly to the student record.

INSTRUCTIONS

This simulation is designed to let you show your ability to prepare ledger balances and an initial trial balance.

This simulation is divided into 10 tasks. You are advised to look through the whole simulation first to gain a general appreciation of your tasks.

The situation is provided on page 266. The tasks to be completed are set out on pages 267 and 268.

Your answers should be set out in the answer booklet provided.

You are allowed **three hours** to complete your work.

A high level of accuracy is required. Check your work carefully.

Correcting fluid may be used but it should be used in moderation. Errors should be crossed out neatly and clearly. You should write in black ink, not pencil.

THE SITUATION

This simulation is concerned with Marples Cookware, a supplier of kitchen hardware to the catering trade.

Your name is Laura Teckworth and you work for Marples Cookware as an accounts assistant. You report to the accounts supervisor, Jim Leslie.

Today's date is 4 August 20X4, and you are dealing with transactions in the month of July 20X4.

All books of account are maintained manually.

Bank account and cash book

A bank statement is received weekly. This is checked by reference to cash book entries, credit transfer details, and a schedule of direct debits and standing orders. Any entries appearing in the bank statement, but not in the cash book, are checked as appropriate and entered in the cash book if correct.

Sales and purchases

All sales and purchases are on credit terms and are subject to VAT at the standard rate. They are recorded in a subsidiary (sales) ledger and a subsidiary (purchase) ledger respectively. A sales ledger control account and a purchase ledger control account are maintained in the main ledger.

Wages and salaries

Wages and salaries are paid monthly by direct credit transfer into the bank accounts of employees. Marples Cookware's bank is informed of the net amounts to be paid by means of a 'Data submission form' submitted each month. These net amounts in turn are extracted from a more detailed 'Wages and salaries analysis' prepared each month by Jim Leslie.

THE TASKS TO BE PERFORMED

Task 1

- Check the entries on the business bank statement for week ending 30 July 20X4 (page 269). You will need to refer to the schedule of standing orders and direct debits on page 270 and to the cash book for week ending 30 July on page 276 in the answer booklet. You can assume that there were no reconciling items on the previous bank reconciliation for the week ending 23 July 20X4.

- Make further entries in the cash book where appropriate.

Task 2

Total the cash book for the week ending 30 July 20X4 and bring down a balance as at start of business on 1 August 20X4.

Task 3

Prepare a bank reconciliation statement as at 31 July 20X4, clearly identifying all discrepancies between the cash book and the bank statement. Use page 277.

Task 4

Jim Leslie has sent you an email shown on page 270

Make appropriate adjustments in the main ledger accounts, dating the entries 31 July 20X4. The main ledger accounts, written up for the month of July 20X4, are on pages 278-283.

Task 5

- Total the list of sales ledger balances as at 31 July 20X4 on page 284, and calculate the balance on the sales ledger control account, on page 281.

- Agree the total of the sales ledger to the balance on the sales ledger control account.

- If you note a discrepancy, explain the cause and the action required in the space provided on page 284.

Task 6

- Total the list of purchase ledger balances as at 31 July 20X4 on page 285, and calculate the balance on the purchase ledger control account, on page 280.

- Agree the total of the purchase ledger balances to the balance on the purchase ledger control account.

- If you note a discrepancy, explain the cause and the action required in the space provided on page 285.

Task 7

Refer to the wages and salaries analyses for June and July 20X4 and the bank data submission form for July 20X4 on pages 271 and 272.

Check the total cash payments in respect of wages and salaries in July 20X4. To do this you should complete the reconciliation form on page 286.

Task 8

The petty cash book has been written up for the week ending 30 July 20X4 on page 287. On the same page you will see a list of the notes and coins in the petty cash tin at close of business on 30 July 20X4, and a reconciliation schedule.

- Total the petty cash book and bring down a balance at close of business on 30 July 20X4.
- Complete the reconciliation schedule on page 288, including a note of any discrepancy.

Task 9

- Total all accounts in the main ledger and bring down balances as at the start of business on 1 August 20X4.
- Enter the balances at 1 August 20X4 in the trial balance on page 289 and total the trial balance. Enter a suspense account to make the total debits and credits balance.

Task 10

Having informed Jim Leslie of the suspense account balance you have now received the email on page 273.

Prepare the journal referred to in the email, including appropriate narrative, using the journal voucher on page 290.

Midnorth Bank plc

14 Bank Buildings, Kendal KE2 9SD

STATEMENT

65-78-78

Account: Marples Cookware

Statement no: 148

Account number: 68431351

Date	Details		Payments £	Receipts £	Balance £
20X4					
26/7	Balance from previous sheet				15,679.32
26/7	Kendal District Council	SO	630.00		
26/7	Cheques/cash received	CC		572.64	15,621.96
27/7	Bank charges for July	CHGS	45.50		
27/7	Cheque 105897		50.00		15,526.46
28/7	Cheques/cash received	CC		10,974.61	
28/7	Bank giro credit from Lardenis Kitchens	BGC		2,789.64	29,290.71
29/7	Cheque 105898		947.62		28,343.09
30/7	Cheque 105899		3,187.69		
30/7	Salaries		11,479.46		
30/7	NorthWest Power Ltd	DD	210.00		13,465.94

Key	SO Standing order	CC Cash and/or cheques	DD Direct debit
	CHGS Bank charges	O/D Overdrawn	BGC Bank Giro Credit

Schedule of standing orders and direct debits (extract)

Payee/reference	Amount	When payable
Kendal District Council	£630.00	April, July, October and January
NorthWest Power Ltd	£210.00	Monthly

From: Jim Leslie

To: Laura Teckworth

Subject: Bad debt/error in purchases day book

Laura

I have just had formal notification from Webster Co that they will be unable to pay us anything in respect of their debt of £980.00 as they have ceased trading. Please write the full amount off as a bad debt.

In the course of my analysis of the purchases day book for July I have noted that the net amount of an invoice from Persimmon Ovens was entered as £540 when it should have been £450.

Please could you draft journals dated 31 July 20X4 to deal with both of these items.

Thanks

Jim

Wages and salaries analysis

Month: June 20X4

Employee name	PAYE £	Employee NIC £	Net pay £	Employer NIC £	Total £
Lydia Akinowe	451.39	130.90	1,805.58	170.18	2,558.05
Desmon Barrett	554.42	160.78	2,217.68	209.02	3,141.90
Justine Horricks	326.65	94.73	1,306.62	123.15	1,851.15
Sam Johnson	144.17	41.81	576.69	54.35	817.02
Jim Leslie	365.07	105.87	1,460.29	137.63	2,068.86
Ann Marple	719.87	156.57	2,159.82	203.55	3,239.81
Laura Teckworth	229.62	66.59	918.48	86.57	1,301.26
	2,791.19	757.25	10,445.16	984.45	14,978.05

Month: July 20X4

Employee name	PAYE £	Employee NIC £	Net pay £	Employer NIC £	Total £
Lydia Akinowe	496.09	143.87	1,984.37	187.03	2,811.36
Desmon Barrett	609.32	176.70	2,437.28	229.71	3,453.02
Justine Horricks	359.00	104.11	1,436.00	135.34	2,034.45
Sam Johnson	158.45	45.95	633.80	59.74	897.94
Jim Leslie	401.22	116.35	1,604.89	151.26	2,273.73
Ann Marple	791.23	172.09	2,373.69	223.72	3,560.73
Laura Teckworth	252.36	73.18	1,009.43	95.14	1,430.11
	3,067.67	832.26	11,479.46	1,081.94	16,461.33

Midnorth Bank plc

Sort code: 64-78-78

Data submission form: net salary payments

Customer name: Marple Cookware & Co
Account number: 68431351
Due date for payments: 30 July 20X4
Total value of payments: £11,479.46

Payee	Sort code	Account no	Amount £
Lydia Akinowe	30-78-45	19867655	1,984.37
Desmon Barrett	20-43-61	54187168	2,437.28
Justine Horricks	10-41-63	71687166	1,436.00
Sam Johnson	45-65-12	05687168	633.80
Jim Leslie	64-78-78	55115721	1,604.89
Ann Marple	20-46-79	68167116	2,373.69
Laura Teckworth	50-22-85	22547168	1,009.43

Signature of customer ……………………………… Date ………………………………

From: Jim Leslie
To: Laura Teckworth
Subject: Collecting the trial balance

You mentioned that the TB for the end of July does not balance. I have looked at the ledgers and have noted one error, which may explain the problem.

In July we posted an amount of £1,134.32 twice from the purchases day book to Administration Overheads.

Please could you draft a journal dated 31 July 20X4 to deal with this item.

Thanks

Jim

FULL SKILLS BASED ASSESSMENT 2

MARPLES COOKWARE

ANSWER BOOKLET

FULL SKILLS BASED ASSESSMENT 2

Tasks 1, 2

Cash book w/e 30 July

| Receipts | | | | | | | Payments | | | |
Debtors £	Other receipts £	Total £	Date	Details	Cheque no	Total £	Creditors £	Other payments £	Salaries & wages £
		15,679.32	26/7	Balance b/f					
572.64		572.64	26/7	Caris & Co					
			26/7	Wrinkles plc	105897	50.00	50.00		
			26/7	Kendal District Council	SO	630.00		630.00	
			27/7	Abacus Ltd	105898	947.62	947.62		
10,974.61		10,974.61	27/7	Jago Hotels plc					
			27/7	Dunmore Co	105899	3,187.69	3,187.69		
			30/7	Salaries		11,479.46			11,479.46
3,473.43		3,473.43	30/7	Tufnell Ltd					
			30/7	NorthWest Power Ltd	DD	210.00		210.00	
			307/7	Mandible Partners	105900	2,782.84	2,782.84		

Task 3

Bank reconciliation at 30 July 20X4

	£
Balance per bank statement	
Balance per cash book	

Tasks 4, 9

ACCOUNT: Administration overheads

DEBIT			CREDIT		
Date	Details	Amount	Date	Details	Amount
20X4		£	20X4		£
01 Jul	Balance b/f	4,357.31			
31 Jul	Purchase ledger control	2,268.64			
31 Jul	Bank	2,656.50			

ACCOUNT: Bad debts

DEBIT			CREDIT		
Date	Details	Amount	Date	Details	Amount
20X4		£	20X4		£
01 Jul	Balance b/f	125.00			

ACCOUNT: Bank control

DEBIT			CREDIT		
Date	Details	Amount	Date	Details	Amount
20X4		£	20X4		£
01 Jul	Balance b/f	6,216.04			
31 Jul	Receipts in month	49,844.91			

ACCOUNT: Capital

DEBIT			CREDIT		
Date	Details	Amount	Date	Details	Amount
20X4		£	20X4		£
			01 Jul	Balance b/f	28,000

ACCOUNT: Fixed assets

DEBIT			CREDIT		
Date	Details	Amount	Date	Details	Amount
20X4		£	20X4		£
01 Jul	Balance b/f	24,000.00			

ACCOUNT: PAYE/NIC liability

DEBIT			CREDIT		
Date	Details	Amount	Date	Details	Amount
20X4		£	20X4		£
31 Jul	Bank	4,532.91	01 Jul	Balance b/f	4,532.91
			31 Jul	Wages/salaries control	4,981.87

ACCOUNT: Petty cash control

DEBIT			CREDIT		
Date	Details	Amount	Date	Details	Amount
20X4		£	20X4		£
01 Jul	Balance b/f	58.00	31 Jul	Sundry expenses	37.52
			31 Jul	VAT	2.67

ACCOUNT: Purchases

DEBIT			CREDIT		
Date	Details	Amount	Date	Details	Amount
20X4		£	20X4		£
01 Jul	Balance b/f	97,645.00			
31 Jul	Purchase ledger control	24,411.25			

ACCOUNT: Purchase ledger control

DEBIT			CREDIT		
Date	Details	Amount	Date	Details	Amount
20X4		£	20X4		£
31 Jul	Bank	23,235.55	01 Jul	Balance b/f	13,617.67
			31 Jul	Purchases/expenses/VAT	31,570.01

ACCOUNT: Sales

DEBIT			CREDIT		
Date	Details	Amount	Date	Details	Amount
20X4		£	20X4		£
			01 Jul	Balance b/f	189,681.76
			31 Jul	Sales ledger control	47,343.81

ACCOUNT: Sales ledger control

DEBIT			CREDIT		
Date	Details	Amount	Date	Details	Amount
20X4		£	20X4		£
01 Jul	Balance b/f	31,562.54	31 Jul	Bank	49,844.91
31 Jul	Sales/VAT	55,628.98			

ACCOUNT: Selling and distribution overheads

DEBIT			CREDIT		
Date	Details	Amount	Date	Details	Amount
20X4		£	20X4		£
01 Jul	Balance b/f	3,642.87			
31 Jul	Purchase ledger control	910.71			

FULL SKILLS BASED ASSESSMENT 2

ACCOUNT: Stock

DEBIT			CREDIT		
Date	Details	Amount	Date	Details	Amount
20X4		£	20X4		£
01 Jul	Balance b/f	5,324.00			

ACCOUNT: Sundry expenses

DEBIT			CREDIT		
Date	Details	Amount	Date	Details	Amount
20X4		£	20X4		£
01 Jul	Balance b/f	1,647.25			
31 Jul	Purchase ledger control	411.81			
31 Jul	Petty cash	37.52			

ACCOUNT: VAT control

DEBIT			CREDIT		
Date	Details	Amount	Date	Details	Amount
20X4		£	20X4		£
31 Jul	Purchase ledger control	4,701.29	01 Jul	Balance b/f	2,761.72
31 Jul	Petty cash	2.67	31 Jul	Sales ledger control	8,285.17

ACCOUNT: Wages/salaries control

DEBIT			CREDIT		
Date	Details	Amount	Date	Details	Amount
20X4		£	20X4		£
31 Jul	Bank	11,479.46	31 Jul	Wages/salaries expenses	16,461.33
31 Jul	PAYE/NIC liability	4,981.87			

ACCOUNT: Wages/salaries expense

DEBIT			CREDIT		
Date	Details	Amount	Date	Details	Amount
20X4		£	20X4		£
01 Jul	Balance b/f	64,016.05			
31 Jul	Wages/salaries control	16,461.33			

Task 5

Sales ledger balances as at 31 July 20X4

Name of debtor	Amount owing as at 31 July 20X4 £
Buzz Ltd	5,921.43
Caris & Co	1,472.05
Hogmanay Enterprises	3,885.00
Landenis Kitchens	7,849.64
Jago Hotels plc	13,677.54
Tufnell Ltd	3,560.95
Webster Co	980.00
Total of sales ledger balances	
Total per control account	
Difference (if any)	

Explanation of difference and action required:

Task 6

Purchase ledger balances as at 31 July 20X4

Name of creditor	Amount owed as at 31 July 20X4 £
Abacus Ltd	5,154.04
Dunmore Co	7,731.07
Mandible Partners	5,291.21
Persimmon Ovens	1,150.00
Wrinkles plc	185.95
Yarnton Ltd	2,439.86
Total of purchase ledger balances	
Total per control account	
Difference (if any)	

Explanation of difference and action required:

Task 7

Reconciliation of wages/salaries payments in month

MONTH: July 20X4 £

Total PAYE June 20X4

Total employees' NIC June 20X4

Total employer's NIC June 20X4 _____

Subtotal (= payments figure in PAYE/NIC control account)

Total net pay in current month (= bank payments figure in wages/salaries control) _____

Total wages/salaries payments in month _____

Task 8

Petty cash book

PCB 19

Receipts £	Date 20X4	Details	Voucher	Total £	VAT £	Sundry expenses £
58.00	1/7	Balance b/f				
	6/7	Postage		4.05		4.05
	12/7	Stationery		5.99	0.89	5.10
	19/7	Postage		6.60		6.60
	21/7	Tea, coffee etc		7.50		7.50
	24/7	Stationery		12.00	1.78	10.22
	29/7	Postage		4.05		4.05
		Totals			2.67	37.52
		Balance c/d				

Notes and coins in the petty cash tin 30 July 20X4

Value	Number	Total value £
£20	0	
£10	0	
£5	1	
£2	2	
£1	6	
50p	3	
20p	4	
10p	3	
5p	3	
2p	2	
1p	2	

FULL SKILLS BASED ASSESSMENT 2

Petty cash reconciliation

DATE: 30 July 20X4

£

Balance per petty cash book
Total of notes and coins
Discrepancy (if any)

Explanation of discrepancy (if any)

Task 9

Trial balance at 31 July 20X4

Account name	Debit £	Credit £
Administration overheads		
Bad debts		
Bank control		
Capital		
Fixed assets		
PAYE/NIC liability		
Petty cash control		
Purchases		
Purchase ledger control		
Sales		
Sales ledger control		
Selling and distribution overheads		
Stock		
Sundry expenses		
VAT control		
Wages/salaries control		
Wages/salaries expense		
Total		

FULL SKILLS BASED ASSESSMENT 2

Task 10

Journal

Date	Account names and narrative	Debit £	Credit £

Answers to Full Skills based Assessments

ANSWERS TO FULL SKILLS BASED ASSESSMENT 1

HURRELL MARKETING

**DO NOT TURN THIS PAGE UNTIL YOU HAVE COMPLETED
THE FULL SKILLS BASED ASSESSMENT**

Task 1

Petty cash book

PCB 39

Receipts £	Date 2005	Details	Voucher	Total £	VAT £	Sundry expenses £
65.21	26/9	Balance b/f				
	27/9	Postage		7.20		7.20
	28/9	Stationery		18.95	2.82	16.13
	29/9	Postage		7.20		7.20
	30/9	Tea, coffee etc		10.58		10.58
		Totals		43.93	2.82	41.11
		Balance c/d		21.28		
65.21				65.21		
21.28						

Notes and coins in the petty cash tin 30 September 2005

Value	Number	Total value £
£20	0	0.00
£10	0	0.00
£5	2	10.00
£2	3	6.00
£1	3	3.00
50p	2	1.00
20p	4	0.80
10p	3	0.30
5p	3	0.15
2p	1	0.02
1p	1	0.01
		21.28

Petty cash reconciliation

Date	30 September 2005	
		£
Balance per petty cash book		21.28
Total of notes and coins		21.28
Discrepancy (if any)		<u>Nil</u>
Explanation of discrepancy (if any)		
N/A		

ANSWERS (Tasks 1 and 4)

Account Administration overheads

Debit			Credit		
Date 2005	Details	Amount £	Date 2005	Details	Amount £
29-Sep	Brought down	50,564.35		
30-Sep	Cash book	20,192.07	30-Sep	Carried down	70,756.42
	70,756.42			70,756.42
01-Oct	Brought down	70,756.42		

Account Bad debts

Debit			Credit		
Date 2005	Details	Amount £	Date 2005	Details	Amount £
29-Sep	Brought down	900.20		
30-Sep	Journal 2	739.76	30-Sep	Carried down	1,639.96
	1,639.96			1,639.96
01-Oct	Brought down	1,639.96		

Account Capital

Debit			Credit		
Date 2005	Details	Amount £	Date 2005	Details	Amount £
30-Sep	Carried down	160,000.00	29-Sep	Brought down	160,000.00
	160,000.00			160,000.00
		01-Oct	Brought down	160,000.00

ANSWERS (Tasks 1 and 4)

Account Distribution costs

Debit			Credit		
Date 2005	Details	Amount £	Date 2005	Details	Amount £
29-Sep	Brought down	18,642.80	30-Sep	Carried down	25,308.97
30-Sep	Cash book	6,666.17			
		25,308.97			25,308.97
01-Oct	Brought down	25,308.97			

Account Fixed assets

Debit			Credit		
Date 2005	Details	Amount £	Date 2005	Details	Amount £
29-Sep	Brought down	174,000.00	30-Sep	Carried down	179,000.00
30-Sep	Journal 1	5,000.00			
		179,000.00			179,000.00
01-Oct	Brought down	179,000.00			

Account PAYE/NIC creditor

Debit			Credit		
Date 2005	Details	Amount £	Date 2005	Details	Amount £
30-Sep	Carried down	1,305.45	29-Sep	Brought down	1,305.45
		1,305.45			1,305.45
			01-Oct	Brought down	1,305.45

ANSWERS (Tasks 1 and 4)

Account Purchases

Debit			Credit		
Date 2005	Details	Amount £	Date 2005	Details	Amount £
29-Sep	Brought down	88,491.46	30-Sep	Journal 1	5,000.00
			30-Sep	Carried down	83,491.46
		88,491.46			88,491.46
01-Oct	Brought down	83,491.46			

Account Purchases ledger control

Debit			Credit		
Date 2005	Details	Amount £	Date 2005	Details	Amount £
30-Sep	Cash book	19,721.30	29-Sep	Brought down	55,436.55
30-Sep	Carried down	35,715.25			
		55,436.55			55,436.55
			01-Oct	Brought down	35,715.25

Account Rental income

Debit			Credit		
Date 2005	Details	Amount £	Date 2005	Details	Amount £
30-Sep	Carried down	10,800.00	29-Sep	Brought down	9,600.00
			30-Sep	Journal 3	1,200.00
		10,800.00			10,800.00
			01-Oct	Brought down	10,800.00

ANSWERS (Tasks 1 and 4)

Account Rent receivable control

Debit			Credit		
Date 2005	Details	Amount £	Date 2005	Details	Amount £
29-Sep	Brought down	800.00	30-Sep	Cash book	1,600.00
30-Sep	Journal 3	1,200.00	30-Sep	Carried down	400.00
		2,000.00			2,000.00
01-Oct	Brought down	400.00			

Account Sales

Debit			Credit		
Date 2005	Details	Amount £	Date 2005	Details	Amount £
30-Sep	Carried down	185,840.55	29-Sep	Brought down	185,840.55
		185,840.55			185,840.55
			01-Oct	Brought down	185,840.55

Account Sales ledger control

Debit			Credit		
Date 2005	Details	Amount £	Date 2005	Details	Amount £
29-Sep	Brought down	75,955.75	30-Sep	Cash book	59,782.86
			30-Sep	Journal 2	739.76
			30-Sep	Carried down	15,433.13
		75,955.75			75,955.75
01-Oct	Brought down	15,433.13			

ANSWERS (Tasks 1 and 4)

Account Stock

Debit			Credit		
Date 2005	Details	Amount £	Date 2005	Details	Amount £
29-Sep	Brought down	3,269.40	30-Sep	Carried down	3,269.40
		3,269.40			3,269.40
01-Oct	Brought down	3,269.40			

Account Sundry expenses

Debit			Credit		
Date 2005	Details	Amount £	Date 2005	Details	Amount £
29-Sep	Brought down	2,693.05	30-Sep	Carried down	2,787.50
30-Sep	Cash book	53.34			
30-Sep	Petty cash book	41.11			
		2,787.50			2,787.50
01-Oct	Brought down	2,787.50			

Account VAT control

Debit			Credit		
Date 2005	Details	Amount £	Date 2005	Details	Amount £
30-Sep	Petty cash book	2.82	29-Sep	Brought down	3,985.05
30-Sep	Carried down	3,982.23			
		3,985.05			3,985.05
			01-Oct	Brought down	3,982.23

ANSWERS (Tasks 2 and 4)

CASH BOOK — CB39

RECEIPTS					PAYMENTS					
Sales ledger £	Rent £	Total £	Date	Details	Cheque no	Total £	Purchase ledger £	Sundry expenses £	Admin overheads £	Distribution costs £
		2,879.34	01-Sep	Balance b/f						
35,231.82	800	36,031.82		TOTALS FOR MONTH TO DATE		32,437.95	7,256.31	2.00	20,192.07	4,987.57
10,675.63		10,675.63	26/9	Paget & Co						
			26/9	Lennox Ltd	456165	5,000.00	5,000.00			
			26/9	Syrillian plc	456166	6,142.01	6,142.01			
			26/9	T Vassell	456167	26.34		26.34		
			26/9	Rendle & Cooper	456168	324.68	324.68			
			26/9	Instis Ltd	456169	720.30	720.30			
2,976.34		2,976.34	29/9	WapWap plc						
4,212.05		4,212.05	30/9	Florin & Co						
			30/9	TransPower plc	STO	158.00	158.00			
			30/9	Salaries	BACS	1,678.60				1,678.60
			30/9	FIXA Insurance Ltd	DD	120.00	120.00			
	400.00	400.00	30/9	Ragoussi Science						
	400.00	400.00	30/9	Farrar & Co						
6,687.02		6,687.02	30/9	MAX Marketing						
			30/9	Bank charges		25.00		25.00		
						46,632.88				
			30/9	Balance c/d		17,629.32				
59,782.86	1,600.00	64,262.20				64,262.20	19,721.30	53.34	20,192.07	6,666.17
		17,629.32	1/10	Balance b/d						

Item not entered in cash book due to lack of supporting documentation: Direct debit of £552.35 to Salem District Council

Action to be taken: Raise query with Dipak Malawi

ANSWERS (Task 3)

Bank reconciliation at 30 September 2005

	£
Balance per bank statement	19,331.61
Outstanding lodgement	4,212.05
Queried DD Salem District Council	552.35
	24,096.01
Unpresented cheque 456166	(6,142.01)
Unpresented cheque 456168	(324.68)
Balance per cash book	17,629.32

ANSWERS (Tasks 5 and 10)

Journals

		DR £	CR £
1	Fixed assets	5,000.00	
	Purchases		5,000.00

Being reclassification of £5,000 purchase from Lennox Ltd as fixed assets

2	Bad debts	739.76	
	Sales ledger control		739.76

Being write off of irrecoverable debt

No journal is needed for the Syrillian plc error as the account is not in the main ledger

3	Rent receivable	1,200.00	
	Rental income		1,200.00

Being rent due for September.

4	Suspense account	2,093.96	
	PAYE/NIC creditor		2,093.96

To correct the incorrect debit of £1,046.98 made to PAYE/NIC creditor on 19 September to a credit, thereby clearing the suspense account

ANSWERS (Task 6)

Sales ledger balances as at 30 September 2005

Account code	Name of debtor	Amount owing as at 30 September 2005 £
B673	Bristol plc	5,678.02
F039	Florin & Co	1,649.28
G182	Gwent Ltd	2,854.11
H004	Hamilton Trading	739.76
M893	MAX Marketing	6,687.02
P678	Paget & Co	1,640.38
W118	WapWap plc	2,108.00
Z365	Zebedee plc	1,503.34
	Total of sales ledger balances	22,859.91
	Total per control account	15,433.13
	Difference (if any)	7,426.78

Explanation of difference and action required:

The sales ledger balances still include that of Hamilton Trading, which has been written off correctly in the control account. They also include a balance of £6,687.02 from MAX Marketing, which we have adjusted in the cash book as having been paid.

Once the balance is written off and the receipt recorded in the sales ledger the reconciliation will work. In the meantime it is the control account figure which is correct.

ANSWERS (Task 7)

Purchases ledger balances as at 30 September 2005

Account code	Name of creditor	Amount owed as at 30 September 2005 £
A902	Armageddon plc	21456.26
D537	Drakes	2,879.64
I839	Instis Ltd	2,458.84
L012	Lennox Ltd	0.00
R643	Rendle & Cooper	5,872.00
S903	Syrillian plc	2,731.06
V555	Vodex plc	1,107.17
	Total of purchases ledger balances	36,504.97 CR
	Total per control account	35,715.25 CR
	Difference (if any)	789.72 CR

Explanation of difference and action required:

The purchases ledger balance for Syrillian plc still includes the credit note posted to the wrong side. To correct this, a debit of 2 x £394.86 = £789.72 must be made to reduce the balance.

Once the adjustment is made in the purchases ledger the reconciliation will work. In the meantime it is the control account figure which is correct.

ANSWERS (Task 8)

Rent receivable ledger balances as at 30 September 2005

Name of tenant	£
Ragoussi Science	0.00
Thompson Training	400.00
Farrar & Co	0.00
Total of rent receivable balances	400.00
Total per control account	400.00
Difference (if any)	0.00

Explanation of difference and action required:

None

ANSWERS (Tasks 9 and 10)

Trial balance at 30 September 2005

Account name	Debit £	Credit £
Administration overheads	70,756.42	
Bad debts	1,639.96	
Cash book	17,629.32	
Capital		160,000.00
Distribution costs	25,308.97	
Fixed assets	179,000.00	
PAYE/NIC liability		1,305.45
Petty cash book	21.28	
Purchases	83,491.46	
Purchases ledger control		35,715.25
Rental income		10,800.00
Rent receivable control	400.00	
Sales		185,840.55
Sales ledger control	15,433.13	
Stock	3,269.40	
Sundry expenses	2,787.50	
VAT control		3,982.23
Suspense account		2,093.96
Totals	399,737.44	399,737.44

Reason for the suspense account:
PAYE/NIC creditor was debited with £1,046.98 employer's NI instead of credited. The imbalance is £1,046.98 x 2 = £2,093.96

ANSWERS (Task 11)

To: Pam Jones
From: Dipak Malawi

Schedule of queries

I have been discussing various matters with Helen Hurrell recently, in connection with her plan to take on her brother as her business partner. Although he is very good at marketing, he has no practical finance or administration background and there are a number of basic issues about which he knows nothing. I have been putting together a checklist for him. Please complete the schedule below, for inclusion in the checklist.

1. When we make a sale to a customer we let them know the amount they have to pay by issuing an **invoice**. This shows the amount that we will **credit** to sales, the amount we will **credit** to VAT, and the amount we will **debit** to their account in the sales ledger. If we agree with them that we have charged too much, we will issue them with a **credit note**.

2. An invoice from a supplier records how much we **owe** them, and is recorded by us in their account in the **purchases** ledger. Until we pay them this money the supplier is a **creditor** of the business.

3. The standard rate for VAT is **17.5%**. VAT appearing in the sales day book is called **output** tax. VAT appearing in the purchases day book is called **input** tax. When there is a credit balance on the VAT control account this means that we **owe** an amount of VAT **to** HM Customs and Excise.

4. Our bank is Avalon Bank plc, which supplies us with regular statements of account. If these show that we are overdrawn, this means that the bank is a **creditor** of our business. When we write a cheque to a supplier, we are the **drawer** of the cheque, the bank is the **drawee** and the supplier is the **payee**. The cheque will take **three** days to clear on our bank account, from the day that the supplier banks it.

5. Our cheques are printed by the bank with two vertical lines (a crossing) with the words 'Account payee' printed between them. This means that **the bank will only pay the amount of the cheque to a bank account in the name of the payee**.

6. Both the sales ledger and the purchases ledger allocate account codes to each account they contain. Referring to the code numbers in the reconciliations for 30 September 2005, the coding system used is **alphanumeric**.

7. The maximum amount of cash our petty cash box is permitted to hold is £200. Every time the box is topped up, it is topped up to £200. This is called the **imprest** amount.

8. We file our weekly bank statements with the relevant bank reconciliation. This is so that **we can check easily that the reconciliation has been done regularly and correctly**.

9. The deeds of our property and the lease agreements that we have with our three tenants are stored at our solicitor's offices. This is to ensure the **security** and **confidentiality** of the documents.

10. In relation to our customers we should aim to keep the following matters confidential:

    1. **their payment record**
    2. **the results of credit checks that we have performed on them when setting up their accounts**.

ANSWERS TO FULL SKILLS BASED ASSESSMENT 1

ANSWERS TO FULL SKILLS BASED ASSESSMENT 2

MARPLES COOKWARE

DO NOT TURN THIS PAGE UNTIL YOU HAVE COMPLETED THE FULL SKILLS BASED ASSESSMENT

COVERAGE OF PERFORMANCE CRITERIA

The following performance criteria are covered in this simulation, except as indicated by an asterisk *

Element	PC Coverage	
3.1	**Balance bank transactions**	
A	Record details from the relevant primary documentation in the cashbook and ledgers.	8
B	Correctly calculate totals and balances of receipts and payments	9
C	Compare individual items on the bank statement and in the cashbook for accuracy	8
D	Identify discrepancies and prepare a bank reconciliation statement.	10
3.2	**Prepare ledger balances and control accounts**	
A	Make and record authorised adjustments	1
B	Total relevant accounts in the main ledger	5
C	Reconcile control accounts with the totals of the balances in the subsidiary ledger	2, 3, 4
D	Reconcile petty cash control account with cash in hand and subsidiary records	11
E	Identify discrepancies arising from the reconciliation of control accounts and either resolve or refer to the appropriate person	3
F	Ensure documentation is stored securely and in line with the organisation's confidentiality requirements	*
3.3	**Draft an initial trial balance**	
A	Prepare the draft initial trial balance in line with the organisation's policies and procedures	6
B	Identify discrepancies in the balancing process	6
C	Identify reasons for imbalance and rectify them	7
D	Balance the trial balance	7

Tasks 1, 2

Receipts							Payments			
Customers £	Other receipts £	Total £	Date	Details	Cheque no	Total £	Suppliers £	Other payments £	Salaries & wages £
		15,679.32	26/7	Balance b/f					
572.64		572.64	26/7	Caris & Co					
			26/7	Wrinkles plc	105897	50.00	50.00		
			26/7	Kendal District Council	SO	630.00		630.00	
			27/7	Abacus Ltd	105898	947.62	947.62		
10,974.61		10,974.61	27/7	Jago Hotels plc					
			27/7	Dunmore Co	105899	3,187.69	3,187.69		
			30/7	Salaries		11,479.46			11,479.46
3,473.43		3,473.43	30/7	Tufnell Ltd					
			30/7	NorthWest Power Ltd	DD	210.00		210.00	
			30/7	Mandible Partners	105900	2,782.84	2,782.84		
			27/7	Bank charges	CHGS	45.50		45.50	
2,789.64		2789.64	28/7	Landenis Kitchens					
						19,333.11			
			30/7	Balance c/d		14,156.53			
		33,489.64				33,489.64	6,968.15	885.50	11,479.46
		14,156.53	1/8	Balance b/d					

Task 3

Bank reconciliation at 30 July 20X4

	£
Balance per bank statement	13,465.94
Outstanding lodgement	3,473.43
	16,939.37
Unpresented cheque 105900	(2,782.84)
Balance per cash book	14,156.53

Tasks 4, 9

ACCOUNT: Administration overheads

DEBIT			CREDIT		
Date 20X4	Details	Amount £	Date 20X4	Details	Amount £
01 Jul	Balance b/f	4,357.31			
31 Jul	Purchase ledger control	2,268.64			
31 Jul	Bank	2,656.50			
			31 Jul	Balance c/d	9,282.45
		9,282.45			9,282.45
01 Aug	Balance b/d	9,282.45			

ACCOUNT: Bad debts

DEBIT			CREDIT		
Date 20X4	Details	Amount £	Date 20X4	Details	Amount £
01 Jul	Balance b/f	125.00			
31 Jul	Sales ledger control	980.00	31 Jul	Balance c/d	1,105.00
		1,105.00			1,105.00
01 Aug	Balance b/d	1,105.00			

ACCOUNT: Bank control

DEBIT			CREDIT		
Date 20X4	Details	Amount £	Date 20X4	Details	Amount £
01 Jul	Balance b/f	6,216.04	31 Jul	Payments in month	41,904.42
31 Jul	Receipts in month	49,844.91			
			31 Jul	Balance c/d	14,156.53
		56,060.95			56,060.95
01 Aug	Balance b/d	14,156.53			

ACCOUNT: Capital

DEBIT			CREDIT		
Date 20X4	Details	Amount £	Date 20X4	Details	Amount £
			01 Jul	Balance b/f	28,000.00
31 Jul	Balance c/d	28,000.00			
		28,000.00			28,000.00
			01 Aug	Balance b/d	28,000.00

ACCOUNT: Fixed assets

DEBIT			CREDIT		
Date 20X4	Details	Amount £	Date 20X4	Details	Amount £
01 Jul	Balance b/f	24,000.00			
			31 Jul	Balance c/d	24,000.00
		24,000.00			24,000.00
01 Aug	Balance b/d	24,000.00			

ACCOUNT: PAYE/NIC liability

DEBIT			CREDIT		
Date 20X4	Details	Amount £	Date 20X4	Details	Amount £
31 Jul	Bank	4,532.91	01 Jul	Balance b/f	4,532.91
			31 Jul	Wages/salaries control	4,981.87
31 Jul	Balance c/d	4,981.87			
		9,514.78			9,514.78
			01 Aug	Balance b/d	4,981.87

ACCOUNT: Petty cash control

DEBIT			CREDIT		
Date 20X4	Details	Amount £	Date 20X4	Details	Amount £
01 Jul	Balance b/f	58.00	31 Jul	Sundry expenses	37.52
			31 Jul	VAT	2.67
			31 Jul	Balance c/d	17.81
		58.00			58.00
01 Aug	Balance b/d	17.81			

ACCOUNT: Purchases

DEBIT			CREDIT		
Date 20X4	Details	Amount £	Date 20X4	Details	Amount £
01 Jul	Balance b/f	97,645.00	31 Jul	Purchase ledger control	90.00
31 Jul	Purchase ledger control	24,411.25			
			31 Jul	Balance c/d	121,966.25
		122,056.25			122,056.25
		121,966.25			

ACCOUNT: Purchase ledger control

DEBIT			CREDIT		
Date 20X4	Details	Amount £	Date 20X4	Details	Amount £
31 Jul	Bank	23,235.55	01 Jul	Balance b/f	13,617.67
31 Jul	Purchases	90.00	31 Jul	Purchases/expenses/VAT	31,570.01
31 Jul	Balance c/d	21,862.13			
		45,187.68			45,187.68
			01 Aug	Balance b/d	21,862.13

ACCOUNT: Sales

DEBIT			CREDIT		
Date 20X4	Details	Amount £	Date 20X4	Details	Amount £
			01 Jul	Balance b/f	189,681.76
			31 Jul	Sales ledger control	47,343.81
31 Jul	Balance c/d	237,025.57			
		237,025.57			237,025.57
			01 Aug	Balance b/d	237,025.57

ACCOUNT: Sales ledger control

DEBIT			CREDIT		
Date 20X4	Details	Amount £	Date 20X4	Details	Amount £
01 Jul	Balance b/f	31,562.54	31 Jul	Bank	49,844.91
31 Jul	Sales/VAT	55,628.98	31 Jul	Bad debts	980.00
			31 Jul	Balance c/d	36,366.61
		87,191.52			87,191.52
01 Aug	Balance b/d	36,366.61			

ACCOUNT: Selling and distribution overheads

DEBIT			CREDIT		
Date 20X4	Details	Amount £	Date 20X4	Details	Amount £
01 Jul	Balance b/f	3,642.87			
31 Jul	Purchase ledger control	910.71			
			31 Jul	Balance c/d	4,553.58
		4,553.58			4,553.58
01 Aug	Balance b/d	4,553.58			

ACCOUNT: Stock

DEBIT			CREDIT		
Date 20X4	Details	Amount £	Date 20X4	Details	Amount £
01 Jul	Balance b/f	5,324.00			
			31 Jul	Balance c/d	5,324.00
		5,324.00			5,324.00
01 Aug	Balance b/d	5,324.00			

ACCOUNT: Sundry expenses

DEBIT			CREDIT		
Date 20X4	Details	Amount £	Date 20X4	Details	Amount £
01 Jul	Balance b/f	1,647.25			
31 Jul	Purchase ledger control	411.81			
31 Jul	Petty cash	37.52			
			31 Jul	Balance c/d	2,096.58
		2,096.58			2,096.58
01 Aug	Balance b/d	2,096.58			

ACCOUNT: VAT control

DEBIT			CREDIT		
Date 20X4	Details	Amount £	Date 20X4	Details	Amount £
31 Jul	Purchase ledger control	4,701.92	01 Jul	Balance b/f	2,761.72
31 Jul	Petty cash	2.67	31 Jul	Sales ledger control	8,285.17
31 Jul	Balance c/d	6,342.30			
		11,046.89			11,046.89
			01 Aug	Balance b/d	6,342.30

ACCOUNT: Wages/salaries control

DEBIT			CREDIT		
Date	Details	Amount	Date	Details	Amount
20X4		£	20X4		£
31 Jul	Bank	11,479.46	31 Jul	Wages/salaries expenses	16,461.33
31 Jul	PAYE/NIC liability	4,981.87			
		16,461.33			16,461.33

ACCOUNT: Wages/salaries expense

DEBIT			CREDIT		
Date	Details	Amount	Date	Details	Amount
20X4		£	20X4		£
01 Jul	Balance b/f	64,016.05			
31 Jul	Wages/salaries control	16,461.33			
			31 Jul	Balance c/d	80,477.38
		80,477.38			80,477.38
01 Aug	Balance b/d	80,477.38			

Task 5

Sales ledger balances as at 31 July 20X4

Name of debtor	Amount owing as at 31 July 20X4 £
Buzz Ltd	5,921.43
Caris & Co	1,472.05
Hogmanay Enterprises	3,885.00
Landenis Kitchens	7,849.64
Jago Hotels plc	13,677.54
Tufnell Ltd	3,560.95
Webster Co	980.00
Total of sales ledger balances	37,346.61
Total per control account	36,366.61
Difference (if any)	980.00

Explanation of difference and action required:

The sales ledger balances still include that of Webster Co, which has been written off correctly in the control account. Once the balance is written off in the sales ledger the reconciliation will work. In the meantime, it is the control account figure which is correct.

Task 6

Purchase ledger balances as at 31 July 20X4

Name of creditor	Amount owed as at 31 July 20X4 £
Abacus Ltd	5,154.04
Dunmore Co	7,731.07
Mandible Partners	5,291.21
Persimmon Ovens	1,150.00
Wrinkles plc	185.95
Yarnton Ltd	2,439.86
Total of purchase ledger balances	21,952.13
Total per control account	21,862.13
Difference (if any)	90.00

Explanation of difference and action required:

The purchase ledger balance for Persimmon still includes the £90 recording error that has been adjusted correctly in the control account. Once the adjustment is made in the purchase ledger the reconciliation will work. In the meantime, it is the control account figure which is correct.

Task 7

Reconciliation of wages/salaries payments in month

MONTH: July 20X4

	£
Total PAYE June 20X4	2,791.21
Total employees' NIC June 20X4	757.26
Total employer's NIC June 20X4	984.44
Subtotal (= payments figure in PAYE/NIC control account)	4,532.91
Total net pay in current month (= bank payments figure in wages/salaries control)	11,479.46
Total wages/salaries payments in month	16,012.37

Task 8

Petty cash book PCB 19

Receipts £	Date 20X4	Details	Voucher	Total £	VAT £	Sundry expenses £
58.00	1/7	Balance b/f				
	6/7	Postage		4.05		4.05
	12/7	Stationery		5.99	0.89	5.10
	19/7	Postage		6.60		6.60
	21/7	Tea, coffee etc		7.50		7.50
	24/7	Stationery		12.00	1.78	10.22
	29/7	Postage		4.05		4.05
		Totals		40.19	2.67	37.52
		Balance c/d		17.81		
58.00				58.00		

Notes and coins in the petty cash tin 30 July 20X4

Value	Number	Total value £
£20	0	0.00
£10	0	0.00
£5	1	5.00
£2	2	4.00
£1	6	6.00
50p	3	1.50
20p	4	0.80
10p	3	0.30
5p	3	0.15
2p	2	0.04
1p	2	0.02
		17.81

Petty cash reconciliation

DATE: 30 July 20X4

	£
Balance per petty cash book	17.81
Total of notes and coins	17.81
Discrepancy (if any)	Nil

Explanation of discrepancy (if any)

N/A

Task 9

Trial balance at 31 July 20X4

Account name	Debit £	Credit £
Administration overheads	9,282.45	
Bad debts	1,105.00	
Bank control	14,156.53	
Capital		28,000.00
Fixed assets	24,000.00	
PAYE/NIC liability		4,981.87
Petty cash control	17.81	
Purchases	121,966.25	
Purchase ledger control		21,862.13
Sales		237,025.57
Sales ledger control	36,366.61	
Selling and distribution overheads	4,553.58	
Stock	5,324.00	
Sundry expenses	2,096.58	
VAT control		6,342.30
Wages/salaries control	–	–
Wages/salaries expense	80,477.38	
Difference		1,134.32
Total	299,346.19	299,346.19

Task 10

Journal

Date	Account names and narrative	Debit £	Credit £
	Suspense account	1,134.32	
	Administration overheads		1,134.32
	Being total from purchases day book posted twice in error		

PART H

Full Exam based Assessments

FULL EXAM BASED ASSESSMENT: JUNE 2004

FULL EXAM BASED ASSESSMENT
JUNE 2004

FOUNDATION STAGE – NVQ/SVQ2

Unit 3

Preparing Ledger Balances and an Initial Trial Balance

DO NOT OPEN THIS PAPER UNTIL YOU ARE READY TO START UNDER EXAM CONDITIONS

FULL EXAM BASED ASSESSMENT: JUNE 2004

FULL EXAM BASED ASSESSMENT: JUNE 2004

This Central Assessment is in two sections.

You have to show competence in both sections, so attempt and aim to complete EVERY task in BOTH sections.

Section 1   Processing exercise
                   Complete all six tasks

Section 2   10 tasks and questions
                   Complete all tasks and questions

You should spend about 90 minutes on each section.

Include all essential workings within your answers, where appropriate.

Sections 1 and 2 both relate to the business described below.

Introduction

- Wendy Mason is the owner of a printing business which trades as WM Printing.
- You are employed by the business as a bookkeeper.
- The business uses a manual accounting system.
- Double entry takes place in the Main (General) ledger. Individual accounts of debtors and creditors are kept in subsidiary ledgers as memorandum accounts.
- Bank payments and receipts are recorded in the Cash Book, which is part of the double entry system.
- Assume today's date is 30 June 2004 unless you are told otherwise.

SECTION 1 – PROCESSING EXERCISE

You should spend about 90 minutes on this section.

Data

Balances at the start of the day on 30 June 2004
The following balances are relevant to you at the start of the day on 30 June 2004:

	£
Credit suppliers	
TGB Ltd	3,000
Compton and Company	8,600
Rowley Associates	10,432
Elton and Lowe Ltd	1,750
Main ledger	
Purchases	285,200
Purchases returns	3,000
Purchases ledger control	40,698
Motor vehicles	5,000
General repairs	200
Insurance	2,900
Motor tax	180
VAT (credit balance)	15,560

Task 1.1

Enter these opening balances into the following accounts, given on pages 332-336.

Subsidiary (Purchases) ledger
    TGB Ltd
    Compton and Company
    Rowley Associates
    Elton and Lowe Ltd
Main (General) ledger
    Purchases
    Purchases returns
    Purchases ledger control
    Motor vehicles
    General repairs
    Insurance
    Motor tax
    VAT

FULL EXAM BASED ASSESSMENT: JUNE 2004

Note. The lines shown in the accounts on pages 332-336 are there to help you present your work neatly and clearly. You may not need to use all of the lines.

Data

Transactions

The following transactions all took place on 30 June 2004 and have been entered into the relevant books of prime entry as shown below. No entries have yet been made into the ledger system. The VAT rate is 17½%.

PURCHASE DAY BOOK

Date 2004	Details	Invoice number	Total £	VAT £	Net £
30 June	TGB Ltd	1602	5,875	875	5,000
30 June	Compton and Company	1011	1,175	525	1,000
30 June	Rowley Associates	P/101	10,575	175	9,000
30 June	Elton and Lowe Ltd	1974	2,350	1,575	2,000
Totals			19,975	2,975	17,000

PURCHASES RETURNS DAY BOOK

Date 2004	Details	Credit note no.	Total £	VAT £	Net £
30 June	TGB Ltd	C042	47	7	40
30 June	Rowley Associates	336	94	14	80
Totals			141	21	120

CASH BOOK

Date 2004	Details	Bank £	Date 2004	Details	VAT £	Bank £
30 June	Balance b/f	21,642	30 June	Motor vehicle		6,000
			30 June	General repairs	28	188
			30 June	Insurance		150
			30 June	Motor tax		90
			30 June	Compton and Company (creditor)		3,000
			30 June	Balance c/f		12,214
		21,642			28	21,642

Task 1.2

From the day books and cash book shown above, make the relevant entries into the accounts in the Subsidiary (Purchases) Ledger and Main (General) Ledger.

Task 1.3

Balance the accounts showing clearly the balances carried down at 30 June (closing balance).

Task 1.4

Now show the balances brought down at 1 July (opening balance).

Subsidiary (Purchases) Ledger

TGB LTD

Date	Details	Amount £	Date	Details	Amount £

COMPTON AND COMPANY

Date	Details	Amount £	Date	Details	Amount £

ROWLEY ASSOCIATES

Date	Details	Amount £	Date	Details	Amount £

ELTON AND LOWE LTD

Date	Details	Amount £	Date	Details	Amount £

Main (General) Ledger

PURCHASES

Date	Details	Amount £	Date	Details	Amount £

PURCHASES RETURNS

Date	Details	Amount £	Date	Details	Amount £

PURCHASES LEDGER CONTROL

Date	Details	Amount £	Date	Details	Amount £

MOTOR VEHICLES

Date	Details	Amount £	Date	Details	Amount £

GENERAL REPAIRS

Date	Details	Amount £	Date	Details	Amount £

INSURANCE

Date	Details	Amount £	Date	Details	Amount £

MOTOR TAX

Date	Details	Amount £	Date	Details	Amount £

		VAT			
Date	Details	Amount £	Date	Details	Amount £

Data

Other balances to be transferred to the trial balance:

	£
Office equipment	15,000
Stock	17,500
Cash	186
Sales ledger control	106,842
Capital	30,710
Sales	418,200
Sales returns	2,605
Discounts allowed	350
Wages	42,181
Rent	3,000
Rates	2,100
Stationery	620
Telephone	800
Heat and light	1,300
Miscellaneous expenses	562

Task 1.5

Transfer the balances that you calculated in Task 1.3, and the bank balance, to the trial balance on page 337.

Task 1.6

Transfer the remaining balances shown above to the trial balance, and total each column.

TRIAL BALANCE AS AT 30 JUNE 2003

	Debit (£)	Credit (£)
Motor vehicles		
Office equipment		
Stock		
Bank		
Cash		
Sales ledger control		
Purchases ledger control		
VAT		
Capital		
Sales		
Sales returns		
Purchases		
Purchases returns		
Discounts allowed		
Motor tax		
General repairs		
Wages		
Insurance		
Rent		
Rates		
Stationery		
Telephone		
Heat and light		
Miscellaneous expenses		
Total		

FULL EXAM BASED ASSESSMENT: JUNE 2004

SECTION 2 – TASKS AND QUESTIONS

You should spend about 90 minutes on this section.

Answer all the questions.

Write your answers in the spaces provided.

Note. You do not need to adjust the accounts in Section 1 as part of any of the following tasks.

Task 2.1

The cheque below has been received today.

```
┌─────────────────────────────────────────────────────────────┐
│  WESTERN BANK plc                              65-29-38     │
│  Bedford Branch                                             │
│  High Street, Bedford, BF15 8ZX        Date  25 June 2004   │
│                                                             │
│  Pay  W M Printing                          £  150—00       │
│       One hundred and five pounds only                      │
│       ..................................                   │
│                                             Design Data Ltd │
│                                                   Director  │
│  00-04-93    65-29-38    82157802                           │
└─────────────────────────────────────────────────────────────┘
```

(a) Give TWO reasons why the cheque will not be honoured by the bank.

_____

_____

_____

(b) What would you do in this situation?

_____

_____

_____

Task 2.2

WM Printing buys goods from and sells goods to Haven Stationers Ltd. It has been agreed to set off a debt of £50 owing between them by a contra entry.

What accounts in the main (general) ledger of WM Printing would be adjusted to record this set off?

                    £   £

_____ _____ _____ _____

Task 2.3

During the last VAT quarter sales amounted to £122,000 plus VAT. Purchases totalled 9,870 including VAT. What would have been the amount payable to H M Customs and Excise at the end of that quarter? Show workings.

_____

_____

_____

Task 2.4

WM Printing offers its customers both trade and cash settlement discounts.

Briefly explain the reason why each of these discounts is offered.

A trade discount is offered _____

_____

_____

A cash settlement discount is offered _____

_____

_____

Task 2.5

Wendy Mason is considering purchasing some new office furniture. The seller is not willing to accept a cheque because of the time it would take to clear.

Briefly explain why it takes time for a cheque to clear.

_____

_____

_____

_____

Task 2.6

WM Printing's transactions in June included the items listed below.

Show whether each is a capital transaction or a revenue transaction by circling the correct answer.

(a) Purchase of office stationery   Capital/Revenue

(b) Decoration of offices   Capital/Revenue

(c) Purchase of a delivery van   Capital/Revenue

(d) Purchase of fuel for the delivery van   Capital/Revenue

Task 2.7

Wendy Mason is considering introducing a computerised accounting system. She has been advised to purchase integrated accounting software.

Briefly explain the meaning of integrated accounting software.

_____

_____

Task 2.8

You are reminded that you do NOT need to adjust, or refer to, the accounts in Section 1 or Section 2.

The following information has become available.

(a) An amount of £78 has been debited to the miscellaneous expenses account instead of the heat and light account.

(b) An amount paid by cheque for rent has been recorded as £50 instead of the correct amount of £500.

(c) An amount of £75 has been credited to the suspense account. The following two errors have now been discovered.

- A payment of £1000 has been recorded as £1100 in the insurance account.
- An amount of £25 has been omitted from the stationery account.

Record the journal entries needed in the Main (General) ledger, to deal with the above. Narratives are not required.

THE JOURNAL

Details	Dr £	Cr £
(a)		
(b)		
(c)		

Task 2.9

This is a summary of transactions with customers during the month of June.

	£
Balance of debtors at 1 June 2004	100,102
Goods sold on credit	40,140
Money received from credit customers	32,250
Discounts allowed	150
Goods returned by credit customers	1,000

(a) Prepare a sales ledger control account from the above details. Show clearly the balance carried down at 30 June (closing balance) and brought down at 1 July (opening balance).

SALES LEDGER CONTROL

Date	Details	Amount £	Date	Details	Amount £

The following closing debit balances were in the Subsidiary (sales) ledger on 30 June.

	£
PDG Commercials	28,333
A B Smith Ltd	15,020
South and Attwood	235
Francis and Company	18,212
Langley and Law	22,400
IJB Ltd	22,792

(b) Reconcile the balances shown above with the sales ledger control account balance you have calculated in part (a).

£

Sales ledger control account balance as at 30 June 2004

Total of subsidiary (sales) ledger accounts as at 30 June 2004 _____

Difference _____

(c) What may have caused the difference you calculated in part (b)?

_____

_____

_____

FULL EXAM BASED ASSESSMENT: JUNE 2004

Task 2.10

On 28 June WM Printing received the following bank statement as at 21 June:

CENTREPOINT BANK plc
High Street, Bedford, BF13 8RF

To: WM Printing Account No 54387299 21 June 2004

STATEMENT OF ACCOUNT

Date 2004	Details	Paid out £	Paid in £	Balance £
2 June	Balance b/f			21,421C
9 June	Cheque No 300175	3,550		17,871C
10 June	Cheque No 300176	368		17,503C
11 June	Cheque No 300178	412		17,091C
14 June	Bank Giro Credit Law and Lodge		12,100	29,191C
21 June	Cheque No 300180	158		29,033C
21 June	Direct Debit Bedford MBC	210		28,823C
21 June	Direct Debit LTM Ltd	4,800		24,023C
21 June	Bank charges	97		23,926C
21 June	Bank Giro Credit BGC Ltd		1,569	25,495C

D = Debit C = Credit

The cash book as at 28 June 2004 is shown below.

CASH BOOK

Date 2004	Details	Bank £	Date 2004	Cheque Number	Details	Bank £
1 June	Balance b/f	21,421	3 June	300175	Mills Ltd	3,550
25 June	Paper Design	1,500	3 June	300176	Baker and Brown	368
27 June	Bate Ltd	2,000	4 June	300177	Legge Ltd	100
			6 June	300178	Parker Papers	412
			17 June	300179	Beta Ltd	300
			17 June	300180	Paper Unlimited	158
			20 June		Bedford MBC	210

(a) Check the items on the bank statement against the items in the cash book.

(b) Update the cash book as needed.

(c) Total the cash book and clearly show the balance carried down at 28 June and brought down at 29 June.

Note. You do not need to adjust the accounts in Section 1.

(d) Using the information on page 343, complete the bank reconciliation statement as at 28 June.

BANK RECONCILIATION STATEMENT AS AT 28 JUNE 2004

£

Balance as per bank statement _____

Add: _____ _____

_____ _____

_____ _____

Less: _____ _____

_____ _____

_____ _____

Balance as per the updated cash book _____

FULL EXAM BASED ASSESSMENT
DECEMBER 2004

FOUNDATION STAGE – NVQ/SVQ2

Unit 3

Preparing Ledger Balances and an Initial Trial Balance

DO NOT OPEN THIS PAPER UNTIL YOU ARE READY TO START UNDER EXAM CONDITIONS

FULL EXAM BASED ASSESSMENT: DECEMBER 2004

FULL EXAM BASED ASSESSMENT: DECEMBER 2004

This Central Assessment is in two sections.

You have to show competence in both sections, so attempt and aim to complete EVERY task in BOTH sections.

Section 1   Processing exercise
Complete all six tasks

Section 2   10 tasks and questions
Complete all tasks and questions

You should spend about 90 minutes on each section.

Include all essential workings within your answers, where appropriate.

Sections 1 and 2 both relate to the business described below.

Introduction

- Keith Boxley is the owner of a catering business called Special Events.
- You are employed by the business as a bookkeeper.
- The business uses a manual accounting system.
- Double entry takes place in the main (general) ledger. Individual accounts of debtors and creditors are kept in subsidiary ledgers as memorandum accounts.
- Bank payments and receipts are recorded in the cash book, which is part of the double entry system.
- Assume today's date is 30 November 2004 unless you are told otherwise.

SECTION 1 – PROCESSING EXERCISE

You should spend about 90 minutes on this section.

Data

Balances at the start of the day on 30 November 2004

The following balances are relevant to you at the start of the day on 30 November 2004:

	£
Credit customers	
Pages Ltd	2,800
Cave and Company	930
PPT Ltd	7,114
Yates and Young	12,600
Motor vehicles	12,900
Sales	285,200
Sales returns	3,000
Sales ledger control	80,698
Discounts allowed	600
Heat and light	2,000
Loan from bank	10,500
VAT (credit balance)	8,560

Task 1.1

Enter these opening balances into the following accounts given on pages 350-354.

Subsidiary (sales) ledger
    Pages Ltd
    Cave and Company
    PPT Ltd
    Yates and Young

Main (general) ledger
    Motor vehicles
    Sales
    Sales returns
    Sales ledger control
    Discounts allowed
    Heat and light
    Loan from bank
    VAT

Note. The lines shown in the accounts on pages 350-354 are there to help you present your work neatly and clearly. You may not need to use all of the lines.

Data

Transactions

The following transactions all took place on 30 November 2004 and have been entered into the relevant books of prime entry as shown below. No entries have yet been made into the ledger system. The VAT rate is 17½%.

SALES DAY BOOK

Date 2004	Details	Invoice number	Total £	VAT £	Net £
30 Nov	Pages Ltd	145	12,220	1,820	10,400
30 Nov	Cave and Company	146	705	105	600
30 Nov	PPT Ltd	147	3,525	525	3,000
30 Nov	Yates and Young	148	1,410	210	1,200
Totals			17,860	2,660	15,200

SALES RETURNS DAY BOOK

Date 2004	Details	Credit note no.	Total £	VAT £	Net £
30 Nov	Pages Ltd	0006	235	35	200
30 Nov	Yates and Young	0007	47	7	40
Totals			282	42	240

CASH BOOK

Date 2004	Details	Discount allowed £	Bank £	Date 2004	Details	Bank £
30 Nov	Balance b/f		15,391	30 Nov	Motor vehicle	8,500
	PPT Ltd	114	4,400	30 Nov	Loan repayment	500
				30 Nov	Electricity	480
				30 Nov	Balance c/f	10,311
			19,791			19,791

Task 1.2

From the day books and cash book shown above, make the relevant entries into the accounts in the subsidiary (sales) ledger and main (general) ledger.

Task 1.3

Balance the accounts showing clearly the balances carried down at 30 November (closing balance).

Task 1.4

Now show the balances brought down at 1 December (opening balance).

Subsidiary (sales) ledger

PAGES LTD

Date	Details	Amount £	Date	Details	Amount £

CAVE AND COMPANY

Date	Details	Amount £	Date	Details	Amount £

FULL EXAM BASED ASSESSMENT: DECEMBER 2004

PPT LTD

Date	Details	Amount £	Date	Details	Amount £

YATES AND YOUNG

Date	Details	Amount £	Date	Details	Amount £

Main (general) ledger

MOTOR VEHICLES

Date	Details	Amount £	Date	Details	Amount £

FULL EXAM BASED ASSESSMENT: DECEMBER 2004

SALES

Date	Details	Amount £	Date	Details	Amount £

SALES RETURNS

Date	Details	Amount £	Date	Details	Amount £

SALES LEDGER CONTROL

Date	Details	Amount £	Date	Details	Amount £

DISCOUNTS ALLOWED

Date	Details	Amount £	Date	Details	Amount £

HEAT AND LIGHT

Date	Details	Amount £	Date	Details	Amount £

LOAN FROM BANK

Date	Details	Amount £	Date	Details	Amount £

VAT

Date	Details	Amount £	Date	Details	Amount £

Task 1.5

Transfer the balances that you calculated in Tasks 1.3 and 1.4, and the bank balance, to the trial balance on page 355.

Data

Other balances to be transferred to the trial balance:

	£
Equipment	20,600
Stock	2,100
Petty cash control	153
Purchases ledger control	32,108
Capital	44,446
Purchases	190,100
Purchases returns	1,400
Discounts received	120
Wages	46,300
Motor expenses	450
Rent and rates	2,600
Stationery	210
Telephone	622
Insurance	3,250
Miscellaneous expenses	1,360

Task 1.6

Transfer the remaining balances shown above to the trial balance, and total each column.

TRIAL BALANCE AS AT 30 NOVEMBER 2004

	Debit £	Credit £
Motor vehicles		
Equipment		
Stock		
Bank		
Petty cash control		
Sales ledger control		
Purchases ledger control		
VAT		
Loan from bank		
Capital		
Sales		
Sales returns		
Purchases		
Purchases returns		
Discounts received		
Discounts allowed		
Heat and light		
Wages		
Motor expenses		
Rent and rates		
Stationery		
Telephone		
Insurance		
Miscellaneous expenses		
Total		

SECTION 2 – TASKS AND QUESTIONS

You should spend about 90 minutes on this section.

Answer all of the following questions on pages o/s.

Write your answers in the spaces provided.

Note. You do not need to adjust the accounts in Section 1 as part of any of the following tasks.

Task 2.1

The following document has been received by Special Events from its customer PKG Ltd.

BACS REMITTANCE ADVICE

To: Special Events   From: PKG Ltd

Your ref: SE102   Our ref: 1650

---

30 November 2004 BACS   **Transfer**   £1410

Payment has been made by BACS and will be paid directly into your bank account on the date shown above.

(a) What accounts in the main (general) ledger will be used to record this transaction?

DEBIT _____

CREDIT _____

(b) Give ONE advantage to Special Events of being paid by BACS transfer.

_____

_____

(c) Give ONE advantage to PKG Ltd of paying by BACS transfer.

_____

_____

Task 2.2

What documents would Special Events send out:

(a) with a cheque to pay an account?

(b) to list unpaid invoices and ask for payment each month?

(c) to correct an overcharge on an invoice issued?

Task 2.3

Special Events keeps a small amount of petty cash in the office to purchase miscellaneous items during the month. The imprest level is £100. The following purchases were made during November.

	£
15 November Window Cleaning	30.00
22 November Postage	25.00
29 November Stationery	28.00

(a) Make the relevant entries in the petty cash control account showing clearly the balance carried down at 30 November (closing balance) and brought down at 1 December (opening balance).

PETTY CASH CONTROL

Date 2004	Details	Amount £	Date 2004	Details	Amount £
1 Nov	Balance c/f	100			

(b) What will be the amount required to restore the imprest level?

(c) Name ONE precaution that should be taken to ensure the petty cash is safe and secure.

_____

_____

_____

Task 2.4

Keith Boxley has just learned that a customer, Bibby and Company, has ceased trading and the outstanding amount on its account will have to be written off as a bad debt.

What accounting entries must you make in the main (general) ledger to write off the net amount of £500 and the VAT?

Account name	Dr £	Cr £
_____	_____	_____
_____	_____	_____
_____	_____	_____

Task 2.5

Keith Boxley needs advice about the most efficient way of organising the filing system.

Suggest one efficient way of filing each of the following documents, giving a different method for each.

(a) Sales invoices _____

(b) Purchase invoices _____

(c) Bank statements _____

Task 2.6

Within a computerised accounting system code numbers will be used, for instance customer account codes.

Give TWO other examples of the use of code numbers in a computerised accounting system.

(i) _____

(ii) _____

Task 2.7

Keith Boxley is purchasing a computer and hopes to change from a manual to a computerised accounting system. He already has a keyboard and mouse.

Name ONE other item of hardware and one item of software that he will also need to operate the system.

Hardware _____

Software _____

Task 2.8

Note: You are reminded that you do NOT need to adjust, or refer to, the accounts in Section 1 or Section 2.

The following information has become available.

(a) An amount of £45 has been credited to the discounts allowed account instead of the discounts received account.
(b) An amount paid by cheque for insurance has been recorded as £120 instead of the correct amount of £180.
(c) A credit purchase of £600 plus VAT for stationery has been incorrectly recorded as £200 plus VAT.

Record the journal entries needed in the main (general) ledger, to deal with the above. Narratives are not required.

THE JOURNAL

Account name	Dr £	Cr £
(a)		
(b)		
(c)		

Task 2.9

This is a summary of transactions with suppliers during the month of November.

	£
Balance of creditors at 1 November 2004	30,260
Goods bought on credit	11,500
Money paid to credit suppliers	9,357
Discounts received	170
Goods returned to credit suppliers	125

(a) Prepare a purchases ledger control account from the above details. Show clearly the balance carried down at 30 November (closing balance) and brought down at 1 December (opening balance).

PURCHASES LEDGER CONTROL

Date	Details	Amount £	Date	Details	Amount £

The following closing credit balances were in the subsidiary (purchases) ledger on 30 November.

	£
Williams and Whale	15,400
Jacksons Ltd	3,500
Conference Caterers	11,218
Fine Foods	1,900
J Wilson	215

(b) Reconcile the balances shown above with the purchases ledger control account balance you have calculated in part (a).

£

Purchases ledger control account balance as at 30 November 2004

Total of subsidiary (purchases) ledger account as at 30 November 2004 _____

Difference ══════

(c) What may have caused the difference you calculated in part (b)?

_____
_____

Task 2.10

On 29 November Special Events received the following bank statement as at 22 November:

CENTREPOINT BANK plc
High Street, Bedford, BF13 8RF

To: Special events   Account No 34287280   22 November 2004

STATEMENT OF ACCOUNT

Date 2004	Details	Paid out £	Paid in £	Balance £
1 Nov	Balance b/f			10,400 C
5 Nov	Cheque No 006165	3,500		6,900 C
8 Nov	Cheque No 006166	2,100		4,800 C
11 Nov	Bank Giro Credit L Smith		5,000	9,800 C
11 Nov	Bank Giro Credit B Roberts		7,500	17,300 C
12 Nov	Cheque 006168	380		16,920 C
15 Nov	Direct Debit Bedford CC	186		16,734 C
19 Nov	Direct Debit Myers Insurance	45		16,689 C
22 Nov	Overdraft facility fee	40		16,649 C
22 Nov	Bank charges	50		16,599 C

D = Debit   C = Credit

The cash book as at 29 November 2004 is shown below.

CASH BOOK

Date 2004	Details	Bank £	Date 2004	Cheque Number	Details	Bank £
1 Nov	Balance b/f	10,400	1 Nov	006165	LLB Ltd	3,500
11 Nov	L Smith	5,000	1 Nov	006166	Down and Daly	2,100
11 Nov	B Roberts	7,500	5 Nov	006167	Hobbs Ltd	4,600
15 Nov	G Brown	1,700	5 Nov	006168	H & H Ltd	380
22 Nov	B Singh	4,550	22 Nov	006169	Eddie's Bar	500

(a) Check the items on the bank statement against the items in the cash book.
(b) Update the cash book as needed.

(c) Total the cash book and clearly show the balance carried down at 29 November (closing balance) and brought down at 30 November (opening balance).

Note. you do not need to adjust the accounts in Section 1.

(d) Using the information on page 361, prepare a bank reconciliation statement as at 29 November.

BANK RECONCILIATION STATEMENT AS AT 29 NOVEMBER 2004

£

Balance as per bank statement _____

Add: _____ _____

_____ _____

_____ _____

Less: _____ _____

_____ _____

_____ _____

Balance as per the updated cash book _____

Answers to Full Exam based Assessments

ANSWERS TO FULL EXAM BASED ASSESSMENT

JUNE 2004 EXAM

DO NOT TURN THIS PAGE UNTIL YOU HAVE COMPLETED THE FULL EXAM BASED ASSESSMENT

ANSWERS TO FULL EXAM BASED ASSESSMENT

SECTION 1 – ANSWERS

Tasks 1.1 to 1.4

Purchases ledger

TGB Ltd

Date 2004	Details	Amount £	Date 2004	Details	Amount £
30 June	Purchase returns	47	30 June	Balance b/f	3,000
30 June	Balance c/d	8,828	30 June	Purchases	5,875
		8,875			8,875
			1 July	Balance b/d	8,828

COMPTON AND COMPANY

Date 2004	Details	Amount £	Date 2004	Details	Amount £
30 June	Cash payment	3,000	30 June	Balance b/f	8,600
30 June	Balance c/d	6,775	30 June	Purchases	1,175
		9,775			9,775
			1 July	Balance b/d	6,775

ROWLEY ASSOCIATES

Date 2004	Details	Amount £	Date 2004	Details	Amount £
30 June	Purchase returns	94	30 June	Balance b/f	10,432
30 June	Balance c/d	20,913	30 June	Purchases	10,575
		21,007			21,007
			1 July	Balance b/d	20,913

ELTON AND LOWE LTD

Date	Details	Amount	Date	Details	Amount
2004		£	2004		£
30 June	Balance c/d	4,100	30 June	Balance b/f	1,750
			30 June	Purchases	2,350
		4,100			4,100
			1 July	Balance b/d	4,100

Main (General) Ledger

PURCHASES

Date	Details	Amount	Date	Details	Amount
2004		£	2004		£
30 June	Balance c/d	285,200	30 June	Balance c/d	302,200
30 June	Purchases	17,000			
		302,200			302,200
1 July	Balance b/d	302,200			

PURCHASES RETURNS

Date	Details	Amount	Date	Details	Amount
2004		£	2004		£
30 June	Balance c/d	3,120	30 June	Balance b/f	3,000
			30 June	Returns	120
		3,120			3,120
			1 July	Balance b/d	3,120

PURCHASES LEDGER CONTROL

Date	Details	Amount	Date	Details	Amount
2004		£	2004		£
30 June	Returns	141	30 June	Balance b/f	40,698
30 June	Payment	3,000	30 June	Purchases	19,975
30 June	Balance c/d	57,532			–
		60,673			60,673
			1 July	Balance b/d	57,532

MOTOR VEHICLES

Date 2004	Details	Amount £	Date 2004	Details	Amount £
30 June	Balance b/f	5,000	30 June	Balance c/d	11,000
30 June	Cash payment	6,000			
		11,000			11,000
1 July	Balance b/d	11,000			

GENERAL REPAIRS

Date 2004	Details	Amount £	Date 2004	Details	Amount £
30 June	Balance b/f	200	30 June	Balance c/d	360
30 June	Cash payment	160			
		360			360
1 July	Balance b/d	360			

INSURANCE

Date 2004	Details	Amount £	Date 2004	Details	Amount £
30 June	Balance b/f	2,900	30 June	Balance c/d	3,050
30 June	Cash payment	150			
		3,050			3,050
1 July	Balance b/d	3,050			

MOTOR TAX

Date 2004	Details	Amount £	Date 2004	Details	Amount £
30 June	Balance b/f	180	30 June	Balance c/d	270
30 June	Cash payment	90			
		270			270
1 July	Balance b/d	270			

ANSWERS TO FULL EXAM BASED ASSESSMENT

VAT

Date 2004	Details	Amount £	Date 2004	Details	Amount £
30 June	Purchases	2,975	30 June	Balance b/f	15,560
30 June	Cash payment	28	30 June	Purchase returns	21
30 June	Balance c/d	12,578			
		15,581			15,581
			1 July	Balance b/d	12,578

Tasks 1.5 and 1.6

TRIAL BALANCE AS AT 30 JUNE 2003

	DR £	CR £
Motor vehicles	11,000	
Office equipment	15,000	
Stock	17,500	
Bank	12,214	
Cash	186	
Sales ledger control	106,842	
Purchases ledger control		57,532
VAT		12,578
Capital		30,710
Sales		418,200
Sales returns	2,605	
Purchases	302,200	
Purchases returns		3,120
Discounts allowed	350	
Motor tax	270	
General repairs	360	
Wages	42,181	
Insurance	3,050	
Rent	3,000	
Rates	2,100	
Stationery	620	
Telephone	800	
Heat and light	1,300	
Miscellaneous expenses	562	
Total	522,140	522,140

SECTION 2 – ANSWERS

Task 2.1

(a) This cheque will not be honoured because the words and figures do not agree and the cheque has not been signed.

(b) I would return the cheque to Design Data Ltd and request a replacement.

Task 2.2

Debit		Credit	
Purchase ledger control account	£50	Sales ledger control account	£50

Task 2.3

	£
Output tax (122,000 × 17.5%)	21,350
Input tax (9,870 × 17.5/117.5)	(1,470)
Payable to H M Customs and Excise	19,880

Task 2.4

A **trade discount** is offered to regular customers or customers placing large orders. The purpose is to secure their business.

A **settlement discount** is offered for prompt payment or for payment in cash. The purpose is to encourage customers to pay more quickly.

Task 2.5

When a cheque payment is made, the person receiving the cheque pays it into his bank. His bank then presents it for payment to the bank of the person issuing the cheque. The issuer's bank verifies that the cheque has been correctly completed and that there are sufficient funds in the account to cover it. It then debits the amount from the issuer's account and transfers the funds to the payee's bank. The payee's bank now credits the payee's account. This is known as the clearing system and it usually takes three days.

Task 2.6

(a) Purchase of office stationery – **Revenue**
(b) Decoration of offices – **Revenue**
(c) Purchase of a delivery van – **Capital**
(d) Purchase of fuel for the delivery van – **Revenue**

Task 2.7

In an integrated accounting software package, the various modules (sales ledger, purchase ledger, main ledger) are interrelated. This means that one entry can automatically update all ledgers.

Task 2.8

		DR £	CR £
(a)	Miscellaneous expenses		78
	Heat and light	78	
(b)	Rent	450	
	Bank		450
(c)	Suspense	75	
	Insurance		100
	Stationery	25	

Task 2.9

(a)

SALES LEDGER CONTROL ACCOUNT

Date 2004	Details	Amount £	Date	Details	Amount £
1 June	Balance b/f	100,102	30 June	Cash received	32,250
30 June	Sales	40,140	30 June	Discounts allowed	150
			30 June	Goods returned	1,000
			30 June	Balance c/d	106,842
		140,242			140,242
1 July	Balance b/d	106,842			

(b)

	£
Sales ledger balance	106,992
Sales ledger control account	(106,842)
Difference	150

(c) This could be caused by discounts not posted to the customers' accounts in the sales ledger.

Task 2.10

(a), (b), (c)

CASH BOOK

Date 2004	Details	Bank £	Date 2004	Cheque Number	Details	Bank £
1 June	Balance b/f	21,421	3 June	300175	Mills Ltd	3,550
25 June	Paper Design	1,500	3 June	300176	Baker and Brown	368
27 June	Bate Ltd	2,000	4 June	300177	Legge Ltd	100
14 June	Law & Lodge	12,100	6 June	300178	Parker Papers	412
21 June	BGC Ltd	1,569	17 June	300179	Beta Ltd	300
			17 June	300180	Paper Unlimited	158
			20 June		Bedford xMBC	210
			21 June		LTM Ltd	4,800
			21 June		Bank charges	97
			28 June		Balance c/d	28,595
		38,590				38,590
29 June	Balance b/d	28,595				

(d) Bank reconciliation statement as at 28 June 2004

		£	£
Balance as per bank statement			25,495
Add:	Paper Design	1,500	
	Bate Ltd	2,000	
			3,500
Less:	300177 Legge Ltd	100	
	300179 Beta Ltd	300	
			(400)
Balance as per the updated cash book			28,595

ANSWERS TO FULL EXAM BASED ASSESSMENT

ANSWERS TO FULL EXAM BASED ASSESSMENT

DECEMBER 2004 EXAM

DO NOT TURN THIS PAGE UNTIL YOU HAVE COMPLETED THE FULL EXAM BASED ASSESSMENT

SECTION 1 – ANSWERS

Tasks 1.1 to 1.4

Subsidiary (sales) ledger

PAGES LTD

Date 2004	Details	Amount £	Date 2004	Details	Amount £
30 Nov	Opening balance	2,800	30 Nov	Credit note 0006	235
30 Nov	Invoice 145	12,220	30 Nov	Balance c/d	14,785
		15,020			15,020
1 Dec	Balance b/d	14,785			

CAVE AND COMPANY

Date 2004	Details	Amount £	Date 2004	Details	Amount £
30 Nov	Opening balance	930	30 Nov	Balance c/d	1,635
30 Nov	Invoice 146	705			
		1,635			1,635
1 Dec	Balance b/d	1,635			

PPT LTD

Date 2004	Details	Amount £	Date 2004	Details	Amount £
30 Nov	Opening balance	7,114	30 Nov	Cash received	4,400
30 Nov	Invoice 147	3,525	30 Nov	Discount allowed	114
			30 Nov	Balance c/d	6,125
		10,639			10,639
1 Dec	Balance b/d	6,125			

YATES AND YOUNG

Date 2004	Details	Amount £	Date 2004	Details	Amount £
30 Nov	Opening balance	12,600	30 Nov	Credit note 0007	47
30 Nov	Invoice 148	1,410	30 Nov	Balance c/d	13,963
		14,010			14,010
1 Dec	Balance b/d	13,963			

Main (general) ledger

MOTOR VEHICLES

Date 2004	Details	Amount £	Date 2004	Details	Amount £
30 Nov	Opening balance	12,900	30 Nov	Balance c/d	21,400
30 Nov	Motor vehicle	8,500			
		21,400			21,400
1 Dec	Balance b/d	21,400			

SALES

Date 2004	Details	Amount £	Date 2004	Details	Amount £
30 Nov	Balance c/d	300,400	30 Nov	Opening balance	285,200
			30 Nov	Invoices	16,200
		300,400			300,400
			1 Dec	Balance b/d	300,400

SALES RETURNS

Date 2004	Details	Amount £	Date 2004	Details	Amount £
30 Nov	Opening balance	3,000	30 Nov	Balance c/d	3,240
30 Nov	Returns	240			
		3,240			3,240
1 Dec	Balance b/d	3,240			

SALES LEDGER CONTROL

Date 2004	Details	Amount £	Date 2004	Details	Amount £
30 Nov	Opening balance	80,698	30 Nov	Cash received	4,400
30 Nov	Invoices	17,860	30 Nov	Credit notes	282
			30 Nov	Discounts allowed	114
				Balance c/d	93,762
		98,558			98,558
1 Dec	Balance b/d	93,762			

DISCOUNTS ALLOWED

Date 2004	Details	Amount £	Date 2004	Details	Amount £
30 Nov	Opening balance	600	30 Nov	Balance c/d	714
30 Nov	PPT Ltd	114			
		714			714
1 Dec	Balance b/d	714			

HEAT AND LIGHT

Date 2004	Details	Amount £	Date 2004	Details	Amount £
30 Nov	Opening balance	2,000	30 Nov	Balance c/d	2,480
30 Nov	Electricity	480			
		2,480			2,480
1 Dec	Balance b/d	2,480			

LOAN FROM BANK

Date 2004	Details	Amount £	Date 2004	Details	Amount £
30 Nov	Loan repayment	500	30 Nov	Opening balance	10,500
30 Nov	Balance c/d	10,000			
		10,500			10,500
			1 Dec	Balance b/d	10,000

VAT

Date 2004	Details	Amount £	Date 2004	Details	Amount £
30 Nov	Sales returns	42	30 Nov	Opening balance	8,560
30 Nov	Balance c/d	11,178	30 Nov	Sales	2,660
		11,220			11,220
			1 Dec	Balance b/d	11,178

Tasks 1.5 and 1.6

TRIAL BALANCE AS AT 30 NOVEMBER 2004

	Debit £	Credit £
Motor vehicles	21,400	
Equipment	20,600	
Stock	2,100	
Bank	10,311	
Petty cash control	153	
Sales ledger control	93,762	
Purchase ledger control		32,108
VAT		11,178
Loan from bank		10,000
Capital		44,446
Sales		300,400
Sales returns	3,240	
Purchases	190,100	
Purchases returns		1,400
Discounts received		120
Discounts allowed	714	
Heat and light	2,480	
Wages	46,300	
Motor expenses	450	
Rent and rates	2,600	
Stationery	210	
Telephone	622	
Insurance	3,250	
Miscellaneous expenses	1,360	
	399,652	399,652

SECTION 2 – ANSWERS

Task 2.1

(a) DEBIT   Bank
    CREDIT   Sales ledger control

(b) Funds transferred into the Special Events account by BACS will be available sooner than funds received by cheque and then paid into the account.

    This also prevents any problems such as cheques being lost in the post.

(c) This is a fast and secure method for PKG to pay its creditors. Cheques do not have to be written out and cannot get lost in the post.

Task 2.2

(a) Special Events would send a remittance advice out with a cheque to pay an account.

(b) A statement will be sent to debtors listing unpaid invoices and asking for payment.

(c) A credit note will be issued to correct an overcharge on an invoice issued.

Task 2.3

(a)

PETTY CASH CONTROL

Date 2004	Details	Amount £	Date 2004	Details	Amount £
1 Nov	Balance c/f	100	15 Nov	Window cleaning	30
			22 Nov	Postage	25
			29 Nov	Stationery	28
			30 Nov	Balance c/d	17
		100			100
1 Dec	Balance b/d	17			

(b) The amount required to restore the imprest will be £83 (100 – 17).

(c) The petty cash should be kept in a locked box.
One person should be responsible for the petty cash.
The petty cash should be regularly reconciled and balanced.

[You only need one of these]

Task 2.4

Account name	Dr £	Cr £
Sales ledger control		587.50
VAT	87.50	
Bad debts	500.00	

Task 2.5

(a) Sales invoices could be filed in numerical order.
(b) Purchase invoices could be filed alphabetically under suppliers.
(c) Bank statements should be filed chronologically.

Task 2.6

(a) Main (general) ledger account codes.
(b) Supplier account codes
(c) Stock account codes
(d) Employee account codes

[You only need two of these]

Task 2.7

Hardware: monitor, hard drive, printer
Software: operating system, accounting package

[You only need one of each]

Task 2.8

THE JOURNAL

	Account name	Dr £	Cr £
(a)	Discounts allowed	45	
	Discounts received		45
(b)	Insurance	60	
	Cash		60
(c)	Stationery	400	
	VAT	70	
	Purchases ledger control account		470

Task 2.9

(a)

PURCHASES LEDGER CONTROL

Date 2004	Details	Amount £	Date 2004	Details	Amount £
30 Nov	Payments	9,357	1 Nov	Balance b/f	30,260
30 Nov	Discounts received	170	30 Nov	Purchases	11,500
30 Nov	Goods returned	125			
30 Nov	Balance c/d	32,108			
		41,760			41,760
			1 Dec		32,108

(b) **Reconciliation**

	£
Purchases ledger control account balance as at 30 November 2004	32,108
Total of subsidiary (purchases) ledger accounts as at 30 November 2004	32,233
Difference	125

(c) The difference may have been caused by the goods returned not having been posted to the suppliers' accounts in the purchases ledger.

Task 2.10

(a) to (c)

CASH BOOK

Date 2004	Details	Bank £	Date 2004	Cheque Number	Details	Bank £
1 Nov	Balance b/f	10,400	1 Nov	006165	LLB Ltd	3,500
11 Nov	L Smith	5,000	1 Nov	006166	Down and Daly	2,100
11 Nov	B Roberts	7,500	5 Nov	006167	Hobbs Ltd	4,600
15 Nov	G Brown	1,700	5 Nov	006168	H & H Ltd	380
22 Nov	B Singh	4,550	22 Nov	006169	Eddie's Bar	500
			15 Nov	DD	Bedford CC	186
			19 Nov	DD	Myers Insurance	45
			22 Nov		O/D facility fee	40
			22 Nov		Bank charges	50
			29 Nov		Balance c/d	17,749
		29,150				29,150
30 Nov	Balance b/d	17,749				

(d) BANK RECONCILIATION STATEMENT AS AT 29 NOVEMBER 2004

	£	£
Balance as per bank statement		16,599
Add: Uncleared lodgements:	1,700	
	4,550	
		6,250
Less: Unpresented cheques:		
006167	4,600	
006169	500	
		(5,100)
Balance as per the updated cash book		17,749

PART I

Lecturers' Resource Pack Activities

Note to Students

The answers to these activities and assessments are provided to your lecturers, who will distribute them in class.

If you are not on a classroom based course, a copy of the answers can be obtained from Customer Services on 020 8740 2211 or e-mail publishing @bpp.com.

Note to Lecturers

The answers to these activities and assessments are included in the Lecturers' Resource Pack, provided free to colleges.

If your college has not received the Lecturers' Resource Pack, please contact Customer Services on 020 8740 2211 or e-mail publishing @bpp.com.

Lecturers' Practice Activities

Chapter 1: Revision of basic bookkeeping

1 Revenue

If revenue expenditure is treated as capital expenditure, then:

(a) the total of the expenses for the period will be:

Too high/Too low/Unaffected

(b) the value of the fixed assets will be:

Too high/Too low/Unaffected

2 Classify

Classify the following ledger accounts according to whether they represent asset, liability, expense or revenue.

(a) Stock

Asset / Liability / Expense / Revenue

(b) Rent received

Asset / Liability / Expense / Revenue

(c) Heat, light and water

Asset / Liability / Expense / Revenue

(d) Bank overdraft

Asset / Liability / Expense / Revenue

3 MEL

MEL Motor Factors Ltd sends a cheque to a supplier. What is the appropriate document to send with the cheque?

Chapter 2: Recording, summarising and posting transactions

4 Primary records

The sales and purchases day books are primary records used for listing data taken from source documents. Double entry is carried out by transferring relevant totals from the day books into the main ledger.

True / False

5 Ledger accounts

The sales ledger and purchase ledger are part of the double entry system.

True / False

Chapter 3: Bank reconciliations

6 Debit or credit

The following bank statement was received from the company's bankers on 2 June 20X3.

Midwest Bank plc

Future Electrical Ltd

Statement of Account

Account No 60413658   Statement Date: 1 June 20X3

Date	Details	Debit £	Credit £	Balance £
1 June	Balance forward			1,791
1 June	Dividend		104	1,895
1 June	Counter credit		7,084	8,979
1 June	GR Insurance DD	89		8,890
1 June	000415	300		8,590

In updating the cash book balance of £4,892:

(a) Which item or items should now be debited to the cash book?

£104/£7,084/£89/£300

(b) Which items or items should now be credited to the cash book?

£104/£7,084/£89/£300

7 Fill in

MMS Textiles Ltd banks at the Moxley branch of the Norwest Bank, sort code no 36-24-41, and its account number is 479836806.

Fill in the paying-in slip and counterfoil given below to bank the cash takings on 1 December which are as follows.

Four	£50 notes
Twenty-three	£20 notes
Thirty-two	£10 notes
Seven	£5 notes
Eight	50 pence coins
Twelve	10 pence coins

LECTURERS' RESOURCE PACK ACTIVITIES

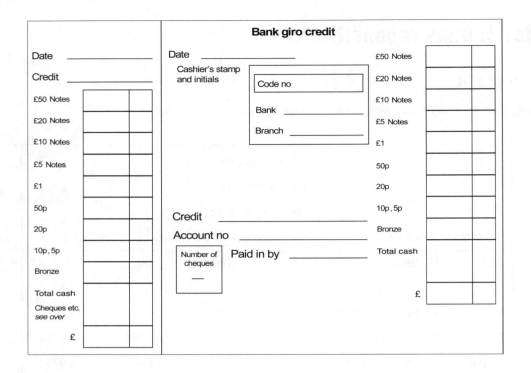

8 Not accepted

Give *two* reasons why the above cheque, received from a debtor, would not be accepted for payment if it was presented to Midwest Bank plc.

(a) _____

(b) _____

Chapter 4: Sales ledger control account

9 Reasons

Give two reasons for maintaining the sales ledger control account.

10 Contra

What double entry would you make in the main ledger in respect of the following.

(a) A set off of £20 is to be made between Tompkinson & Co's accounts in the sales ledger and in the purchases ledger.

Debit   *Amount*   *Credit*   *Amount*

(b) The account of D L Mason who owes £1,214 is to be written off as a bad debt.

Debit   *Amount*   *Credit*   *Amount*

Chapter 5: Purchase ledger control account

11 One reason

Give one reason for maintaining a purchase ledger control account.

12 Control account

This is a summary of transactions with suppliers during December 20X4

	£
Balance on purchase ledger control account at 1 December 20X4	20,356
Money paid to suppliers	23,417
Discount received	321
Goods purchased on credit	35,128
Goods returned to suppliers	414

Calculate the balance on the purchase ledger control account at 31 December 20X4.

Chapter 6: Other control accounts

13 Imprest

The company operates its petty cash using the imprest system. The imprest amount is £250.00. At the end of a particular period the five analysis columns were totalled to give the following amounts.

Column 1	£26.19
Column 2	£45.27
Column 3	£6.94
Column 4	£12.81
Column 5	£14.38

How much cash would be required to restore the imprest amount for the following period?

£........................

Chapter 7: The correction of errors

14 Correction

Journals are used to correct an error which breaks the rules of double entry.

True / False

Chapter 8: From ledger accounts to initial trial balance

15 Suspense

(a) A trial balance has debits totalling £50,000 and credits totalling £45,000. Set up a suspense account so that the final balance balances.

(b) You discover that the cash balance is £5,000 too high in the list of balance. Clear the suspense account.

Chapter 9: Filing

16 Codes

The cheque numbers in a cheque book are an example of:

A sequential code / a hierarchical code

17 Methods

List two classification methods for filing documents and files.

(a) _____

(b) _____

18 Documents

Suggest one classification method of filing each of the following documents. Your answer should suggest a different classification method for each document.

(a) General correspondence
(b) Invoices
(c) Insurance policies

Lecturers' Skills based Assessment

FULL SKILLS BASED ASSESSMENT
T S STATIONERY

FOUNDATION STAGE – NVQ/SVQ2

Unit 3

Preparing Ledger Balances and an Initial Trial Balance

The purpose of this Full Skills Based Assessment is to give you an idea of what an AAT simulation looks like. It is not intended as a definitive guide to the tasks you may be required to perform.

The suggested time allowance for this Assessment is **three hours**. Up to 30 minutes extra time may be permitted in an AAT simulation. Breaks in assessment will be allowed in the AAT simulation, but it must normally be completed in one day.

Calculators may be used but no reference material is permitted.

**DO NOT OPEN THIS PAPER UNTIL YOU ARE READY TO START
UNDER EXAM CONDITIONS**

COVERAGE OF PERFORMANCE CRITERIA

All performance criteria in Unit 3 are covered by this full skills based assessment.

Element	PC Coverage
3.1	**Balance bank transactions**
	Record details from the relevant primary documentation in the cash book and ledger.
	Correctly calculate totals and balances of receipts and payments.
	Compare individual items on the bank statement and in the cash book for accuracy.
	Identify discrepancies and prepare a bank reconciliation statement.
3.2	**Prepare ledger balances and control accounts**
	Make and record authorised adjustments.
	Total relevant accounts in the main ledger.
	Reconcile control accounts with the total of the balance in the subsidiary ledger.
	Reconcile petty cash control account with cash in hand and subsidiary records.
	Identify discrepancies arising from the reconciliation of control accounts and either resolve or refer to the appropriate person.
	Ensure documentation is stored securely and in line with the organisation's confidentiality requirements.
3.3	**Draft an initial trial balance**
	Prepare the draft initial trial balance in line with the organisation's policies and procedures.
	Identify discrepancies in the balancing process.
	Identify reasons for imbalance and rectify them.
	Balance the trial balance.

Knowledge and understanding

Whilst some areas of knowledge and understanding can be inferred through performance, there will be gaps in evidence which should be plugged by other assessment methods, eg questioning.

Centres are reminded that there should be a mix of evidence across the unit, simulations cannot stand alone as evidence of competent performance, and the evidence in the portfolio should be mapped clearly to the student record.

TS STATIONERY

INSTRUCTIONS

This Assessment is designed to test your ability to prepare ledger balances and an initial trial balance.

The situation is provided on page 404.

The tasks you are to perform are set out within the data.

You are allowed three hours to complete your work.

A high level of accuracy is required. Check your work carefully.

Correcting fluid may be used but should be used in moderation. Errors should be crossed out neatly and clearly. You should write in black ink, not pencil.

You are advised to read the whole of the Assessment before commencing, as all of the information may be of value and is not necessarily supplied in the sequence in which you might wish to deal with it.

INTRODUCTION

- You are the bookkeeper for a small business supplying decorative and unusual stationery and cards called T S Stationery.

- The accounting system is a manual system with all double entry taking place in the main ledger and subsidiary ledgers kept for debtors and creditors.

- Today is 2 April 20X1 and you are trying to prepare the trial balance for the year ended 31 March 20X1.

- Before preparing the trial balance there are a number of accounting tasks for the last few days of March that must be undertaken.

Task 1

The purchases day book and purchases returns day book has not yet been posted for the last week in March. The two day books are given below, together with the relevant main ledger accounts and subsidiary ledger accounts. You are required to update the ledger accounts to reflect the entries in the day books.

PURCHASES DAY BOOK

Supplier	Gross £	VAT £	Net £
FP Paper	188	28	160
Gift Products Ltd	235	35	200
Harper Bros	141	21	120
J S Traders	282	42	240
	846	126	720

PURCHASES RETURNS DAY BOOK

Supplier	Gross £	VAT £	Net £
Gift Products Ltd	94	14	80
Harper Bros	47	7	40
	141	21	120

MAIN LEDGER ACCOUNTS

PURCHASE LEDGER CONTROL ACCOUNT

	£			£
		27 Mar	Opening balance	14,325

PURCHASES ACCOUNT

		£		£
27 Mar	Opening balance	166,280		

PURCHASES RETURNS ACCOUNT

£			£
	27 Mar	Opening balance	4,180

VAT ACCOUNT

£			£
	27 Mar	Opening balance	1,405

SUBSIDIARY LEDGER ACCOUNTS

F P PAPER

£			£
	27 Mar	Opening balance	3,825

GIFT PRODUCTS LIMITED

	£			£
		27 Mar	Opening balance	4,661

HARPER BROS

	£			£
		27 Mar	Opening balance	3,702

J S TRADERS

	£			£
		27 Mar	Opening balance	2,137

Task 2

Reconcile the balance on the purchase ledger control account with the total of the four creditor balances (these are the only credit suppliers of the business).

You should now balance the purchases account, purchases returns account and VAT account.

Task 3

Journal number 336

	£	£
Bad debts expense	400	
Sales ledger control		400

Being write off of bad debt from C Cummings

Journal number 337

	£	£
Sales ledger control	100	
Sales		100

Being undercast of sales day book

The relevant main ledger accounts are given below. You are also given all of the individual debtor accounts from the subsidiary ledger.

Enter the journal entries in the relevant main ledger and subsidiary ledger accounts and then reconcile the balance on the sales ledger control account to the total of the individual debtor accounts in the subsidiary ledger.

You can now balance the sales account and the bad debts expense account.

MAIN LEDGER

SALES LEDGER CONTROL ACCOUNT

		£			£
31 Mar	Balance b/d	23,230			

TS STATIONERY

SALES ACCOUNT

	£			£
		31 Mar	Balance b/d	255,810

BAD DEBTS EXPENSE ACCOUNT

	£		£

SUBSIDIARY LEDGER

RETAIL ENTERPRISES

		£		£
31 Mar	Balance b/d	5,114		

C CUMMINGS

		£		£
31 Mar	Balance b/d	400		

PALMER LIMITED

		£		£
31 Mar	Balance b/d	6,248		

REAPERS STORES

		£		£
31 Mar	Balance b/d	5,993		

KNIGHT RETAIL

		£		£
31 Mar	Balance b/d	5,575		

Task 4

Given below is the cash receipts and payments book for the business for the month of March 20X1. You are also given the bank statement for the month.

You are required to check the cash book carefully to the bank statement and adjust the cash book for any missing entries.

CASH BOOK

RECEIPTS			PAYMENTS			
Date	Detail	£	Date	Detail	Cheque no	£
1 Mar	Balance b/d	3,668	5 Mar	Harper Bros	002643	2,558
7 Mar	Palmer Ltd	2,557	12 Mar	Gift Products	002644	3,119
15 Mar	Retail Engineering	4,110	18 Mar	F P Paper	002645	2,553
20 Mar	Reapers Stores	4,782	24 Mar	J S Traders	002646	983
28 Mar	Knight Retail	3,765	31 Mar	BACS – wages		3,405

NORTHERN BANK
Royal Bank House
Trestle Square
Sandefield
SF2 3HS

Cheque account: T S Stationery   Account number 10364382

SHEET 0124

		Paid out £	Paid in £	Balance £
1 Mar	Balance b/d			3,668
10 Mar	Credit		2,557	6,225
16 Mar	Cheque 002644	3,119		3,106
20 Mar	Credit		4,110	7,216
22 Mar	Cheque 002643	2,558		
	SO – District Council: rates	200		4,458
25 Mar	Credit		4,782	9,240
26 Mar	Cheque 002645	2,553		
	SO – Loan repayment	400		6,287
30 Mar	Interest		20	6,307
31 Mar	BACS	3,405		2,902

Task 5

Total and balance the adjusted cash book and complete the double entry in the ledger accounts given. You can then balance each of the ledger accounts.

RATES ACCOUNT

		£			£
31 Mar	Balance b/d	2,200			

LOAN ACCOUNT

		£			£
			31 Mar	Balance b/d	6,400

BANK INTEREST RECEIVABLE

		£			£
			31 Mar	Balance b/d	100

Task 6

Prepare a bank reconciliation statement, in the following format.

£

Balance per bank statement
Add:

_____

Less:

_____

Balance per adjusted cash book

=========

Task 7

T S Stationery sublets part of its premises and has three tenants. The rent book for March is given below. The details have not yet been entered into the ledger accounts, although the payment of the rent has been entered in the cash receipts book. You are required to enter the totals in the relevant ledger accounts given and to balance the accounts.

	Rent due £	Overdue rent b/f £	Payment received £	Outstanding rent £
M Savage	2,000	350	2,350	–
T Stiles	1,500	–	1,000	500
L Fraser	1,000	130	750	380
	4,500	480	4,100	880

NON-TRADE DEBTORS CONTROL ACCOUNT

	£		£
1 Mar Balance b/d	480		

RENT RECEIVABLE ACCOUNT

	£		£
		1 Mar Balance b/d	45,000

Task 8

The petty cash is run on an imprest system of £100 per month.

The petty cash vouchers in the petty cash box at 31 March were:

Voucher number	£
0264	3.67
0265	9.48
0266	6.70
0267	13.20
0268	2.36
0269	1.55
0270	10.46
0271	4.89
0272	3.69

The cash in the petty cash box was:

Note/coin	Number
£10	1
£5	4
£2	2
£1	7
50p	3
20p	4
10p	5
5p	1
2p	7
1p	1

Reconcile the petty cash vouchers and the petty cash and determine the amount that will appear in the trial balance for petty cash.

TS STATIONERY

Task 9

You are now ready to prepare the initial balance at the year end, 31 March 20X1. Given below are the ledger balances at 31 March 20X1 which must be completed with the balances from the ledger accounts dealt with in earlier tasks.

You are required to prepare the initial trial balance at 31 March 20X1.

	£
Building	100,000
Motor vehicles	34,500
Office equipment	13,000
Purchases	Own figure
Purchases returns	Own figure
Capital	53,855
Sales	Own figure
Sales returns	6,800
Discounts allowed	300
Stock	16,000
Loan	Own figure
Discount received	600
Debtors (SLCA)	Own figure
Petty cash	Own figure
Creditors (PLCA)	Own figure
VAT	Own figure
Bank	Own figure
Non-trade debtors	Own figure
Rent receivable	Own figure
Motor expenses	4,297
Telephone	4,850
Electricity	3,630
Rates	Own figure
Miscellaneous expenses	3,900
Bad debts expense	Own figure
Bank interest receivable	Own figure

Task 10

The owner of the business is delighted that the initial trial balance does in fact balance and has said to you that he therefore assumes this means that all of the accounting entries are correct.

You are required to write a memo to the owner explaining what types of errors there may be in the accounting records that are not shown up by the trial balance, using examples of how these errors could take place in T S Stationery's books but still not cause an imbalance on the trial balance.

FULL SKILLS BASED ASSESSMENT

FULL EXAM BASED ASSESSMENT: DECEMBER 2003

FULL EXAM BASED ASSESSMENT DECEMBER 2003 (AMENDED)

FOUNDATION STAGE – NVQ/SVQ2

Unit 3

Preparing Ledger Balances and an Initial Trial Balance

DO NOT OPEN THIS PAPER UNTIL YOU ARE READY TO START UNDER EXAM CONDITIONS

FULL EXAM BASED ASSESSMENT: DECEMBER 2003

FULL EXAM BASED ASSESSMENT: DECEMBER 2003

This assessment is in two sections.

You have to show competence in both sections, so attempt and aim to complete EVERY task in BOTH sections.

Section 1 Processing exercise
Complete all five tasks

Section 2 10 tasks and questions
Complete all tasks and questions

You should spend about 90 minutes on each section.

Include all essential workings within your answers, where appropriate.

The original paper contained two blank pages for workings.

Sections 1 and 2 both relate to the business described below.

Introduction

- Ben Hooper is the owner of The Little Fabric Warehouse, a business that supplies curtain and upholstery material.
- You are employed by the business as a bookkeeper.
- The business uses a manual accounting system.
- Double entry takes place in the main (general) ledger. Individual accounts of debtors and creditors are kept in subsidiary ledgers as memorandum accounts.
- Assume today's date is 30 November 20X3 unless you are told otherwise.

FULL EXAM BASED ASSESSMENT: DECEMBER 2003

SECTION 1 – PROCESSING EXERCISE

You should spend about 90 minutes on this section.

Data

Balances at the start of the day on 30 November 20X3

The following balances are relevant to you at the start of the day on 30 November 20X3.

	£
Credit suppliers:	
Lee Ltd	2,016
Ball and McGee	5,200
Horner and Company	8,308
H & H Ltd	652
Purchases	139,300
Purchases returns	258
Purchases ledger control	30,405
Loan	10,000
Travel expenses	569
Rates	3,200
Stationery	475
VAT (credit balance)	11,309

Task 1.1

Enter these opening balances into the following accounts, given on pages 422-426.

Subsidiary (Purchases) Ledger
    Lee Ltd
    Ball and McGee
    Horner and Company
    H & H Ltd

Main (General) Ledger
    Purchases
    Purchases returns
    Purchases ledger control
    Loan
    Travel expenses
    Rates
    Stationery
    VAT

FULL EXAM BASED ASSESSMENT: DECEMBER 2003

Data

Transactions

The following transactions all took place on 30 November 20X3 and have been entered into the relevant books of prime entry as shown below. No entries have yet been made into the ledger system. The VAT rate is 17½%.

PURCHASES DAY BOOK

Date	Details	Invoice number	Total £	VAT £	Net £
20X3					
30 Nov	Lee Ltd	P31621	3,525	525	3,000
30 Nov	Ball and McGee	402	1,410	210	1,200
30 Nov	Horner and Company	8714	12,690	1,890	10,800
30 Nov	H & H Ltd	667	4,700	700	4,000
Totals			22,325	3,325	19,000

PURCHASES RETURNS DAY BOOK

Date	Details	Credit Number	Total £	VAT £	Net £
20X3					
30 Nov	Lee Ltd	041	235	35	200
30 Nov	H & H Ltd	162	940	140	800
Totals			1,175	175	1,000

CASH BOOK

Date	Details	VAT £	Bank £	Date	Details	VAT £	Bank £
20X3				20X3			
30 Nov	Balance b/f		12,842	30 Nov	Loan repayment		700
				30 Nov	Travel expenses		50
				30 Nov	Rates		3,200
				30 Nov	Stationery	14	94
				30 Nov	Ball and McGee (creditor)		3,445
				30 Nov	Horner and Company (creditor)		2,200
				30 Nov	Balance c/f		3,153
Totals			12,842			14	12,842

Task 1.2

From the day books and cash book shown above, make the relevant entries into the accounts in the subsidiary (purchases) ledger and main (general) ledger

Task 1.3

Balance the accounts showing clearly the balances carried down at 30 November (closing balance).

Task 1.4

Now show the balances brought down at 1 December (opening balance).

Subsidiary (Purchases) Ledger

LEE LTD

Date	Details	Amount £	Date	Details	Amount £

BALL AND MCGEE

Date	Details	Amount £	Date	Details	Amount £

HORNER AND COMPANY

Date	Details	Amount £	Date	Details	Amount £

H & H LTD

Date	Details	Amount £	Date	Details	Amount £

Main (General) Ledger

PURCHASES

Date	Details	Amount £	Date	Details	Amount £

FULL EXAM BASED ASSESSMENT: DECEMBER 2003

PURCHASES RETURNS

Date	Details	Amount £	Date	Details	Amount £

PURCHASE LEDGER CONTROL

Date	Details	Amount £	Date	Details	Amount £

LOAN

Date	Details	Amount £	Date	Details	Amount £

TRAVEL EXPENSES

Date	Details	Amount £	Date	Details	Amount £

RATES

Date	Details	Amount £	Date	Details	Amount £

STATIONERY

Date	Details	Amount £	Date	Details	Amount £

VAT

Date	Details	Amount £	Date	Details	Amount £

Data

Other balances to be transferred to the trial balance:

	£
Motor vehicles	25,650
Office equipment	7,320
Stock	15,860
Petty cash control	210
Sales ledger control	125,385
Capital	14,818
Sales	310,600
Sales returns	850
Discounts allowed	100
Wages	28,604
Insurance	2,400
Rent	7,200
Telephone	2,400
Heat and light	3,175
Miscellaneous expenses	1,850

FULL EXAM BASED ASSESSMENT: DECEMBER 2003

Task 1.5

Transfer the balances that you calculated in Task 1.4, and the bank balance, to the trial balance on this page.

Task 1.6

Transfer the remaining balances shown above to the trial balance, and total each column.

TRIAL BALANCE AS AT 30 NOVEMBER 20X3

	Debit £	Credit £
Motor vehicles		
Office equipment		
Stock		
Bank		
Cash		
Sales ledger control		
Purchase ledger control		
VAT		
Capital		
Sales		
Sales returns		
Purchases		
Purchases returns		
Loan payable		
Wages		
Insurance		
Heat and light		
Rent		
Rates		
Telephone		
Motor expenses		
Stationery		
Hotel expenses		
Miscellaneous expenses		
Total		

FULL EXAM BASED ASSESSMENT: DECEMBER 2003

SECTION 2 – TASKS AND QUESTIONS

You should spend about 90 minutes on this section.

Answer all of the following questions.

Write your answers in the spaces provided.

Note. You do not need to adjust the accounts in Section 1 as part of any of the following tasks.

Task 2.1

The Little Fabric Warehouse has the following cash and cheques to bank on 1 December:

Cash		Cheques	
Three	£20 notes	L Gower Ltd	£352.50
Ten	£10 notes	Upholstery World	£176.25
Eight	£5 notes	B Wood	£100.00
Five	£1 coins		
Six	50p coins		

Complete both sides of the paying-in slip shown below.

Date_____ **bank giro credit** Notes £50

Cashier's stamp Notes £20

Paid in by.. Notes £10

Notes £5

Middleway Bank plc £2

£1

50p

20p

Cheques 10p, 5p

2p, 1p

Total Cash

Cheques, Pos

Branch Sort Code: 32-09-39   Account Number: 34027476   85   £

Please do not write or mark below this line or fold this voucher

Details of cheques, etc.   Sub-total b/f

Carried forward £ _____   Total carried over £ _____

In view of the risk of loss in course of clearing, customers are advised to keep an independent record of the drawers of cheques
Please do not write or mark below this line

FULL EXAM BASED ASSESSMENT: DECEMBER 2003

Task 2.2

The Little Fabric Warehouse has sold goods to a credit customer for £810.75, including VAT. What is the amount of VAT included in this figure?

Show your workings.

Task 2.3

The Little Fabric Warehouse has given a customer a settlement discount of £50.

What will be the accounting entries needed in the main (general) ledger of The Little Fabric Warehouse to record this transaction? (Ignore VAT.)

Debit _____ £ _____

Credit _____ £ _____

Task 2.4

The Bank Manager has contacted Ben Hooper and reminded him of the range of services offered by the bank, including the night safe facility.

(a) Briefly describe the night safe service offered by the bank.

_____
_____
_____

(b) Why might a business wish to use this service?

_____
_____
_____

Task 2.5

What entries would be needed in the main (general) ledger to record a contra transfer between The Little Fabric Warehouse and its customer, Parish Fabrics?

Circle the correct answer.

(a) Debit: Sales ledger control account
    Credit: Purchases ledger control account

(b) Debit: Sales ledger control account
    Credit: Parish Fabrics

(c) Debit: Purchases ledger control account
    Credit: Sales ledger control account

Task 2.6

Ben Hooper wants to computerise the accounting system and is particularly interested in the printed reports and documents the computer could produce automatically and more efficiently.

(a) Name TWO reports that could be produced more efficiently by computer.

_____

_____

(b) Name TWO types of document sent to customers, which currently have to be typed or hand written, that could be produced more efficiently by computer.

_____

_____

Task 2.7

The petty cash control account shown below is in the main (general) ledger of The Little Fabric Warehouse. The imprest level of £500 was restored from the bank and put in the petty cash box on 1 December, one day after the month end.

PETTY CASH CONTROL

Date 20X3	Details	Amount £	Date 20X3	Details	Amount £
1 Nov	Balance b/f	321	30 Nov	Stationery	75
			30 Nov	Milk	10
			30 Nov	Stamps	26

(a) Balance the petty cash control account at 30 November, showing clearly the balances carried down and brought down.

(b) Enter the restored imprest amount on 1 December.

(c) Balance the account at 1 December, showing clearly the balance carried down and brought down.

(d) Name TWO precautions that should be taken to ensure the security and accuracy of the petty cash.

Task 2.8

The following information has become available.

(a) A cash purchase of office stationery has been entered in the petty cash book as £30 instead of the correct amount of £36. (Ignore VAT.)

(b) An amount of £75 has been credited to the suspense account. The following two errors have now been discovered:

- rent paid has been understated by £10
- a figure in the heat and light account has been overstated by £85.

(c) A cheque for £500 has been received from a customer, J Wright and Company, and has been incorrectly debited to the sales ledger control account and credited to the bank account.

Record the journal entries needed in the main (general) ledger to correct the errors shown above. You do not need to give dates or narratives.

Note. You do NOT need to adjust the accounts in any previous tasks in Section 1 or Section 2.

JOURNAL

Details	Dr £	Cr £

Task 2.9

The following is a summary of transactions with credit customers during the month of November.

	£
Balance of debtors at 1 November 2003	£130,680
Goods sold on credit	30,600
Money received from credit customers	35,150
Discount allowed	400
Goods returned by customers	345

(a) Prepare a sales ledger control account from the details shown above. Show clearly the balance carried down at 30 November and brought down at 1 December.

SALES LEDGER CONTROL

Date	Details	Amount £	Date	Details	Amount £

The following closing debit balances were in the subsidiary (sales) ledger on 30 November.

	£
Parish Fabrics	18,500
Colourway Decor	22,305
Innes and Company	7,500
Seeley Sofas	20,000
BKJ Ltd	31,120
Baber & Jones	11,160
Interior Designs	15,200

(b) Reconcile the balances shown above with the sales ledger control account balance you have calculated in part (a).

	£
Sales ledger control account balance as at 30 November 20X3	
Total of subsidiary (sales) ledger accounts as at 30 November 20X3	
Difference	

(c) What may have caused the difference you calculated in part (b)?

___

___

___

___

Task 2.10

On 28 November The Little Fabric Warehouse received the following bank statement as at 21 November.

MIDDLEWAY BANK PLC
The Stand, Hadley, H16 9QT

To: The Little Fabric Warehouse   Account No: 34027476   21 November 2003

STATEMENT OF ACCOUNT

Date	Details	Paid out	Paid in	Balance
20X3		£	£	£
1 Nov	Balance b/f			2,577C
7 Nov	Cheque No 400189	600		1,977C
10 Nov	Cheque No 400190	201		1,776C
11 Nov	Cheque No 400188	250		1,526C
14 Nov	Bank Giro Credit L Green		8,000	9,526C
17 Nov	Cheque No 400191	817		8,709C
19 Nov	Direct Debit Hadley MB	1,870		6,839C
21 Nov	Direct Debit			
	District Cleansing	200		6,639C
21 Nov	Bank charges	97		6,542C

D = Debit   C = Credit

The cash book as at 28 November 20X3 is shown below.

FULL EXAM BASED ASSESSMENT: DECEMBER 2003

CASH BOOK

Date 20X3	Details	Bank £	Date 20X3	Cheque number	Details	Bank £
1 Nov	Balance b/f	2,577	3 Nov	400188	Taylors Ltd	250
27 Nov	Hi Trading	3,100	3 Nov	400189	McCracken Ltd	600
28 Nov	Silk Sales	387	4 Nov	400190	P Bowen	201
			13 Nov	400191	Parkes & Company	817
			19 Nov		Hadley MB	1,870
			26 Nov	400192	KOK & Company	85
			27 Nov	400193	Magda Fabrics	320

(a) Check the items on the bank statement against the items in the cash book.

(b) Update the cash book as needed.

(c) Total the cash book and clearly show the balance carried down at 28 November and brought down at 29 November.

(d) Using the information on page 433 and 434, prepare a bank reconciliation statement as at 28 November. The bank reconciliation statement should start with the balance as per the bank statement and reconcile to the balance as per the cash book.

Note. You do not need to adjust the accounts in Section 1.

The lines in the bank reconciliation statement below are there to help you present

your work neatly and clearly. You may not need to use all the lines.

Bank reconciliation statement as at 28 November 20X3

£

Balance as per bank statement _____

Add: _____ _____

_____ _____

_____ _____

Less: _____ _____

_____ _____

_____ _____

Balance as per cash book _____

Glossary and Index

Glossary of International Terms

UK	International
Sales ledger	Accounts receivable/ Receivables ledger
Purchase ledger/ bought ledger	Accounts payable/ Payables ledger
Balance sheet items	
Fixed assets	Non-current assets
Tangible fixed assets	Property, plant and equipment
Intangible fixed assets	Intangible non-current assets
Stock	Inventory
Debtors	Receivables
Creditors	Payables
Long term liabilities	Non-current liabilities
Debenture	Loan stock
Capital and reserves	Equity
Capital and reserves (consolidated accounts)	Equity attributable to equity holders of the parent
Profit and loss account (in the balance sheet)/ Accumulated profits	Retained earnings
Profit and loss account items	
Profit and loss account	Income statement
Turnover/sales	Revenue
Taxation	Tax expense
Other items	
Statement of total recognised gains and losses	Statement of recognised income and expense

Glossary

Bad debt – Where a customer has gone bankrupt or is otherwise not expected to pay, the debt will be written off as a bad debt. The accounting entry will be:

DR Bad debts ; CR Sales ledger (and SLCA)

Bank statement – A document sent out every month by banks to all of their customers, showing movements on their account. Large organisations usually arrange for a weekly statement, so that they can monitor their cash more closely. This is the record of the customer's account in the bank's books so, when compared to the bank account in the general ledger, the entries will be reversed.

Capital expenditure – Expenditure to acquire or improve fixed assets – eg. property, plant, vehicles.

Cash book – The cash book records the movement of funds into, and out of, the organisation's bank account. Cheques written and cash banked will be recorded in the cash book, and it will then be updated to reflect items which have gone directly to or from the bank account – cash transfers received, direct debits and standing orders going out. At regular intervals, usually once a month, it will be reconciled to the bank statement.

Control account – An impersonal account in the general (main) ledger which acts as a summary of personal accounts. For instance, the sales ledger control account acts as a summary of all the accounts in the sales ledger.

Journal – This is used to used to record unusual entries or to make corrections or amendments to existing entries in the general (main) ledger. The entries are recorded on a journal voucher. Any entry into the general ledger which does not come from one of the books of prime entry will be made by journal.

Provision for doubtful debts – Where no particular debt is thought to be bad, but the business knows from experience that, for instance, 5% of it's debtors will not pay, a provision can be made against 5% of it's total debtors. The accounting entry will be:

DR Bad debts (or Bad and doubtful debts) ; CR Provision for doubtful debts

Revenue expenditure – Expenditure other than for the acquisition or improvement of fixed assets. This expenditure covers the normal expenses of the business – eg. rent and rates, salaries and wages, materials, fuel, repairs and maintenance.

Suspense account – Where it is not known how an item should be posted, it can be posted to suspense until a decision is made. For instance, if an unexplained amount of money was transferred into the bank account, it could be posted to suspense while waiting for the bank to explain where it came from. Nothing can be left in suspense at the end of the year. A difference in the trial balance can be posted temporarily to a suspense account, but must be investigated and transferred out before the accounts are prepared.

Trial balance – A list of all the general ledger balances shown in debit and credit columns. If the totals of the debit and credit columns are not the same, an error must be looked for – possibly more than one.

Unpresented cheque – Where a cheque has been issued but has not been presented for payment, it will appear in the cash book but not on the bank statement. This will have to be adjusted for in preparing the bank reconciliation statement.

GLOSSARY

INDEX

Accession register, 133
Active file, 129
Alphabetical classification, 131
Alpha-numeric classification, 133

Bad debt relief, 66
Bad debts, 65
Bad debts and VAT, 66
Balance sheet, 6
Balancing ledger accounts, 116
Balancing the cash book, 23
Bank charges, 42
Bank reconciliations, 42
Bank statements, 25, 43
Batch processing, 122
Books of prime entry, 17
Business accounts, 53
Business finance services, 54

Capital and revenue expenditure, 7
Capital items, 7
Cash books, 22
Cash control account, 95
CHAPS, 54
Characteristics of a filing system, 129
Classification, 131
Classified, 138
Classifying information, 131
Compensating errors, 102, 104, 117
Competition, 53
Confidentiality, 138
Control accounts, 62
Control totals, 122
Correction of errors, 104
Credit note, 9
Credits, 4, 116

Debits, 4, 116
Direct debit, 44
Discount, 10
Documents, 9
Double entry, 4, 27, 117
Double entry bookkeeping, 5

Environment, 136
Errors, 42
Errors of commission, 102, 104
Errors of omission, 102, 103
Errors of principle, 102, 103, 117
Errors of transposition, 102

File, 128
File security, 138
Files, 128
Filing cabinets
   lateral suspension, 137
   vertical suspension, 137
Filing system, 128
Folio numbers, 70
Foreign exchange, 54
Format of a ledger account, 26
Frequency of the reconciliation, 49

Geographical classification, 134

Home banking, 54

Income statement, 6
Information
   classifying, 131
   cross-referencing, 131
   indexing, 131
Information storage, 128
Insurance services, 54
Integrated accounting systems, 78
In-tray, 137
Invoice, 9

Journals, 104

Ledger account, 26
List of balances, 114
Location, 137

Main ledger, 17, 25
Manila folders, 137

INDEX

Master files, 129
Microfiche, 138
Microfilm, 138

Non-active file, 129
Non-trade receivables, 96
Numerical classification, 133

Omission of a transaction, 117
Out of date cheques, 50
Outstanding lodgements, 47

Payables ledger control account, 35, 82, 86
Payables, 30
Pensions, 54
Permanent files, 128
Personal accounts, 63
Petty cash, 25, 94
Physical storage, 137
Pigeon-hole, 137
Posting from the day books, 33
Programme controls, 52
Provision for doubtful debts, 67
Purchase day book, 21
Purchase returns day book, 21

Receivables, 30
Receivables ledger control account, 33

Reference files, 129
Revenue items, 7

Safe, 137
Safe custody services, 54
Sales analysis, 20
Sales day book, 18
Sales returns day book, 20
Standing order, 44
Standing orders and direct debit schedule, 50
Stopped cheques, 50
Subject classification, 134
Subsidiary ledger, 17
Suspense account, 106, 108, 109

T accounts, 26
Temporary files, 128
Timing differences, 42
Transaction files, 129
Trial balance, 114
Types of error, 102

Unpresented cheques, 47

Value added tax (VAT), 10

Wrong account, 117

Review Form & Free Prize Draw – Unit 3 Ledger Balances and Initial Trial Balance (4/05)

All original review forms from the entire BPP range, completed with genuine comments, will be entered into one of two draws on 31 January 2006 and 31 July 2006. The names on the first four forms picked out on each occasion will be sent a cheque for £50.

Name: _____ Address: _____

How have you used this Combined Text and Kit?
(Tick one box only)

☐ Home study (book only)
☐ On a course: college _____
☐ With 'correspondence' package
☐ Other _____

Why did you decide to purchase this Combined Text and Kit? *(Tick one box only)*

☐ Have used BPP Texts in the past
☐ Recommendation by friend/colleague
☐ Recommendation by a lecturer at college
☐ Saw advertising
☐ Other _____

During the past six months do you recall seeing/receiving any of the following?
(Tick as many boxes as are relevant)

☐ Our advertisement in *Accounting Technician* magazine
☐ Our advertisement in *Pass*
☐ Our brochure with a letter through the post

Which (if any) aspects of our advertising do you find useful?
(Tick as many boxes as are relevant)

☐ Prices and publication dates of new editions
☐ Information on Interactive Text content
☐ Facility to order books off-the-page
☐ None of the above

Your ratings, comments and suggestions would be appreciated on the following areas

	Very useful	Useful	Not useful
Introduction	☐	☐	☐
Chapter contents lists	☐	☐	☐
Activities and answers	☐	☐	☐
Key learning points	☐	☐	☐
Quick quizzes and answers	☐	☐	☐
Practice activities	☐	☐	☐
Full skills based assessments	☐	☐	☐
Full exam based assessments	☐	☐	☐
Lecturers' Resource Section	☐	☐	☐

	Excellent	Good	Adequate	Poor
Overall opinion of this Combined Text and Kit	☐	☐	☐	☐

Do you intend to continue using BPP Interactive Texts/Assessment Kits?   ☐ Yes   ☐ No

The BPP author of this edition can be e-mailed at: marymaclean@bpp.com

Please return this form to: Janice Ross, BPP Professional Education, FREEPOST, London, W12 8BR

Review Form & Free Prize Draw (continued)

Please note any further comments and suggestions/errors below

Free Prize Draw Rules

1   Closing date for 31 January 2006 draw is 31 December 2005. Closing date for 31 July 2006 draw is 30 June 2006.

2   Restricted to entries with UK and Eire addresses only. BPP employees, their families and business associates are excluded.

3   No purchase necessary. Entry forms are available upon request from BPP Professional Education. No more than one entry per title, per person. Draw restricted to persons aged 16 and over.

4   Winners will be notified by post and receive their cheques not later than 6 weeks after the relevant draw date.

5   The decision of the promoter in all matters is final and binding. No correspondence will be entered into.

See overleaf for information on other
BPP products and how to order

AAT Order

To BPP Professional Education, Aldine Place, London W12 8AW
Tel: 020 8740 2211. Fax: 020 8740 1184
E-mail: Publishing@bpp.com Web: www.bpp.com

Mr/Mrs/Ms (Full name) _____
Daytime delivery address _____
Postcode _____
Daytime Tel _____ E-mail _____

	5/05 Texts	5/05 Kits	Special offer	8/05 Passcards	Success CDs
FOUNDATION (£14.95 except as indicated)				Foundation	
Units 1 & 2 Receipts and Payments	☐	☐	Foundation Sage Bookeeping and Excel Spreadsheets CD-ROM free if ordering all Foundation Text and Kits, including Units 21 and 22/23 ☐	£6.95 ☐	£14.95 ☐
Unit 3 Ledger Balances and Initial Trial Balance	☐	(Combined Text & Kit)			
Unit 4 Supplying Information for Mgmt Control	☐	(Combined Text & Kit)			
Unit 21 Working with Computers (£9.95)	☐				
Unit 22/23 Healthy Workplace/Personal Effectiveness (£9.95)	☐				
Sage and Excel for Foundation (Workbook with CD-ROM £9.95)	☐				
INTERMEDIATE (£9.95 except as indicated)					
Unit 5 Financial Records and Accounts (for 06/06 exams)	☐	☐		£5.95 ☐	£14.95 ☐
Unit 6/7 Costs and Reports (Combined Text £14.95)	☐			£5.95 ☐	
Unit 6 Costs and Revenues		☐			£14.95 ☐
Unit 7 Reports and Returns		☐			
TECHNICIAN (£9.95 except as indicated)					
Unit 8/9 Core Managing Performance and Controlling Resources	☐	☐		£5.95 ☐	£14.95 ☐
Spreadsheets for Technician (Workbook with CD-ROM)	☐		Spreadsheets for Technicians CD-ROM free if take Unit 8/9 Text and Kit ☐		
Unit 10 Core Managing Systems and People (£14.95)	☐	(Combined Text & Kit)		£5.95 ☐	£14.95 ☐
Unit 11 Option Financial Statements (A/c Practice) (for 06/06 exams)	☐	☐		£5.95 ☐	
Unit 12 Option Financial Statements (Central Govnmt)	☐	☐		£5.95 ☐	
Unit 15 Option Cash Management and Credit Control	☐	☐		£5.95 ☐	
Unit 17 Option Implementing Audit Procedures	☐	☐		£5.95 ☐	
Unit 18 Option Business Tax FA05 (8/05) (£14.95)	☐	(Combined Text & Kit)		£5.95 ☐	
Unit 19 Option Personal Tax FA05 (8/05) (£14.95)	☐	(Combined Text & Kit)		£5.95 ☐	
INTERMEDIATE 2004 (£9.95 except as indicated)					
Unit 5 Financial Records and Accounts (for 12/05 exams)	☐	☐			
TECHNICIAN 2004 (£9.95 except as indicated)					
Unit 11 Option Financial Statements (A/c Practice) (for 12/05 exams)	☐	☐		£5.95 ☐	
Unit 18 Option Business Tax FA04 (8/04)	☐	(Combined Text & Kit)		£5.95 ☐	
Unit 19 Option Personal Tax FA04 (8/04)	☐	(Combined Text & Kit)		£5.95 ☐	
SUBTOTAL	£	£	£	£	£

TOTAL FOR PRODUCTS £ _____

POSTAGE & PACKING

Texts/Kits	First	Each extra	
UK	£3.00	£3.00	£ ___
Europe*	£6.00	£4.00	£ ___
Rest of world	£20.00	£10.00	£ ___

Passcards			
UK	£2.00	£1.00	£ ___
Europe*	£3.00	£2.00	£ ___
Rest of world	£8.00	£8.00	£ ___

Success CDs			
UK	£2.00	£1.00	£ ___
Europe*	£3.00	£2.00	£ ___
Rest of world	£8.00	£8.00	£ ___

TOTAL FOR POSTAGE & PACKING £ _____
(Max £12 Texts/Kits/Passcards - deliveries in UK)

Grand Total (Cheques to *BPP Professional Education*)
I enclose a cheque for (incl. Postage) £ _____
Or charge to Access/Visa/Switch
Card Number ☐☐☐☐ ☐☐☐☐ ☐☐☐☐ ☐☐☐☐   CV2 No ☐☐☐ last 3 digits on signature strip

Expiry date _____   Start Date _____

Issue Number (Switch Only) ☐☐

Signature _____

We aim to deliver to all UK addresses inside 5 working days; a signature will be required. Orders to all EU addresses should be delivered within 6 working days. All other orders to overseas addresses should be delivered within 8 working days. * Europe includes the Republic of Ireland and the Channel Islands.

See overleaf for information on other
BPP products and how to order

AAT Order

To BPP Professional Education, Aldine Place, London W12 8AW
Tel: 020 8740 2211. Fax: 020 8740 1184
E-mail: Publishing@bpp.com Web:www.bpp.com

Mr/Mrs/Ms (Full name) _____
Daytime delivery address _____
_____ Postcode _____
Daytime Tel _____ E-mail _____

OTHER MATERIAL FOR AAT STUDENTS

| | 8/04 Texts | 6/04 Text | 3/03 Text | 3/04 Text |

FOUNDATION (£5.95)
Basic Maths and English ☐

COMPUTER BASED TRAINING
AAT Bookkeeping Certificate (CD-ROM plus manual) £130 ☐

INTERMEDIATE (£5.95)
Basic Bookkeeping (for students exempt from Foundation) ☐
Business Maths and English
(higher level Maths and English, also useful for ACCA/CIMA) £9.95 ☐

FOR ALL STUDENTS (£5.95)
Building Your Portfolio (old standards)
Building Your Portfolio (2003 standards)
Basic Costing ☐

TOTAL FOR PRODUCTS £ ☐

POSTAGE & PACKING

	First	Each extra
Texts/Kits		
UK	£3.00	£3.00 £___
Europe*	£6.00	£4.00 £___
Rest of world	£20.00	£10.00 £___
Passcards		
UK	£2.00	£1.00 £___
Europe*	£3.00	£2.00 £___
Rest of world	£8.00	£8.00 £___
Tapes		
UK	£2.00	£1.00 £___
Europe*	£3.00	£2.00 £___
Rest of world	£8.00	£8.00 £___

TOTAL FOR POSTAGE & PACKING £___
(Max £12 Texts/Kits/Passcards - deliveries in UK)

AAT PAYROLL

Finance Act 2005
8/05
December 2005 and June 2006 assessments

Special offer
Take Text and Kit together £44.95 ☐

☐
For assessments in 2006
☐ £44.95 ☐

Finance Act 2004
8/04
June 2005 exams only

Special offer
Take Text and Kit together £44.95 ☐

☐
☐
For assessments in 2005
☐ £44.95 ☐

		£___		£___
LEVEL 2 Text (£29.95)				
LEVEL 2 Kit (£19.95)				
LEVEL 3 Text (£29.95)				
LEVEL 3 Kit (£19.95)				
SUBTOTAL		£___		£___

Grand Total (Cheques to *BPP Professional Education*) £___

I enclose a cheque for (incl. Postage) ☐
Or charge to Access/Visa/Switch

Card Number [_____] CV2 No [___] *last 3 digits on signature strip*

Expiry date [____]   Start Date [____]

Issue Number (Switch Only) [____]

Signature _____

We aim to deliver to all UK addresses inside 5 working days; a signature will be required. Orders to all EU addresses should be delivered within 6 working days. All other orders to overseas addresses should be delivered within 8 working days. * Europe includes the Republic of Ireland and the Channel Islands.